THRU·THE GRAPEVINE

FINGER LAKES REGION COOKBOOK

Cover Design by Sally Gwin & Carol Stemski
Graphic Solutions   Corning, NY

JUNIOR LEAGUE OF GREATER ELMIRA-CORNING, INC.
ELMIRA, NEW YORK
1991

ISBN: 9609980
Library of Congress Catalog Card Number: 82-83914

First Printing	MAY, 1983	5,000 Copies
Second Printing	OCT., 1983	10,000 Copies
Third Printing	NOV., 1984	10,000 Copies
Fourth Printing	DEC., 1987	10,000 Copies
Fifth Printing	NOV., 1991	10,000 Copies
Sixth Printing*	NOV., 1993	20,000 Copies

(*Southern Living® **Hall of Fame** edition)

Over 1,000 recipes were submitted by members of the Junior League of Greater Elmira-Corning, Inc. The 635 recipes contained in this book were tested and retested for quality, selected and edited for clarity by Elmira-Corning Junior League members. However, this book is not only a cookbook, but a reflection of our Finger Lakes Region. We hope that after reading THRU THE GRAPEVINE, you will appreciate the many fine aspects of this region that we have grown to love!

COOKBOOK COMMITTEE
JUNIOR LEAGUE OF GREATER ELMIRA-CORNING, INC.

THRU THE GRAPEVINE
may be obtained by addressing:

THRU THE GRAPEVINE
Junior League of Greater Elmira-Corning, Inc.
P.O. Box 3150
Elmira, New York 14905

For your convenience, an order blank may be found
in the back of the book.

CONTRIBUTORS
Those who spread recipes Thru The Grapevine!

June Ainey
Phyllis Albee
Marian Ambrose
Jean Aronson
Margaret Ashbridge
Connie Barone
Joanne Beecher
Jane Benedict
Pat Boatwright
Jane Booth
Peg Bosley
Dorrie Brand
Norma Brooks
Sage Bryner
Jeanne Bucher
Jan Butts
Jane Cadwallader
Monica Campanella
Lynn Canter
Jan Carlson
Kathy Carozza
Kathy Carpenter
Sharron Chimley
Jackie Chotkowski
Sue Condit
Suzanne Connelly
Debbie Courtney
Fran Crew
Pat Cusick
Betsy Dalrymple
Jean Davidson
Marilyn DeFilippo
Susan DeFilippo
Janice DeLaney
Hollace Donner
Bette Evans
Joan Featherman
Sue Fennell
Cecie Fitzpatrick
Judy Frandsen
Brigid Galusha
Ann Gear
Sue Geise
Margaret Geraghty
Bonnie Gestwicki
Ellen Gibbs
Babette Glauner
Hope Goodsite
Kathy Graham
Karla Greenwald
Lois Grund
Cindy Haigh
Carol Halliday
Sue Hamlin
Lois Hart
Denise Hayes

Katherine Heanue
Peggy Higginbotham
Darcy Hopko
Pat Houghton
Janet Howell
Libby Howell
Karin Howland
Susan Hughes
Pat Hunt
Margie Ingram
Carol Kacala
Nancy Kaemmerer
Jane Kelleher
Cyndee Kennedy
Anita Kimball
Marcia Kimball
Nancy Kimball
Eileen Kingsbury
Jan Kline
Judy Koehn
Diana Konkle
Myrna Lamberton
Sue Lentz
Betty Loomis
Lois Manes
Lyce Martin
Fran McKinnon
Alberta McLaud
Beverly McLeod
Nancy McLeod
Mary Jane McMillan
Ann Meacham
Jeanne Meacham
Sue Mearns
Lynda Moore
Cora Jo Morgan
Fran Morrisey
Margaret Morse
Ann Mortimer
Terry Nicklaus
Margaret Nye
Katie Oakleaf
Martha Olmstead
Jean O'Neill
Cheryl Parente
Ann Paton
Debbie Perry
Linda Peterson
Nan Peterson
Martha Pierce
Cindy Pollard
Joan Popovich
Linda Porter
Trudi Porter
Trudy Potter
Janet Proudfoot

Alice Rahill
Ann Rees
Dede Reynolds
Georgia Reynolds
Betsy Risen
Mary Booth Roberts
Hazel Robinson
Elaine Rothberg
Marilyn Ruffer
Kathy Rurak
Barbara Ryan
Kathy Scaringe
Dot Schott
Sue Schrader
Lucy Schweizer
Margaret Seem
Kaye Shannon
Gretchen Sharlow
Pam Shaw
Mary Ann Sheen
Mary Shoemaker
Ann Sigel
Christine Sinko
Edie Skinner
Jo Ann Smith
Mary Welles Smith
Priscilla Smith
Susie Smith
Hatsy Sophia
Ann Streeter
Claribell Streeter
Janice Streeter
Peggy Streeter
Marilynn Sullivan
Sarah Tipton
Lucia Underhill
Mimi Updegraff
Judy Valicenti
Patt Vernon
Janet Webb
Phiddy Webb
Shirley Weiermiller
Lori Welliver
Ann Wenzl
Marge Wert
Wendy Wheadon
Nancy Willwerth
Suzanne Winkler
Jackie Woltjen
Joanne Woodin
Sandy Wright
Joanna Wurtele
Linda Yenawine
Joanne Zimmer

FOREWORD

Welcome to the celebration! Of course it's a celebration of food and wine, but it's also a celebration of place — the beautiful Finger Lakes area of New York State.

If you subscribe to O'Donnell's Gastronomic Observation No. 1, you'll agree that wherever vineyards bloom, an interest in good food flourishes. Now I don't necessarily mean restaurant food, although our area boasts many fine eating establishments. I'm talking about the food folks cook and serve at home — good, honest meals prepared with care and with the freshest of ingredients.

Just by picking up this cookbook, you've signalled **your** interest in this sort of good cooking, and you'll find within these pages more than 600 recipes to whet your appetite. In fact, we owe a big "thank you" to all the people who have shared their culinary ideas and inspirations in *Thru The Grapevine*, and to the many others who tested and tasted and selected only the best for publication.

Now, I have a confession to make here — I'm a cookbook-aholic, a compulsive condition shared by numbers of other good folks, as I've discovered in my wanderings around the country. I'd rather stick my nose in a good batch of recipes than in a Faulkner, Hemingway or Christie classic — and I have the cookbook collection to prove it! I lost count after 500, old and new.

During those wanderings (I conduct cooking demonstrations all over the U.S.), I'm drawn, like nutmeg to spinach, to the "local" cookbook section in bookstores. Why? Where else can you find the tried and true favorites that reflect the food preferences and sophistication of a particular area? Unhappily, not all of these books, however well-intentioned, are as successful as the book you have in your hands.

Putting a cookbook together is hard work. I should know. I've just had my first book published by Random House, *Cooking With Cornelius: The Corning Cookbook*. To me, many "area" cookbooks are just recipes strung together with little thought given to practicality or accuracy, or whether the menus balance food flavors, colors and textures to produce harmonious meals. Even worse: Many times I've been intrigued by a recipe and then realized, sometimes by reading it, oftentimes by making it, that it surely had never been tested!

So many friends of mine have devoted priceless hours to this labor of love that I know you'll treasure your copy of *Thru The Grapevine* as much as I do mine. The recipes are tested, the text readable — and in type large enough even for me to read easily — and it's sprinkled with touches of humor, just like life in the kitchen of any busy cook.

I especially like the "rating system" that helps you gauge the usability of a recipe by the cook's level of expertise. Bravo to the cookbook committee!

Finally, *Thru The Grapevine* is the kind of book that, by virtue of its menu suggestions alone, makes me long to fling off my blazer, don an apron and get cooking! Join me in the celebration!

Cornelius

Cook and Author

TABLE OF CONTENTS

ILLUSTRATIONS

WINERY
The Finger Lakes Region has large and small wineries which produce acclaimed vintage wines.

WINE SECTION

Wine Committee

Bernard J. Feinberg
Donald L. Brooks Jr.
Martha and C. Brent Olmstead
Nils W. Peterson
Barbara Kelly
Pat Cusick

b

A HISTORIC TRIP *THRU THE GRAPEVINE* REGION

The history of viti-culture, or grape growing, in New York State's Finger Lakes region goes back to the early 19th century. In 1829, the Rev. Mr. Bostwick brought grapes from the Hudson Valley to his rectory in Hammondsport at the southern end of Lake Keuka. The soil drainage and climate of this area are said to be similar to that of the French Champagne region. Soon farmers in the area realized the softening effect of the lakes' waters on the harsh upstate climate and planted grapes on the glacially formed slopes. Thus began the exciting wine industry of Central New York.

The vines planted were those of vitis labrusca, the native American grape. These grapes traditionally produce the distinctive "grapy" wines for which Eastern varietals have become known. The New York sparkling wines made from these grapes have been internationally recognized since 1873. They are still the backbone of New York grape production, and include Concord, Catawba, Niagara, Delaware, Diamond, Dutchess, Elvira, Isabella, Ives and Missouri Reisling (not a vinifera but a varietal nomenclature.)

The great phylloxera (or root louse) infestation in the European vineyards took place in the mid 19th century. In the early 20th century, the French developed grapes which were grafted on native American disease-resistant root stock and termed French hybrids. These vines grow very well in the Finger Lakes region. Some of our finest wines come from these varieties. The more popular of these are Seyval Blanc, Aurora, Vidal Blanc, Baco, Foch and Chelois. Also grown in the area are Chancellor, Cascade, Colobel, Landot, Millot, Rougeon, Verdelet, Ravat and Vincent.

In the 1950's Dr. Konstantin Frank, with the encouragement of Charles Fournier, introduced the vitis vinifera or "great grapes", the classic European wine grapes, to the Finger Lakes region. These grapes, coupled with the Farm Wineries Act of 1977, have brought about the mushrooming of small wineries along the shores. A tour of the Finger Lakes area is now a lakes' oenophile's dream come true.

The vinifera grapes are the world's oldest cultivated variety. In this area the Chardonnay and the Riesling grapes do particularly well, and plantings have been made of Cabernet Sauvignon, Gamay Beaujolais, Gewurztraminer, Merlot, Pinot Gris and Pinot Noir.

The Farm Wineries Act enables grape growers to make and market their own wines. Many of these small wineries are producing wines that rival, and occasionally exceed, in quality those coming from California and Europe.

New York State licenses wineries in two ways — commercial wineries, which have no production limit; and farm wineries which have a limit of 50,000 gallons of wine a year.

COMMERCIAL WINERIES

The oldest of the wineries with a commercial license is Taylor Great Western. It started as the Pleasant Valley Wine Company in Hammondsport in 1860. Their fine champagnes, deemed "the Greatest in the West", resulted in the popular name, Great Western. In 1880, Walter Taylor, a cooper from Halsey Valley, Tioga County, came to make barrels for the burgeoning wine business in Hammondsport. Soon he was growing grapes and producing wines.

During Prohibition Taylor marketed grape juice in barrels, with very explicit instructions how **not** to make wine, how much sugar **not** to add, how long **not** to let the juice ferment, because unless the instructions were carefully followed, illegal wine would result. Taylor's business was **not** hurt by this marketing method.

In 1961, Taylor Wines and Great Western merged, and in 1977 were acquired by Coca-Cola. They are now part of the Wine Spectrum, a massive wine marketing division of Coca-Cola.

Taylor-Great Western owns 1200 acres of vineyards around the lakes which produce 10% of their needs. Their additional requirements are filled by 450 grape growers with 37 grape varieties. These grapes are from an area that extends to the western borders of New York State. Taylor-Great Western makes 68 wines, which include Varietals, fortified dessert wines, proprietary wines and the famous sparkling wines. They are particularly known for the Lake Country series (Red, White, Pink and Gold), and the new Lake Country Soft series, which is slightly sweet, faintly effervescent and lower in alcohol.

Taylor-Great Western operates as two separate wineries but shares the management process. They have a strong commitment to the tourism aspect of the wine industry and their tours and tastings are excellent. They support a series of summer concerts on Cayuga, Seneca and Keuka Lakes. In 1982 they sponsored the Wineglass Marathon Run, which is expected to become an annual event.

Gold Seal Vineyards is the descendent of the Urbana Wine Company, founded in 1865. The Champagne of Urbana was a gold medal winner at the Paris Exposition of 1876 and became known as Gold Seal Champagne from the medal replica on the label. Like many other wineries, Urbana was dealt a severe blow by Prohibition. After Repeal in 1934, Charles Fournier came from France to bring new life to the faltering winery.

It was Charles Fournier who encouraged Dr. Konstantin Frank to grow the vinifera grape in the Finger Lakes region. He then accepted and implemented Dr. Frank's results on a commercial basis.

Gold Seal, a name adopted in 1957, is now a wholly owned subsidiary of Seagram Company Ltd. The 500 acres owned by Gold Seal includes the largest vinifera vineyards on the East Coast and provide 25% of the Winery's needs. The vintage varietals, Rieslings and Chardonnays, and especially the late harvest Riesling under the Charles Fournier label, are excellent wines at reasonable prices. The generic wines of Gold Seal, especially the Chablis, are fine everyday table wines. Certainly, the Champagnes cannot be recommended highly enough. The Blanc de Noir, a very dry Champagne made from the Pinot Noir grape, is outstanding not only for taste but for color.

The Barry Wine Company on Hemlock Lake was founded in 1872 by the Roman Catholic Dioceses of Rochester to produce a sacramental wine. In 1979 it was purchased from a missionary order, which had also used the winery facilities, by Ted and Skip Cribari. The Cribaris came from California with a family tradition of wine making.

The grapes grown in the immediate area are labrusca, the native American grape, and the wines produced from these carry generic names. Barry also produces wines from French hybrid grapes grown by other Finger Lakes' growers, along with fortified wines, a port and a cream sherry. Since two-thirds of their wines are still produced for sacramental purposes, only 10,000 cases of wine are available to the public, and their award-winning reserve wine production is very limited.

Widmers Wine Cellars of Naples markets wines with wide popular appeal. The winery was founded in 1888 by John Jacob Widmer, a Swiss, whose fellow immigrants on the East Coast provided a ready market. Prohibition turned production to grape juice, fruit jellies, syrups, sacramental and medicinal wines. Their good management during this national wine disaster found them well-equipped to re-enter the popular wine business after Repeal.

Widmers produce generic, proprietary, dessert and champagne type wines. Their Lake Series of proprietary wines are very successful, as is the crackling Lake Niagara.

Canandaigua Wine Company located at the north end of Canandaigua Lake markets over 16,000,000 gallons of popular wines, placing it among the 10 top wineries in the world in production. Among the brands made here are Richard's Wild Irish Rose, J. Roget Champagnes, Canada Muscrat, New York State Table Wines and the Canandaigua Seyval and Chardonnay. The Sands family runs Canandaigua and has wineries in South Carolina, Virginia and California. The wines are made from grapes grown all over the United States and are available nationally.

Bully Hill Winery on Keuka Lake was started in 1970 by Walter S. Taylor, a member of the Taylor Winery family. Bully Hill produces widely marketed wines from French hybrid grapes grown in the Finger Lakes and neighboring areas. Among the wines are Seyval Blanc, Bully Hill Red, Vidal Blanc and a Sparkling Seyval. Mr. Taylor's legal difficulties over the name of his wine have brought the winery into national prominence.

Chateau Esperanza is at the head of Keuka Lake, just east of Branchport. Owned by two women, Angela Lombardi and Sherry LeBeck, Esperanza opened in 1979, "when the time was ripe." The wines of Esperanza are made from French hybrid and vinfera grapes from Finger Lakes' growers. These are soon to be joined by grapes from the Chateau's own growing vineyard holdings. All the wines of Esperanza are vintage (dated by year) and use a vineyard designation (the name of the grape grower is used on the label).

Villa D'Ingianni Winery is on the east side of Keuka Lake, near Keuka Landing. The winery makes 140,000 gallons of wine a year and the wine is largely marketed under a liquor store's own label as generic jug wine. It also bottles what it refers to as premium wines under the Villa label.

Penn Yan Wine Cellars of Penn Yan is like Villa D'Ingianni in that they bottle generic jug wines for liquor stores.

FARM WINERIES

The small "boutique" wineries of the Finger Lakes started to appear in 1977 after the passage of the Farm Wineries Act. The wineries are, or can be, open seven days a week, can sell wine to credit card purchasers and can ship by United Parcel Service within the state. In addition, they have the impetus to experiment with blending and creating some innovative wines. This creativity produces great variations in taste, so wines should be sampled and chosen with care.

Among the first of the wineries to open in 1977 was Glenora, on the west side of Seneca Lake. Owned by a group of local grape growers, Glenora has been a leader in the evolution of premium quality wines in the East. In the past, they produced a variety of red and white wines but now have limited their offerings to the highly successful Chardonnay, Riesling, Cayuga, Seyval, Ravat and Champagne. These wines have won numerous medals in various regional, national and international competitions, and are striking examples of what New York State grapes and knowledgeable wine makers can achieve.

Next comes the Wagner Estate Winery on the east side of Seneca Lake. The unique octagonal winery sits above the lake as if it had been there forever. The traditions of three generations of grape growers have culminated in this striking building and some even more striking wines. Wagner is also one of the very few estate wineries in the Finger Lakes area. This designation applies to a winery which produces wine only from grapes grown on its own land. Bill Wagner produces 18-20 varieties of still and sparking wines among which his Chardonnay, Riesling and Seyval have been consistent champions. Soon Champagne will join his inventory of fine wines. Wagner's Winery sponsors a series of summer festivals at the winery, with music, dancing, and Wagner's red wines.

Heron Hill, north of Hammondsport, on the west side of Keuka Lake is another of the early farm wineries. Peter Johnstone, co-owner, was in advertising, and his frequent travels to France fostered an unquenchable interst in fine food and wine. This interest could only be served by making his own fine wines, which include Riesling, Chardonnay and Ravat. The Otter Spring Wines, his premium label, are outstanding. His continuing interest in fine food is evidenced by the menu display, in the tasting room of restaurants which serve his wines and also by an award program for achievement by Finger Lakes area restaurants.

Vinifera Wine Cellars is the home of Dr. Konstantin Frank, the father of the vinifera grape in the Northeast. Dr. Frank's conviction that the "Noble Grapes" could survive our harsh winters with the aid of the climate-tempering lakes, has brought a revolution to wine production in New York State. The Chardonnays, Rieslings, Pinots, Gewurztraminers and Cabernets of which we are so proud might have been long delayed, or never come at all, without Dr. Frank's dedication and his encouragement by Charles Fournier of Gold Seal. Dr. Frank grows over 65 varieties of grapes, most of them grown experimentally. He sells his grape juice to home wine makers so that you may try to match his lovely Rieslings and Chardonnays.

The DeMay Wine Cellars, just south of Hammondsport, is a tiny section of the Beaune vineyards of France transported to upstate New

York. The old stone winery turns out wine made in the 250 year old tradition of the DeMay family. The Merlot and Vin Rose are unusual offerings, and the DeMay Champagne, made in the classic "methode champenoise", is delicious.

McGregor Vineyards is perched high above the east side of Keuka Lake overlooking Bluff Point. The grapes of McGregor were bottled by others and produced such good wine that the McGregors were encouraged to make their own wines. They offer Cayuga, Chardonnay, Riesling, Gewurztraminer and an outstanding red wine, Pinot Noir.

Hermann J. Wiemer Vineyards lie on the west side of Seneca Lake. Mr. Wiemer's training in Germany as a vintner and his background in grape growing grants his customers the assurance of delicious wines, and growers in the area a source of fine root stock. His winery's hills show not only the beautiful Riesling, Chardonnay and Gewurtztraminer vines, but also rows of tiny shoots that will be the vinifera grape vines of the future.

Casa Larga Vineyards of Fairport, southwest of Rochester, is the realization of Andrew Colaruotolo's life long dream. Perched atop the highest hill in Monroe County, the idyllic rural scene is in dreamlike contrast to the distant view of the Rochester skyline. Here the new vines are grafted and nurtured next to the family's garden of tomatoes, peppers, onions and eggplant. The charming winery holds Italian wine making equipment, bright with the colors of the Italian flag as well as the original family wine press. What started as a suburban subdivision is now a vineyard with a potential of 40 acres. Mr. Colaruotolo's childhood, spent in the vineyards on the western coast of Italy, south of Rome, is being revived here on the rolling hills with their lovely views. The vines of Casa Larga produce Gewurztraminer, Chardonnay, Riesling, Cabernet, Pinot Noir, Delaware, Aurora and De Chaunac wines as well as a line of red, white and rose, marketed under a proprietary label.

The Lucas Vineyard, on the western side of Cayuga Lake just north of Interlaken, markets wine from French hybrid grapes with vinifera grapes planted, but not yet producing. Bill Lucas, a tugboat captain in New York City, also worked as a grape grower until seized by the winemaking fever so prevalent in this area. His efforts were so successful that Lucas is now one of our newer farm wineries. Cayuga, Aurora, De Chaunac and Interlaken Red are among their wines as well as the Tugboat series, whose motto is "Wine if by land, Tug if by sea."

In 1982, the farm winery scene was enlarged by the addition of eight new wineries. Each has a different philosophy and approach to the art of wine making and can only enhance the Finger Lakes reputation for fine wine.

Americana Vineyards at Covert, south of Interlaken on the west side of Cayuga Lake, is the long-hoped for dream of James and Mary Ann Treble. Jim returned from the midwest to grow grapes, fired by the tales of his grandfather, a retired grower. The Trebles make what they call "Classic" wines, Seyval, Aurora, Catawba, a November Harvest wine and a Rhine wine from the vinifera, French hybrid grapes grown at the vineyard. Only at harvest are these grapes touched by workers outside the family and that is only for the handpicking used at Americana. The Trebles aim to produce wines that are both enjoyable and reasonably priced.

5

Finger Lakes Wine Cellars just west of Branchport is the 100 year old farm of Arthur and Joyce Hunt, the sixth generation to farm the slopes overlooking Keuka Lake. 75 acres yield French hybrid and native grapes that make charming wines, among which is a Niagara that carries the scent of harvest throughout the year. The juice of their grapes is available to home winemakers and their winery tours are given on horse-drawn hay wagons.

Four Chimneys Farm Winery, on the west side of Seneca at Himrod, is the only organic winery in the United States and is certified by the New York State Natural Food Associates. Their offerings of Cabernet Sauvignon, Pinot Noir, Chenin Blanc, Chardonnay, Riesling and Gamay are an impressive selection of varieties for this Eastern climate.

Plane's Cayuga Vineyard, on the west side of Cayuga just north of Ovid, is the home of Dr. Robert Plane and his wife, Mary. Dr. Plane's background in chemistry (he is President of Clarkson University in Potsdam, New York) explains his scientific approach to the growing of their French hybrid, vinifera and American stock. Soil analysis and climatic conditions determine the choice of grapes to be grown. Mrs. Plane manages the vineyard and sells their quality grapes to other wineries. As evidence of their growing skills, Glenora Winery used their grapes to make its spectacular 1978 Glenora Chardonnay Robert Plane Vineyard, and also the award winning 1980. Such success for the grapes encouraged them to make their own wines, and now we have the Plane's Chardonnay, Chancellor, Cayuga, Rose, as well as a House Red and House White.

Poplar Ridge, on the east side of Seneca just north of Valois, is the end result of David Bagley's love affair with wine. Winemaker for five wineries and consultant for an equal number, he now has his own winery which offers Marechal Foch, Chelois, Vidal, Cayuga, Riesling, Ravat, Seyval and Aurora. David's grapes go to New York City's home winemakers through the Green Market Program.

Rolling Vineyards, north of Watkins Glen on the east side of Seneca Lake, has the most beautiful view of all the wineries. Ed Grow and Joanne Beligotti are making some classic wines in this tiny facility. The Seyval and Riesling are outstanding. The Aurora, Chelois and Foch are joined by the Seneca Lake proprietary series — Red and Rose, a blend of native and hybrid grapes.

Rotolo and Romeo of Avon, southwest of Rochester, are at present limiting their wine production to what they hope will be the perfect De Chaunac. When this is achieved, they hope to go on to produce and market additional varieties, one by one.

The Wickham Winery, at Hector on the east side of Seneca Lake, is owned by a family which first settled here in the late 1700's and has been active on the local and state level for almost 200 years. The Wickhams have long been grape growers and are now part of the growing wine community. The native and French hybrid grapes from their large farm produce Dry and Semi-Dry Aurora, Cayuga, Delaware, Marechal Foch, Rose and Catawba. Each year will bring challenges and changes as weather and grape quality determine what wines will be produced.

In October of 1982, wineries of the Finger Lakes area were given the right to use "Finger Lakes" as designation. The wineries had been lobbying for this decision for some time. Since this is comparable to the French "Appellation controllee" and a mark of quality and standards, the wines of the Finger Lakes now carry their banners even higher and more proudly than before. The wines of New York State Finger Lakes region need bow to no one in excellence nor in variety. There is something for everyone in the wines of the Finger Lakes and we hope you'll try them all!

Update — Harvest 1983

The Barry Wine Company recently became Eagle Crest Vineyards Inc. It is named for the resting site of the bald eagle at the southern end of Hemlock Lake. In the fall of 1984, Eagle Crest will be releasing premium Foch, Cayuga and Ravat wines to the restaurant market, under the Eagle Crest label. Barry wines will still be on the retail market.

"Tam splendidum marmor quam merum vinum Marmora" — "As splendid as marble, so pure are the wines of Marmora" so says the label of Fair Haven Winery. Perched on the eastern slope of Seneca Lake, above Valois, John Marmora's tiny estate winery is the focus of great plans. Mr. Marmora has traveled widely in Europe and returned to Lake Country to make hearty table wines from his Niagara, Aurora and Concord grapes. Plans for the 1984 season include "Bed and Breakfast" accommodations at his farmhouse adjoining the beautiful Hector land-use area, as well as a Blanc de Noir (white wine from red grapes) to join his Lake Hill Red and Seneca Vista Red. The guests at Fair Haven will have a swimming pond and a nature preserve to enhance the enjoyment of their stay.

Just east of Trumansburg on Rt. 89 is Frontenac Point, the Vineyard and winery of Jim and Carol Doolittle. The Doolittles' devotion to the philosophy of the farm winery has been demonstrated by their involvement in the drafting of the Farm Winery Act and the formation of the State Fair competition which includes wineries from all of New York. The wines of Frontenac are dinner wines individually fermented in wood and this year include Blanc Sec, Chelois Rose, Nouveau Red and a tiny amount of a Trockenbeerenauslese. 1984's releases will include a Chardonnay aged in French Oak and a Proprietars Reserve, blended Chelois and Pinot Noir — very French in concept. The wines of Frontenac are available only in regional restaurants and liquor stores as the winery is not open to the public.

Lakeshore Winery is the northern most winery on the Cayuga Wine Trail. Three acres of vinifera grapes on the western shore of Cayuga Lake lie directly behind a 150 year-old post and beam barn turned winery. Many hours of loving labor have restored the barn to glowing charm, a fitting home for well displayed farm implements of the past, the warm rag rugs on the shiny concrete floors and the quality craft items shown in the loft gift shop. Best of all are the handmade wines from hand picked grapes. Riesling, Chardonnay Cabernet and a Baco Noir that is definitely worth tasting. The special charm of Lakeshore is the style of the equipment: all the pressing, bottling, and corking equipment is just what you would use at home to make your own wine, even to the sour mash barrels used for aging. Lakeshore buys some grapes from neighboring grape growers (the Baco Noir) so it cannot claim the estate designation, but its wines can claim equality with any in the Finger Lakes Region. See back pages for Update 1987.

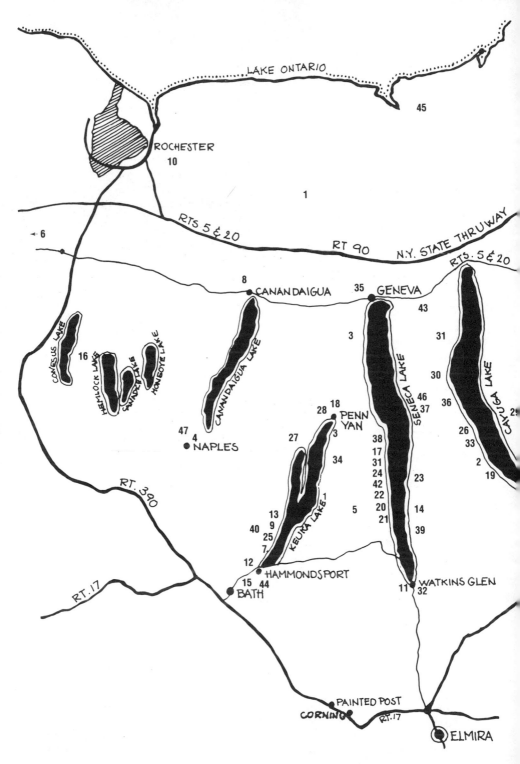

1. Amberg Wine Cellars
2. Americana Vineyards
3. Anthony Road Wine Company
4. Arbor Hill Grapery
5. Barrington Champagne Company
6. Batavia Wine Cellars
7. Bully Hill Vineyards
8. Canandaigua Wine Company
9. Cana Vineyards Winery
10. Casa Larga Vineyards
11. Castel Grisch Winery & Restaurant
12. Chateau de Rheims Winery
13. Chateau Frank
14. Chateau LaFayette Reneau
15. Dr. Frank's Vinifera Wine Cellars
16. Eagle Crest Vineyards
17. Four Chimneys Farm Winery
18. Fox Run Vineyards
19. Frontenac Point Vineyard
20. Fulkerson Wine Cellars
21. Giasi Winery
22. Glenora Wine Cellars
23. Hazlitt 1852 Vineyards
24. Herman J. Wiemer Vineyard
25. Heron Hill Vineyards
26. Hosmer
27. Hunt County Vineyards
28. Keuka Spring Vineyards
29. King Ferry Winery (Treleaven)
30. Knapp Vineyards
31. Lakeshore Winery
32. Lakewood Vineyards
33. Lucas Vineyards
34. McGregor Vineyard Winery
35. Newland Vineyard
36. Plane's Cayuga Vineyard
37. Poplar Ridge Vineyards
38. Prejean Winery
39. Rolling Vineyards Farm Winery
40. St. Walter de Bully Wine Company
41. Six Mile Creek Vineyard
42. Squaw Point Winery
43. Swedish Hill Vineyard
44. Taylor – Great Western – Golden Seal Winery
45. Thorpe Vineyards
46. Wagner Vineyards
47. Widmer's Wine Cellars Manischewitz Wines

GENERAL WINE SUGGESTIONS

Wines to serve with appetizers:

Cocktail sherry, champagne or a good white table wine is suitable to use with all appetizers which might include spicy snacks, seafood, cheese, fruit or shellfish.

White wine suggestions: Seyval, Ravat, Riesling, Aurora or Cayuga

Wines to serve with soup as main meal:

Wine suggestions: inexpensive jug type wine, red or white, compatible with the main soup ingredient

Wines to use with luncheon salads:

Chicken or turkey salad	Because of the vinegar or may-
Crab or shrimp salad	onnaise used in salad dressings, a
Chef's salad	less expensive white wine is
	suggested such as a jug type
	Chablis or Rhine wine.
Fruit salad	A nice sparkling white wine.

Wines to use with eggs, omelets and cheese dishes:

Eggs Benedict, eggs with cheese or mushroom sauce	Use a dry, white wine or perhaps a rose. White wines suggestions:
Omelets	Verdelet, Cayuga, Johannisberg
Scrambled eggs with bacon, ham or sausage	Riesling or Ravat. For a special treat or Sunday brunch, a cham-
Cheese fondue	pagne or Chardonnay.
Cheese souffle	
Quiche	

Wines to use with pasta dishes:

Macaroni, spaghetti or rice with mushrooms, cheese or light sauces	Seyval, Ravat or Cayuga
Spaghetti, lasagne, ravioli or manicotti with tomato or meat sauces	Red, Burgundy type wine
Pasta with seafood: clams, crab, shrimp, etc.	Dry, white wine
Curried rice dishes	Gewurztraminer

Wines to use with meats:

Beef:	
Prime ribs of beef or fillet of beef	Cabernet Sauvignon, Chancellor, DeChaunac or Pinot Noir

Barbecued short ribs, stews or pot roast	Pinot Noir, Chelois or Baco Noir
Ground beef dishes, meat loaf or hamburgers	Inexpensive red table wine

Veal:

Veal roast or veal Marsala	Riesling or Ravat
Veal chops	Baco Noir, Pinot Noir or Chelois
Veal Scallopini	Seyval or Verdelet
Veal Parmesan	Foch or Seyval Blanc

Lamb:

Roast leg of lamb or lamb chops	Cabernet Sauvignon or Pinot Noir
Lamb stews, shish kebobs, or barbecued lamb ribs	Chelois, Baco Noir, Chancellor or DeChaunac

Ham:	Gewurztraminer, Rose, Ravat or Dutchess

Pork:

Pork roast, chops or spareribs	Rose, Gewurztraminer, Riesling or Aurora
Venison or game meats	Full bodied red wine: Cabernet Sauvignon, Chelois or Baco Noir

Wines to use with poultry:

Roast turkey, roast chicken or Cornish game hens	Seyval, Ravat, Riesling, Cayuga or Aurora
Poultry with herb, sausage or other spicy stuffing	Gewurztraminer or Pinot Noir
Chicken breasts, casseroles, creamed chicken, chicken a la king or bland sauces	Seyval, Ravat, Riesling, Cayuga or Aurora
Curried or barbecue sauces	Delaware or Aurora

Wines to use with fish and seafood:

Baked or Poached: trout, snapper, salmon, flounder, sole, swordfish or scallops	Use a fine, dry white wine such as Chardonnay, Riesling, Ravat or Seyval Blanc
Shellfish: crab, shrimp, oysters, lobster	Aurora, Riesling, Cayuga or Chardonnay
Note: if served with a rice sauce such as a Newburg	A rose or light red wine

Wines to use with casserole dishes:

Beef and lamb casseroles	Red, Burgundy type
Seafood and chicken casseroles	White wine

Wines to use with a dessert or after dinner:

Sweet wines are suitable such as Muscat, cream sherry and occasionally special bottlings such as Vidal Ice wine.

The Finger Lakes wines suggested in this cookbook fall into the following categories:

1. **Vinifera Vitis vinifera** is a species of grape introduced in the United States from Europe. Some of the vinifera varieties are:
Pinot Chardonnay — crisp, dry, white
Gewurtztraminer — spicy, white
Johannisberg Riesling — crisp, dry, full-bodied, white
Pinot Noir — dry, red
Cabernet Sauvignon — dry, red

2. **Hybrids or French American Varietals** are made predominately from the grape variety named on the label. The wine has a characteristic aroma and flavor from that grape. Some of the varietals are:
Seyval Blanc — dry, white
Aurora — fresh, crisp, white
Ravat — crisp, white
Verdelet — dry, white
Cayuga — dry, medium-bodied white
Baco Noir — full-bodied, dry, red
Marechal Foch — dry, deep to ruby red
Chelois — dry, red
De Chaunac — dry, dark red
Chancellor — dry, dark red

3. **Native** or **Labrusca** type:
Delaware — fruity, semi-dry, white
Dutchess — medium dry, white
Niagara — fruity, medium dry, white
Diamond — very dry, white
Pink Catawba — sweet, fruity, light rose

The following are jug-type or generic wines, which are blends of other grapes and not characteristic of the European names:
Chablis
Sauterne
Rhine
Rose
Burgundy

Criteria of good wine quality:

1. Variety of grape
2. The producer
3. Year
4. Area of Origin

GLOSSARY OF WINE TERMS

Commercial Winery: a winery producing over 50,000 gallons a year. (New York State regulations)

Estate Winery: a winery producing wines from grapes grown only on its own land.

Farm Winery: a winery producing less than 50,000 gallons a year. (New York State regulations)

French Hybrid Grape: varieties which have resulted from the grafting of French grape vines onto phylloxera resistant grape stock from America.

Generic Wine: a term which is used to identify wines as a class; red table wine, Chablis and Burgundy are examples. This is used most often with unidentified wines in a blend.

Ice wines: made from grapes which have matured through the Fall season, and are then frozen on the vine and harvested in the winter. The flavor and sugar of the wine is concentrated. Serve well chilled. This wine is special for a Thanksgiving or Christmas after dinner wine.

Labrusca grape: the native American grape, the "Fox" grape, used primarlly for fruit production. It tends to produce a very intense, fruity or "grapy" wine.

Proprietary wines: wines which carry a "brand" name, such as Lake Country, or the Tugboat series; the name of the winery's brand.

Varietal: wine which takes its characteristics from a specific grape such as Delaware. The varietal term is useful because it identifies a recognizable, distinctive quality in the wine derived from the specific grape.

Vinifera grapes: used to produce vinifera wines (the "great grapes"). Over 150 varieties are cultivated world wide. They have existed for over 5,000 years. The "classic" wines are produced from these. They include the Chardonnay, Riesling, Gewurtztraminer, Cabernet Sauvignon, Gamay Beaujolais, Merlot and Zinfandel.

WINE HELPFUL HINTS

Uses for Leftover Wines:

— Salad dressings
— Cakes and breads — makes them moist and enhances the flavor
— Fondue (white only)
— Marinade for meats
— Barbecue sauce for spareribs, chicken and shish kebobs
— Dips for appetizers
— Summer drinks, such as wine coolers
— Sauces for basting roasts and game hens
— Served over fresh fruit

To Chill or Not to Chill?

Red wines should be served at room temperature (55°-60°). White and rose wines are best when served chilled. Be careful not to over-chill good white wines because the bouquet and sweetness is adversely affected. Sweeter white wines are served cooler than dry white wines. Rose wines will taste less sweet, if well chilled. In general, open a red wine 30 minutes to an hour before serving. A red wine will be aereated more effectively if properly decanted. Open a white or a rose wine when you are ready to drink it.

When serving champagne, use a dry glass. Crushed ice chills the glass, but leaves moisture which breaks down the bubbles.

SPRING MENUS

Men's Night to Cook After a Visit to the National Woman's Hall of Fame, Seneca Falls, N.Y.

Skillet Sausage Italiano
Caesar Salad
Chocolate Ribbon Dessert

Wine suggestion: Chateau Esperanza Foch

Cocktail Party to Follow a Tour of the George Eastman House, Rochester, N.Y.

Cheese Stuffed Mushrooms
Scallop Blankets
Crab Melba
Pate Maison
Pineapple-Pecan Spread
Stuffed Grape Leaves

Wine suggestions:
Hot Appetizers — Dr. Frank's Gewurtztraminer
Cold Appetizers — Herman Weimer's Late Harvest
Riesling

Ladies Luncheon to Kick-off the L.P.G.A., Corning, New York

Crab and Avocado Elegant
Creamy Spinach Salad
Peach Macaroon Mousse

Wine suggestion: Gold Seal Dry Riesling

Brunch Before a Day at The Finger Lakes Race Track, Farmington, N.Y.

Oranges in Liqueur
Sausage Brunch Eggs
Cheddar Chipped Beef
Buttermilk Bran Muffins
Peach Rum Jam

Wine suggestion: Great Western Natural Champagne

SUMMER MENUS

Dinner on the Boat While Cruising the Erie Canal, Liverpool, N.Y.

Summer Meatloaf
Marinated Broccoli and Mushrooms
Copper Pennies Salad
Dilly Bread
Granola Dessert with Fresh Berries

Wine suggestion: Wagner's Riesling

Outdoor Barbecue at Harris Hill After a Visit to the National Soaring Museum, Elmira, N.Y.

Herb-Curry Dip with Fresh Vegetables
Oriental Shrimp
Grilled Leg of Lamb
Ratatouille
7 Layer Salad
Herb Pita Toast
Lemon Mousse

Wine suggestions:
Appetizers — Wickham Cayuga White
Lamb — McGregor's Pinot Noir

After Theatre Supper Following the Hill Cumorah Pageant, Palmyra, N.Y.

Fettuccine A La Carbonara
Mixed Greens with Light Italian Salad Dressing
Hot Herb Bread
Orange Galliano Pie

Wine suggestion: Heron Hill Aurora

Lawn Party at Quarry Farm to Kick-off the Mark Twain Festival, Elmira, N.Y.

Artichoke Quiche
Mushroom and Swiss Cheese Quiche
Salmon Quiche
Sweet and Sour Sausage
Rumakis
Beef Fillet with Horseradish Sauce
Red Raspberry Salad
Cold Cauliflower Salad with Mustard Sauce
French Bread
Brownie Confections
Sherry-Poppy Seed Cake
Fresh Fruit

Wine suggestions:
Quiches, Rumakis and Sausage — Otter Spring Riesling (Heron Hill)
Beef Fillet With Horseradish Sauce — Chateau Esperanza Cabernet
Sauvignon
Sherry-Poppy Seed Cake, Fresh Fruit — Dr. Frank's Muscat Ottonel

16

AUTUMN MENUS

Brunch Before a Tour of Seneca and Keuka Lake Wineries

Lemon Champagne Punch
Easiest Cheese Souffle
Scotch Eggs
Hot Fruit Compote
Apple Sour Cream Coffee Cake
Creme A La Creme with Almonds and Maple Syrup

Wine suggestion: Wagner's Chardonnay

Mexican Buffet After a Visit to the Corning Glass Center and Rockwell Museum, Corning, N.Y.

Chili Rellenos
Guacamole with Tortilla Chips
Monterey Cheese Enchiladas
Mexican Salad
Veracruz Tomatoes
Mexican Corn Bread
Flan

Beverage suggestion: Beer

Tailgate Picnic Before a Cornell Football Game, Ithaca, N.Y.

Marinated Mushroom Antipasto
Chinese Chicken Wings
Ham Loaf
New York Deli Potato Salad
French Bread
Graham Cracker Brownies
Apricot Bars

Wine suggestion: Johnson's Cascade Rose

Hunters' Dinner

Clam Stuffed Mushrooms
Egg Dip with Melba Rounds
Cream of Carrot and Tomato Soup
Canard au Nicaise
Wild Rice and Wine Casserole
Green Beans Parisienne
Cranberry Salad Mold
Grape Streusel Pie
Pear Crumble Pie

Wine suggestions:
Appetizers — Great Western Verdelet
Duck, Wild Rice, Salad and Beans — Glenora Ravat
Fruit Pies — Widmer's Niagara

WINTER MENUS

Apres Ski Party

Hot Buttered Rye and Ginger
Rolled Sausage Snacks
Spinach Boat
Hamburger Soup
Tomato Cheese Bisque
Beer Bread
Goodie Bread
New England Butter Crunch Loaf

Wine suggestion: Bully Hill Red or Hot Mulled wine, using a jug wine such as Chablis, Rhine or Burgundy

Children's Skating Party

Hot Chocolate
Bumsteads
Barbecued Beef Bundles
Potato Chips
Carrot Sticks
Bread and Butter Pickles
No Fuss Fruit Salad
Frosted Brownies
Lemon Squares

Beverage suggestion: Double martinis for the adults

New Year's Eve Formal Dinner

American Boursin Cheese with English Biscuits and Grapes
Artichoke Crab Ambrosia
Mushroom Bisque
Chicken Cordon Bleu
Creamy Garlic potatoes
Carrots and Water Chestnuts
Asparagus Vinaigrette
Frozen Egg Nog Mousse

Wine suggestions:
Appetizers — Rolling Vineyard Seyval
Chicken, Potatoes, Carrots and Asparagus — Glenora Chardonnay
Egg Nog Mousse — Serve at midnight with Gold Seal Blanc de Blanc Champagne

Super Bowl Party

Beer Sharp Cheese Spread with Sesame Sticks
Miniature Reuben Sandwiches
Shrimp Chutney Spread with Assorted Crackers
Boeuf Bourguigonne
Noodles
Korean Salad
Gruyere Bread
Caramel Surprise

Wine suggestion: Four Chimneys Cabernet

MARK TWAIN'S STUDY

Mark Twain's sister-in-law had a study, which was a replica of a Mississippi steamboat pilot house, built near their summer home in Elmira. In this study Mark Twain wrote most of *Tom Sawyer, Huckleberry Finn*, and many of his other works.

BEVERAGES AND APPETIZERS

Vegetables

Other

HOLIDAY PUNCH RECIPE

**COMPLIMENTS OF SENECA FALLS HISTORICAL SOCIETY,
SENECA FALLS, N.Y.**

Easy **3 Quarts**

1 cup granulated sugar
2 cups lemon juice
1 46 oz. can red
   fruit-flavored punch,
   chilled
1 28 oz. bottle club soda
   or ginger ale, chilled
Cherries and orange slices
   (optional)

In quart measure or medium bowl, stir sugar into lemon juice until dissolved. Place ice cubes in large punch bowl. Pour lemon juice-sugar mixture and fruit punch over ice. Slowly add club soda or ginger ale. Stir. If desired, garnish with cherries and orange slices, and enjoy.

PARTY PUNCH

Easy **14 Cups**

1 6 oz. can frozen orange
   juice concentrate,
   thawed
1 6 oz. can frozen
   lemonade concentrate,
   thawed
1 quart apple juice
2 quarts ginger ale
2 pints rainbow sherbet

In large punch bowl, combine concentrates and apple juice. Mix in ginger ale. Spoon in 1 pint sherbet. Keep adding more sherbet as it melts.

LEMON CHAMPAGNE PUNCH

Be careful — this one sneaks up on you!

Easy   **50 Punch Cups**

1 12 oz. can frozen
lemonade
1 46 oz. can unsweetened
pineapple juice
1 fifth Rhine wine
Ice Mold (pretty with whole
strawberries frozen in
ice)
2 fifths inexpensive
champagne
1 10 oz. pkg. frozen whole
strawberries

Mix lemonade, pineapple juice and Rhine wine in punch bowl. Add ice mold. Add champagne and strawberries just before serving.

JUMPING JULIUS

Easy   **2 Servings**

1 scoop orange sherbet
1 scoop vanilla ice cream
3 oz. half and half
3 oz. gin or vodka
4 oz. orange juice
4 oz. club soda

Mix in blender.

KAHLUA

                                                   2 Quarts

Easy   **Make Ahead**

3½ cups sugar
2 cups boiling water
1 2 oz. jar instant coffee
1 quart vodka
1 vanilla bean, cut up

Dissolve sugar in boiling water. Add coffee. Pour into ½ gallon bottle and add vodka and vanilla bean. Keep tightly closed for 30 days.

20

HOT BUTTERED RYE AND GINGER

Easy

20 oz. apple juice
5 oz. ginger brandy
7 oz. whiskey or bourbon
5 tsp. butter
5 dashes cinnamon
5 dashes nutmeg

Heat apple juice. Add brandy, whiskey and butter. Season with cinnamon and nutmeg. Serve hot. This is great for cold winter activities.

DILL BOAT

Easy

**1½ Cups
Make Ahead**

1 lb. loaf pumpernickel
  bread, unsliced
6 oz. cream cheese,
  softened
2 Tbsp. pimiento-stuffed
  green olives, finely
  chopped
2 tsp. onion, grated
½ tsp. dried dillweed
Dash salt
5 Tbsp. light cream

Hollow out loaf of bread and put pieces aside for dipping. Mix all ingredients, except bread. Chill several hours. When ready to serve, fill shell with dip.

DILL WEED DIP

Easy

**1 Cup
Make Ahead**

½ cup sour cream
½ cup mayonnaise
2 Tbsp. onion, grated *or* 1
  tsp. dried onion
1 Tbsp. dill weed
1 Tbsp. Accent

Mix well; chill several hours or overnight. Serve with fresh vegetables, crackers or in a hollowed out loaf of bread.

HELPFUL HINT
Every kitchen should have an aloe plant to treat burns.

HERB-CURRY DIP

Easy

2 Cups
Make Ahead

1 cup mayonnaise
½ cup sour cream
1 tsp. crushed mixed
  herbs
¼ tsp. salt
⅛ tsp. curry powder
1 Tbsp. parsley, snipped
1 Tbsp. onion, grated
1½ tsp. lemon juice
½ tsp. Worcestershire
  sauce
2 tsp. capers (optional)

Blend all ingredients and chill well. Serve with carrot and celery sticks and cauliflower florets.

VEGETABLE DIP

Easy

2½ Cups
Make Ahead

1 cup mayonnaise
1 cup sour cream
2 tsp. celery seed
1 pkg. dry garlic salad
  dressing mix (Good
  Seasons preferred)

Mix all ingredients; chill. Use with fresh vegetables such as carrot sticks, celery, cauliflower and green pepper.

BLEU CHEESE DIP

Delicious as dip or salad dressing!

Easy

3 Cups
Make Ahead

1 cup mayonnaise
1 cup sour cream
1 cup Bleu cheese,
  crumbled
Juice of 1 whole lemon

Mix all ingredients together and chill. Serve with fresh vegetables as dip or salad dressing.

23

MONTEREY JACK CHEESE DIP

Easy

2 Cups
Make Ahead

4-5 scallions, finely
  chopped
1 4 oz. can green chilies,
  drained and diced
½ cup pitted ripe olives,
  diced
1-2 tomatoes, peeled and
  chopped
8 oz. Monterey Jack
  cheese, shredded
½ cup Italian salad
  dressing
Tortilla chips

Mix all ingredients together, except tortilla chips. Refrigerate at least 2 hours. Serve with tortilla chips.

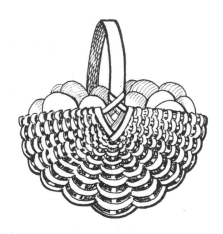

EGG DIP

Super light and smooth!

Average

2 Cups
Make Ahead

2 eggs, beaten
2 Tbsp. sugar
Dash of salt
1 Tbsp. butter
8 oz. cream cheese
Minced onion to taste
2 hard-boiled eggs,
  chopped

In double boiler, combine 2 raw eggs, sugar, salt and butter. Stir constantly over hot water until thick. Add cream cheese. Remove from stove. Add onion and hard-boiled eggs; mix well. Refrigerate. Bring to room temperature 1 hour before serving. Serve with melba rounds or firm crackers.

CLAM DIP

Easy

2½ to 3 Cups
Make Ahead

16 oz. cream cheese,
  softened
2 6 ½ oz. cans minced
  clams, drained
1 Tbsp. mayonnaise
¾ tsp. sugar
½ tsp. parsley, chopped
1 Tbsp. chives, snipped
½ tsp. Worcestershire
  sauce
½ tsp. prepared mustard
¼ tsp. curry powder
1 tsp. sweet pickle relish

Mix all ingredients together. Chill well. Serve with crackers.

PARTY FISH DIP

Easy

3 Cups
Make Ahead

2 cups sour cream
1 pkg. Good Season salad
  dressing (any kind)
1 7 oz. can tuna fish,
  drained

Mix all ingredients together and chill well before serving. Serve with potato chips, crackers or raw vegetables.

SHRIMP DIP

Easy

2 Cups
Make Ahead

1 6 oz. can tiny shrimp,
  drained
8 oz. cream cheese,
  softened
½ cup mayonnaise
Onion powder
½ onion, finely chopped
Seasoned salt (optional)

Combine all ingredients and chill several hours or overnight. Serve with assorted crackers.

GREEN CHILI DIP

Easy

2½ Cups
Make Ahead

8 oz. cream cheese,
   softened
½ cup mayonnaise
½ cup cottage cheese
2 tsp. dried chives
½ tsp. garlic salt
1 4 oz. can green chilies,
   drained and diced (2
   cans make a very hot
   dip)

Mix all ingredients together and re-frigerate. Serve with tortilla chips, corn chips or firm crackers.

GUACAMOLE

Average

1½ to 2 Cups
Make Ahead

2 large ripe avocados
2-3 Tbsp. lemon or lime
   juice (to prevent
   discoloration)
Salt to taste
½ tsp. ground coriander
   seed or 2 tsp. parsley,
   minced
2-4 green chilies, chopped
   or liquid hot pepper
1 clove garlic, minced
   and/or 2-3 tsp. minced
   onions, blended in
   mayonnaise to make
   smooth (optional)
1 Tbsp. pimiento, chopped
   (optional)

Cut avocados in half, remove seeds and scoop out pulp with a spoon. Mash pulp with a fork, while blending in lemon or lime juice. Add salt and parsley or co-riander. Add chilies or hot pepper. Add optional ingredients, if desired. Serve this mixture as a dip with tortilla tri-angles, a salad, or serve with chips.

SPINACH BOAT

A sure hit for a cocktail party!

Easy

**3 Cups
Make Ahead**

1 10 oz. pkg. frozen
chopped spinach,
thawed and *drained*
½ cup scallions, finely
sliced
½ cup fresh parsley,
minced
2 cups mayonnaise
1 tsp. salt
½ tsp. pepper
1 loaf unsliced
pumpernickel or rye
bread

Combine all ingredients, except bread.
Hollow out bread, reserving bread
cubes for dipping. Place spinach mixture into bread boat. Serve with bread
cubes and raw vegetables. May be
made ahead, covered, and refrigerated
before being put into bread boat.

SPINACH DIP

Easy

**3½ Cups
Make Ahead**

1 10 oz. pkg. frozen
chopped spinach
1 pkg. vegetable soup mix
(Knorr's preferred)
1 cup sour cream
1 cup mayonnaise (or less,
if desired)
1 6 oz. can water
chestnuts, drained and
chopped
Dash of garlic salt

Thaw and drain spinach. Mix all ingredients and chill overnight. Serve with
crackers, vegetables or pretzels.

SPRING GARDEN DIP

Easy

2½ Cups
Make Ahead

1 cup sour cream
½ cup mayonnaise
1 Tbsp. sugar
1 tsp. salt
Dash of pepper
¼ cup *each* green onions,
   radishes, cucumbers,
   green peppers, all
   minced
1 clove garlic, minced

Blend first 5 ingredients. Stir in minced vegetables. Serve in bowl with carrot sticks, celery, cauliflower florets, cherry tomatoes and cucumbers.

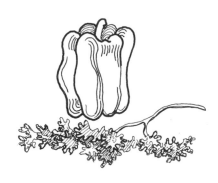

CHILI CON QUESO DIP

Easy

3 Cups
Make Ahead

2 lbs. Velveeta or
   Monterey Jack cheese,
   cubed
1 4 oz. can chili peppers,
   or 2 hot peppers, diced
1 tomato, diced
¼ cup onion, diced
1 Tbsp. Worcestershire
   sauce
⅛ tsp. garlic powder
¼ tsp. oregano
Dash of hot pepper

Combine all ingredients and simmer for 1-2 hours in double boiler. Serve with taco or corn chips.

HOT CHILI DIP

Easy

4 Cups
Make Ahead

1 lb. ground beef
1 green pepper, chopped
1 envelope (1¾ oz.) chili
  mix
1 6 oz. can tomato paste
3 oz. cream cheese
1 cup water
King-size corn chips

Cook beef and green pepper in skillet, stirring to crumble, until beef browns; drain off excess fat. Stir in chili mix, tomato paste, cream cheese and water. Cook over medium heat, stirring occasionally, until mixture comes to a boil. Serve with king-size corn chips.

HOT CLAM DIP

Easy

2 Cups
Make Ahead

11 oz. cream cheese,
  softened
⅛ tsp. garlic powder
1 tsp. Worcestershire
  sauce
3 Tbsp. mayonnaise
Dash of tabasco sauce
1 7 oz. can minced claims,
  drained

Whip all ingredients together with an electric mixer. Place in a ½ quart baking dish and bake at 350° for 15 minutes. Serve with chips or crackers.

HOT ARTICHOKE DIP

Easy

5½ Cups
Make Ahead
Freeze

8 oz. cream cheese,
  softened
1 8 oz. can artichoke
  hearts, drained
1¾ cups Parmesan
  cheese, grated
2 cups mayonnaise

Mash artichokes with fork and combine with other ingredients. Put in ovenproof dish. Bake at 350° for 20 minutes or until heated through. Serve with chips or crackers.

MEXICALI DIP

Easy

3 Cups
Make Ahead

1 4 oz. can green chilies,
   drained and chopped
1 8½ oz. can artichoke
   hearts packed in water,
   drained and slightly
   mashed
1¼ cups Parmesan
   cheese
1 cup mayonnaise
Tortilla or nacho chips

Combine chilies, artichoke hearts, cheese and mayonnaise. Transfer to an 8 inch pie plate. Bake at 350° for 20 minutes. Serve with chips.

BEER SHARP CHEESE SPREAD

Easy

2 Cups
Make Ahead

8 oz. cream cheese,
   softened
¾ cup beer
8 oz. sharp Cheddar
   cheese, softened
   (Cracker Barrel
   preferred)
1 clove garlic

Blend cream cheese in blender on high 20 seconds. Add beer, Cheddar cheese and garlic. Cover and blend 20 seconds more or until smooth. Chill. Serve with sesame seed crackers.

BLEU CHEESE SPREAD

Easy

1½ Cups
Make Ahead

¾ cup sour cream
6 oz. Bleu cheese
1 Tbsp. mayonnaise
Salt, pepper and garlic salt
   to taste
½ cup pecans, chopped

Mix all ingredients well. Refrigerate several hours. Serve with crackers.

CREAM CHEESE AND MARMALADE

2 Cups
Make Ahead

Easy

8 oz. cream cheese,
  softened
1½ Tbsp. mayonnaise
1½ tsp. Worcestershire
  sauce
½ cup pecans, chopped
1 Tbsp. dried parsley
½-1 cup apricot or orange
  marmalade

Mix all ingredients, except marmalade. Shape as desired; refrigerate. When ready to serve, spread marmalade on top.

PINEAPPLE-PECAN SPREAD

Especially attractive for summer entertaining!

4 Cups
Make Ahead

Easy

2 8 oz. pkgs. cream
  cheese, softened
1 8½ oz. can crushed
  pineapple, drained
2 cups pecans, chopped
Dash garlic
Dash chives
Dash salt
½ fresh pineapple

Combine all ingredients and serve in a fresh pineapple. Best when made ahead and allowed to marinate in fresh pineapple overnight. Serve with crackers.

SNOW CAP SPREAD

8-10 Servings
Make Ahead

Easy

2 4½ oz. cans deviled
  ham
1 Tbsp. onion, minced

Frost Mound with:
8 oz. cream cheese
¼ cup sour cream
2½ tsp. prepared sharp
  mustard

Mix together and mound on serving plate.

Mix together and frost mound. Serve with crackers.

CRAB MEAT SPREAD

Easy

1½ Cups
Make Ahead

1 6 oz. can crab meat,
    picked over well
¼ cup mayonnaise
1 tsp. lemon juice
½ Tbsp. parsley, chopped
½-1 Tbsp. chives, chopped
1 tsp. Worcestershire
    sauce
Ground black pepper to
    taste
Tabasco sauce to taste

Combine all ingredients and serve with crackers or toast rounds. Best served at room temperature.

CREAM CHEESE AND CRAB MEAT

Easy

2 Cups
Make Ahead

1 7 oz. can crab meat
¾ cup catsup
2 Tbsp. horseradish
8 oz. cream cheese

Combine crab meat, catsup and horseradish and let chill. Put cream cheese on dish and spread mixture on top. Serve on rye crackers.

SHRIMP SPREAD

Both lovely and delicious!

2 Cups
Make Ahead

Easy

1 jar frozen shrimp
    cocktail, (Sau-Sea
    preferred)
1 6¼ oz. can tiny shrimp,
    drained
1 Tbsp. horseradish
8 oz. cream cheese

Thaw frozen shrimp cocktail. Cut shrimp from the frozen cocktail and can into bite-size pieces. Combine frozen cocktail sauce, shrimp and horseradish together. Spread over bar of cream cheese. Serve with crackers.

SHRIMP CHUTNEY SPREAD

A sensational spread you'll use often!

4 Cups
Make Ahead

Easy

16 oz. cream cheese,
   softened
½ cup sour cream
1 lb. shrimp, cut into small
   pieces
½ tsp. curry powder
1 cup chutney
Garlic powder to taste
Salt to taste
Parsley for garnish

Combine all ingredients; garnish with parsley. Use as spread on crackers.

RADISH AND CREAM CHEESE SPREAD

1½ Cups
Make Ahead

Easy

8 oz. cream cheese
4 Tbsp. butter, softened
½ tsp. celery salt
Dash paprika
½ tsp. Worcestershire
   sauce
¼ cup green onions, finely
   chopped
1 cup radishes, finely
   chopped

Mix cheese, butter, celery salt, paprika and Worcestershire sauce together until smooth. Stir in radishes and onions. Chill several hours or overnight to blend flavors. Spread on crackers or serve with vegetables.

CHEESE SPREAD

Easy

4 Cups
Make Ahead
Freeze

1 lb. margarine, softened
  and whipped
½ lb. sharp Cheddar
  cheese, grated
¼ lb. Romano cheese,
  grated
1 tsp. Worcestershire
  sauce
¼ tsp. garlic powder
½ tsp. paprika
English muffins or French
  bread

Whip all ingredients, except bread, with mixer until fluffy. Spread on English muffins or French bread and broil.

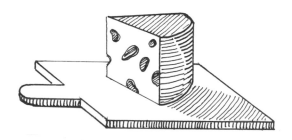

CHIPPED BEEF SPREAD

Easy

2 Cups
Make Ahead

8 oz. cream cheese
2 Tbsp. milk
4 oz. dried beef, rinsed
  and shredded
½ tsp. garlic powder
¼ tsp. pepper
½ cup sour cream
2 Tbsp. onion, finely
  chopped
¼ cup green pepper,
  finely chopped
2 Tbsp. butter, melted
½ cup pecans, chopped

Soften cream cheese and blend all ingredients, except butter and pecans. Place in casserole dish. Mix butter and pecans and put on top of cream cheese mixture. Bake at 350° for 20 minutes. Serve with party rye or firm crackers.

34

SUPER CONCOCTION ON PARTY RYE

Easy

2 Party Rye Loaves
Make Ahead
Freeze

1 lb. lean uncooked
  bacon, cut up into *tiny*
  pieces
½ cup green pepper,
  finely chopped
⅔ cup onion, finely diced
1 egg, beaten
2 garlic cloves, mashed
⅓ cup Worcestershire
  sauce
¾ cup sharp cheese,
  grated
Dash of pepper
2 loaves party rye

Combine all ingredients, except party rye, and put into blender or food processor until it is difficult to define ingredients. Spread on party rye. Bake at 350° for 12-15 minutes. To freeze, put uncooked pieces onto cookie sheet until frozen and then store in plastic bags.

CLAM PARMESAN SPREAD

Deliciously different!

6-8 Servings
Make Ahead

Easy

6 strips bacon
1 small clove garlic, thinly
  sliced
2 7 oz. cans minced
  clams, drained
1 tsp. dry basil
4 tsp. cornstarch
½ to ¾ cup tomato puree
½ tsp. salt
½ tsp. pepper
4 tsp. parsley flakes
2 4 oz. cans mushroom
  pieces, drained
4 Tbsp. Parmesan cheese,
  grated

Cut bacon into ½ inch strips, saute over low heat in skillet with garlic until lightly browned and slightly crisp. Drain off excess drippings, but reserve **3 Tbsp. drippings.** Add remaining ingredients including reserved drippings, except Parmesan cheese. Cook mixture until thickened and bubbly; add Parmesan cheese. This is very thick. Serve on crackers or rye bread.

HOT CRAB COCKTAIL SPREAD

Easy

4-8 Servings
Make Ahead
Freeze

8 oz. cream cheese, softened
1 Tbsp. milk
2 tsp. Worcestershire sauce
1 7½ oz. can crab meat
2 Tbsp. green onion, chopped
2 Tbsp. slivered almonds, toasted

Combine cream cheese, milk and Worcestershire sauce. Drain and flake crab meat; add to mixture along with onion. Turn into greased pie plate and top with almonds. Bake at 350° for 15 minutes or until heated through. Serve with assorted crackers.

BLEU CHEESE BALL

Easy

2 Cheese Balls
Make Ahead
Freeze

2 lbs. cream cheese, softened
1 9 oz. wedge Danish Bleu cheese
1 medium onion, finely chopped
1 cup pecans, chopped

Mix cheeses with onion and shape into 2 large or 4 small balls. Roll in nuts and store in refrigerator.

PARTY CHEESE BALL

Easy

1 Ball
Make Ahead
Freeze

16 oz. cream cheese,
  softened
2 cups sharp Cheddar
  cheese, shredded
1 Tbsp. pimiento, chopped
1 Tbsp. onion, chopped
1 Tbsp. green pepper,
  chopped
2 tsp. Worcestershire
  sauce
1 tsp. lemon juice
Pecans, finely chopped

Combine cream cheese and Cheddar cheese mixing until well blended. Add remaining ingredients; mix well. Chill. Shape into a ball; roll in pecans. Serve with assortment of crackers. May make into 2 or 3 smaller balls.

PINEAPPLE CHEESE BALL

Always complimented!

Easy

1 Ball
Make Ahead
Freeze

2 cups pecans, chopped
16 oz. cream cheese
1 8½ oz. can crushed
  pineapple, drained
1 Tbsp. seasoned salt
3 Tbsp. green pepper,
  finely chopped
2 Tbsp. onion, finely
  chopped

Blend all ingredients, except 1 cup pecans, with fork or spoon. Do not use blender or mixer. Shape into ball and roll in 1 cup pecans. Chill 2-4 hours. Serve with crackers.

AMERICAN BOURSIN CHEESE

Fools even the most discerning palate!

Easy

**1½ Cups
Make Ahead**

4 Tbsp. butter, softened
  (not margarine)
Approximately ⅓ cup
  Green Goddess salad
  dressing
8 oz. cream cheese,
  softened
1 clove garlic, finely
  minced
2-4 Tbsp. parsley,
  chopped

Mix all ingredients and chill for 3 hours. Serve with crackers.

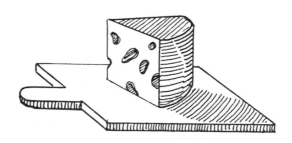

HOT PEPPER CHEESE

This will add some spice to your life!

Easy

**3 Pounds
Make Ahead
Freeze**

2 lbs. New York State
  sharp Cheddar cheese,
  grated
1 12 oz. jar hot cherry
  peppers in oil (Progresso
  preferred)
1 four inch diameter sweet
  onion, grated
Mayonnaise

Bring cheese to room temperature. Drain oil from peppers into cheese. Wearing rubber gloves, finely chop peppers; add to cheese mixture. Add onion. Add enough mayonnaise to make cheese spreadable. Store in plastic containers. Serve with crackers or French bread.

BLEU CHEESE MOUSSE

Average

1 Quart Mold
Make Ahead

6 eggs, separated
6 Tbsp. heavy cream
1½ Tbsp. unflavored
   gelatin
4 Tbsp. cold water
¾ lb. Bleu cheese
1½ cups heavy cream

Beat 6 egg yolks with cream in saucepan, over low heat, until creamy. Soften gelatin in cold water. Dissolve gelatin over hot water. Add to eggs. Force Bleu cheese through sieve into gelatin mixture. Whip heavy cream. Beat 3 egg whites until stiff; reserve remaining egg whites for another use. Fold whipped cream and beaten egg whites into gelatin mixture. Pour mixture into an oiled 1 quart mold. Refrigerate until set. Serve with crackers.

STUFFED GOUDA

Especially good garnished with whole almonds!

Average

8 Servings
Make Ahead

8 oz. Gouda cheese, at
   room temperature
½ cup sour cream
1½ tsp. dry Italian salad
   dressing mix
1 Tbsp. white wine

Cut circle from top of Gouda and reserve any cut off cheese. Hollow out rest of cheese leaving a rind of about ¼ inch on all sides. Combine cheese, sour cream, dry salad dressing mix and wine. Beat until smooth and spoon mixture back into shell. Cover and chill. Serve with crackers.

CHEESE BITES

Easy

4 Dozen
Make Ahead
Freeze

1 cup Cheddar cheese,
   shredded and at room
   temperature
½ cup butter, softened
½ tsp. tabasco sauce
1 cup flour
⅛ tsp. salt
1 cup Rice Krispies

Mix all ingredients well, adding cereal last. Pinch off marble-size pieces and place on greased baking sheet. Bake at 350° for 10-15 minutes. Store in airtight container. To restore to oven-baked freshness, heat in a moderate oven for a few minutes before serving.

CHEESE MUFFIN WEDGES

Easy

**3 Dozen
Make Ahead**

2 cups Cheddar cheese,
   shredded
3 green onions, chopped
1 6 oz. can pitted black
   olives, drained and
   chopped
½ tsp. curry powder
4 English muffins

Combine cheese, green onion, olives and curry powder; mix well. Separate muffins and spread with mixture. Bake at 350° for 10 minutes, then broil until bubbly. Cut into bite-size wedges.

HOT CHEESE HORS D'OEUVRES

Compliments guaranteed!

Easy

**2 Dozen
Make Ahead**

1 cup sharp cheese
5 slices bacon
1 medium onion
1 small clove garlic
2 Tbsp. mayonnaise
1 Tbsp. prepared mustard
24 slices party rye bread

Grind cheese, bacon, onion, and garlic together. Combine with mayonnaise and mustard until well mixed. Spread generously on bread. Place on cookie sheet and broil 6-7 minutes, 5 inches from heat.

PUFFED CHEESIES

Average

1½ cups Swiss cheese, grated
½ cup Parmesan cheese, grated
½ cup butter, softened
¾ cup flour
¾ tsp. salt
⅛ tsp. cayenne pepper
⅛ tsp. nutmeg
1 egg
1 tsp. water
½ cup Swiss cheese, grated

Combine first seven ingredients. Form into ball and chill at least 15 minutes. Break off tablespoonfuls and form each into ball, then flatten into circle about ¼ inch thick. Arrange on baking sheet, leaving space between. Brush tops with egg mixed with water. Sprinkle with ½ cup grated Swiss cheese. Bake at 425° for 10 minutes or until puffed and lightly browned.

 # SWISS PARTY PUFFS

Easy

2½ Dozen
Make Ahead

½ cup mayonnaise
¼ cup onion, chopped
2 Tbsp. parsley, snipped
30 party rye slices, toasted
Swiss cheese

Combine mayonnaise, onion and parsley. Spread onto 30 party rye slices. Top each with ¼ slice Swiss cheese. Broil 2-3 minutes. May refrigerate and broil when ready to serve.

CHILI RELLENOS

Muy Bueno!

Easy

2 4 oz. cans green chilies,
   drained
1½ cups sharp Cheddar
   cheese, grated
3 cups Monterey Jack
   cheese, shredded
2 eggs
2 Tbsp. milk
1 Tbsp. flour

Cut chilies into thin strips or use chopped chilies. In a lightly greased 9 inch square pan, make layers of cheese, chilies, cheese, chilies, cheese. Beat eggs, flour and milk together. Pour over layered ingredients. Bake at 375° for 50-60 minutes or until firm. Cool; cut into squares and reheat when ready to serve. Can be made ahead and frozen and then heated in microwave or oven when ready to serve.

MINIATURE QUICHE

Small in size, but grand in taste!

Easy

1½ Dozen
Make Ahead
Freeze

1 8 oz. pkg. butterflake
   rolls
Small pieces of shrimp,
   bacon, boiled ham or
   mushrooms
1 egg, beaten
½ tsp. salt
Dash of pepper
½ cup light cream
1 tsp. brandy or sherry
1 cup Swiss cheese,
   grated

Grease small muffin tins. Separate rolls into "petals" and press one into each muffin cup. On dough in pans, place small pieces of cut up shrimp, crumbled crisp bacon, small pieces boiled ham or chopped mushrooms. Combine egg, salt, cream and brandy. Add about 1 Tbsp. liquid to each quiche, filling half way. Top with grated or cut up Swiss cheese. Bake at 375° for 20 minutes. When cooled, they may be wrapped in foil and frozen. To reheat, bake, wrapped in foil, at 375° for about 12-15 minutes.

LIVER PATE

Easy

8 oz. cream cheese,
  softened
8 oz. liver sausage
1 generous Tbsp. onion,
  chopped
1 tsp. lemon juice
1 tsp. Worcestershire
  sauce
Dash of salt and pepper

Combine cream cheese and liver sausage, mixing until well blended. Add remaining ingredients and mix well. Chill until ready to serve. Serve with assorted crackers and mustard sauce, if desired.

PATE MAISON

Just serve, sit back and wait for the raves!

Average

1 medium onion
1 clove garlic
½ cup butter
8 oz. chicken livers
1 bouquet garni (parsley,
  chervil, bay leaves,
  marjoram, and thyme)
Salt and pepper
1½ Tbsp. brandy
Butter, clarified

Finely chop onion and garlic, and cook in 2 Tbsp. butter until just turning color. Add livers, herbs and seasoning and fry together for 3-5 minutes. Cool, then chop very finely or process in blender until smooth. Cream remaining butter; add liver mixture to butter and mix well. Add brandy. Turn mixture into 1 large china bowl or individual pots. Smooth top and cover with layer of clarified butter. Refrigerate. Best when made day before. Serve with fresh melba toast or crackers.

BAKED ITALIAN MEATBALLS

Average

4½ Dozen
Make Ahead
Freeze

1 lb. ground chuck
½ lb. bulk hot sausage
½ cup fine bread crumbs
1 egg, beaten
½ tsp. onion powder
¼ tsp. garlic powder
1 tsp. parsley flakes
1 16 oz. jar spaghetti
    sauce

Mix all ingredients, except spaghetti sauce, and form into walnut-size meatballs. Bake, on a rack over a tray with edges, at 350° for 25-30 minutes. (Saves the mess of frying and also gets rid of excess fat.) Pour fat off tray and scrape meat drippings into warmed spaghetti sauce. Stir thoroughly and add meatballs. Serve in chafing dish or warmer. This recipe may also be used as a main course.

GLAZED MEATBALLS

Easy

20 Servings
Make Ahead
Freeze

MEATBALLS:
1 lb. ground chuck
1 tsp. garlic salt
Salt and pepper to taste

Mix together and shape into 1 inch balls. Drop into boiling glaze.

GLAZE:
1 14 oz. bottle catsup
1 10 oz. jar grape jelly
2 Tbsp. brown sugar
1 onion, diced
2 Tbsp. vinegar or sherry

Mix and cook to boiling point. Add meatballs and simmer until glaze is very thick (2-3 hours). Serve while hot.

HELPFUL HINT

For a less greasy cocktail meatball, that holds its shape, bake on rack, over a tray, at 350° for 25 to 30 minutes, instead of frying.

44

SWEET AND SOUR MEATBALLS

Average

4 Dozen
Make Ahead

1½ lbs. ground chuck
½ cup bread crumbs
1 tsp. salt
¼ tsp. pepper
1 egg, slightly beaten
½ cup milk
¼ cup shortening

Combine all ingredients, except shortening, and make into small meatballs. Melt shortening in oblong baking dish in 350° oven. Bake meatballs for 30 minutes. Drain. Leave meatballs in dish:

SAUCE:
2 cups tomato juice
2 Tbsp. flour
¾ cup barbecue sauce
¼ cup water
1 16 oz. can pineapple chunks, drained

Mix tomato juice. flour, barbecue sauce and water. Add to drained meatballs and bake 45 minutes longer. Add pineapple and heat through in warm oven. Sausage or cocktail hot dogs may be added to the sauce with meatballs. May also be used as a buffet dish.

MINIATURE REUBEN SANDWICHES

Perfect for a Super Bowl party!

Easy

1½ Dozen

1 loaf party rye or
  pumpernickel bread
¼ lb. corned beef, sliced
4 oz. can sauerkraut,
  drained
3 slices Swiss cheese, cut
  into 1x2 inch rectangles
2 Tbsp. butter or
  margarine

Top half of bread slices with sliced corned beef; top each with some of the sauerkraut and a rectangle of cheese. Cover with remaining bread slices. In skillet over moderate heat melt 2 Tbsp. butter. Add sandwiches a few at a time and grill about 2 minutes on each side until lightly browned and cheese is melted. Add additional butter as needed. Serve hot.

REUBEN APPETIZERS

Average

3 oz. cream cheese,
    softened
1 tsp. instant minced onion
1 16 oz. can sauerkraut,
    well drained and
    chopped
1 12 oz. can corned beef
1 cup bread crumbs
½ cup flour
½ cup evaporated milk
Salad oil
1 tsp. salt

Combine cream cheese and onion. Add sauerkraut, corned beef and ¼ cup bread crumbs; mix well. Shape into 1 inch balls. Roll in flour; dip into milk, then in remaining ¾ cup bread crumbs. Heat salad oil to 375°. Add salt. With appetizers at room temperature, fry 1-2 minutes. These are great for fondue parties.

FOIE DE POULET
(CHICKEN LIVERS FLAMED IN BRANDY)

Average

4 Servings

2 Tbsp. butter
½ yellow onion, finely
    chopped
1 carrot, finely chopped
1 lb. chicken livers
3 slices boiled ham, diced
3 mushrooms, thinly sliced
    or 1 3 oz. can
    mushrooms, drained
2 Tbsp. brandy
2 Tbsp. flour
½ cup white wine
½ cup beef broth
1 cup seedless green
    grapes
Parsley

Heat butter in large skillet. Saute onion for 3 minutes, then add carrot and continue cooking for 2 minutes. Add livers and stir over high heat until almost tender. Add ham and mushrooms and cook 2 minutes. Add brandy and light it with a match immediately. When flames have died down, stir in flour and add wine and broth gradually, to form a medium-thick sauce. Add grapes and cook just until the grapes have heated through. Garnish with parsley.

MARINATED CHICKEN LIVERS

Average

½ tsp. Accent
½ tsp. salt
⅛ tsp. pepper
1 Tbsp. onion, minced
1 tsp. oregano
1 Tbsp. parsley
2 Tbsp. oil
2 Tbsp. white wine or
  sherry
1 pint chicken livers
Flour
Butter

Mix all ingredients, except flour and butter. Marinate at least ½ hour. Dip chicken livers into flour and fry in butter 2-3 minutes or until browned.

RUMAKIS

Average

**1½ Dozen
Make Ahead**

BASIC RECIPE:
6 chicken livers
18 whole water chestnuts
9 slices bacon, cut in half
1 Tbsp. soy sauce
1 Tbsp. sherry

Cut chicken livers into three pieces. Fold each piece over a water chestnut and then wrap with a bacon strip, securing with toothpick. Combine soy sauce and sherry (using equal amounts of each, depending on quantity needed) and marinate rumakis for 1 hour or longer (even overnight). Grill or broil until bacon is crisp. May partially cook ahead, then refrigerate and finish cooking, before serving.

When using marinade variations, double basic recipe, eliminating soy sauce and sherry in basic recipe.

MARINADE VARIATION #1:
½ cup soy sauce
¼ tsp. ginger
¼ tsp. curry powder

Combine ingredients and continue as above. If desired, a sauce of catsup and horseradish may be made for dipping.

MARINADE VARIATION #2:
¼ cup vegetable oil
¼ cup soy sauce
2 Tbsp. catsup
1 tsp. vinegar
¼ tsp. pepper
2 Tbsp. Worcestershire
   sauce
Dash of garlic powder

Combine ingredients and continue as above.

48

CHINESE CHICKEN WINGS

Easily multiplied for a large party!

Easy

**2½ Dozen
Make Ahead
Freeze**

3 lbs. chicken wings, with
   tips cut off
Salt and pepper
2 Tbsp. oil
1 cup honey
½ cup soy sauce
1 clove garlic, mashed
2 Tbsp. catsup

Preheat oven to 375°. Cut chicken wings into 2 parts. Place in 9x12 inch shallow baking pan. Sprinkle with salt, pepper and oil. Combine honey, soy sauce, garlic and catsup; pour over wings. Baked at 375° for 50 minutes. These may be frozen or refrigerated. They may be wrapped in foil and reheated on top of grill for 10 minutes.

BACON-CHEESE PUFFS

Complicated

**2½ Dozen
Make Ahead
Freeze**

1 4 oz. container whipped
   cream cheese
1 egg
1 tsp. lemon juice
1 tsp. chives, chopped
Dash of pepper
½ cup sharp white natural
   Cheddar cheese,
   shredded
4 slices bacon, crisply
   fried and crumbled
4 frozen patty shells,
   thawed (Pepperidge
   Farm preferred)
Milk

Combine cream cheese, egg, lemon juice, chives and pepper. Beat well. Stir in cheese and bacon. Chill. Roll one patty shell into 8x4 inch rectangle. Cut into 2 inch squares. Top each square with filling. Brush edges with milk. Fold into triangle. Place on baking sheet. Repeat with remaining shells and filling. Chill until baking time. Preheat oven to 450°, reduce to 400°, and bake for 12-15 minutes. Any leftover cheese mixture is great broiled on top of toast points or crackers.

49

BACON DUMPLINGS

Average

1 to 1½ Dozen
Make Ahead

½ cup bacon, finely diced
2 cups ½ inch bread
   cubes, made from day
   old bread
2 Tbsp. onion, finely
   chopped
2 Tbsp. mushrooms, finely
   chopped (optional)
¼ cup milk
2 Tbsp. parsley, chopped
½ cup flour
Salt to taste
1 10½ oz. can beef broth

Brown bacon and save fat. Put 4 Tbsp. fat back into skillet and reheat until a light haze forms. Add bread cubes. Brown on all sides and remove. Add 2 more Tbsp. bacon fat, heat and add onion and mushrooms. Cook for 8-10 minutes. Add to bread cubes in bowl. Add milk and parsley and stir in flour. Let mixture stand for 10 minutes. Gently mix in bacon and salt to taste. Dampen hands and form into 1½ inch balls. Bring beef broth to a boil in a small to medium-size pan. Drop dumplings into it. Reduce heat to medium and cook, uncovered, for 12-14 minutes, or until firm to the touch. If made ahead, these may be gently reheated with melted butter poured over so as not to dry out.

BACON ROLL-UPS

Easy

2 Dozen
Make Ahead
Freeze

1 8 oz. pkg. crescent
   refrigerator rolls
½ cup sour cream
Onion salt
½ lb. bacon, cooked and
   crumbled

Unroll rolls, spread with sour cream. Sprinkle with onion salt and bacon. Cut each roll lengthwise into 3 equal wedges; roll up each, starting at point of wedge. Bake at 375° for 12-15 minutes.

FRISKY WHISKEY DOGS

Surprisingly great!

Easy

8-10 Servings
Make Ahead
Freeze

1 lb. hot dogs or 1-2 pkgs.
small cocktail hot dogs
¾ cup, or more, bourbon
or rye
½ cup catsup
½ cup brown sugar
1 Tbsp. onion, grated

Cut hot dogs into bite-size pieces. Put in frying pan with all the ingredients. Simmer for 1 hour; if liquid dries too much, add more whiskey. Serve hot with toothpicks.

ROLLED SAUSAGE SNACKS

Easy

2½ Dozen
Make Ahead

1 8 oz. can refrigerated
crescent rolls
2 Tbsp. butter or
margarine, melted
¼ cup Parmesan cheese,
grated
1 tsp. oregano
8 brown n' serve sausages
(Swift's Original Recipe
preferred)

Separate crescent dough into 4 rectangles. Press perforations to seal. Brush each with butter. Combine cheese and oregano and sprinkle over dough. Cut each rectangle crosswise to form 2 squares. Place a sausage link on each square and roll up. Cut each roll into 4 pieces and secure with a wooden toothpick. Place cut-side down on an ungreased broiler tray. Refrigerate until ready to serve. Bake at 375° for 12-15 minutes or until golden brown. Serve hot.

SAUSAGE BALLS

Easy

3 Dozen
Make Ahead
Freeze

1 lb. ground hot sausage
2 cups biscuit mix
2 cups sharp Cheddar
cheese, grated
Garlic powder (optional)

Add water as necessary to mix all ingredients well. Roll in 1 inch balls. Sprinkle with garlic powder, if desired. Bake at 350° for 15-20 minutes. These can be cooked on a broiler pan so fat can drain off. Be sure and watch — don't let them burn on the bottom!

SAUSAGE ROLLS

Average

1-2 Dozen
Make Ahead

1 lb. ground pork sausage
1 lb. flaky pastry or 1 pkg.
  Pepperidge Farm flaky
  pastry or 1 8 oz. pkg.
  crescent rolls
1 egg, beaten
1 Tbsp. flour

Flour sausage and roll into 2 rolls about 14 inches long. Roll out pastry to 14 inches long, and wide enough to roll around both sausage pieces. Divide pastry in half lengthwise. Brush edges with egg, put sausage roll on each strip. Roll up and press securely to seal. Cut each roll into 6 pieces, or more, if smaller cocktail-size required. Make slit across top, brush with egg and place on ungreased baking sheet. Bake at 400° for 20 minutes.

SHRIMP PUFFS

Average

4 Dozen
Make Ahead
Freeze Puffs

PUFF SHELLS:
1 cup water
½ cup butter or margarine
1 cup flour
4 eggs

Heat oven to 400°. Heat water and butter to a rolling boll in saucepan. Reduce heat to low; stir in flour vigorously until mixture forms a ball. Remove from heat. Beat in eggs thoroughly, one at a time. Beat until smooth. Drop by teaspoon onto ungreased baking sheet into mounds 3 inches apart. Bake for 45 minutes or until golden brown and dry. Cool, cut off tops and fill with shrimp salad.

SHRIMP SALAD:
1 cup shrimp, chopped
1 cup celery, diced
1 tsp. lemon juice
1 tsp. onion, minced
Salt and pepper to taste
Dash white wine
Mayonnaise
Paprika for garnish
  (optional)

Mix all ingredients with mayonnaise to moisten. Stuff shells.

TUNA-CHEESE LOG

Average

3x5 Inch Log
Make Ahead

6 oz. cream cheese,
  softened
1 oz. Bleu cheese,
  crumbled
2 Tbsp. celery, finely
  chopped
1 Tbsp. onion, finely
  chopped
1 Tbsp. mayonnaise
Few drops tabasco sauce
1 6½ oz. can tuna, drained
  and flaked
½ cup pecans or walnuts,
  chopped

In small mixer bowl, beat together cream cheese and Bleu cheese. Stir in celery, onion, mayonnaise, tabasco sauce and tuna. Shape mixture into log. Chill several hours or overnight. Before serving, roll in chopped nuts. Serve with crackers.

TUNA PATE

Easy

6 Servings
Make Ahead

1 10 oz. can tomato soup
8 oz. cream cheese
2 envelopes unflavored
  gelatin
2 6½ oz. cans tuna (or
  equivalent amount of
  other cooked fish)
½ cup celery, diced
1 medium onion, grated
Dash tabasco sauce

Heat soup; add cream cheese and stir until melted. Put into blender, stir in gelatin and blend until dissolved. Blend in other ingredients and pour into 6 cup mold. Refrigerate until set. Serve with crackers or pretzels. Can also be served as a salad.

CRAB MEAT-BACON ROLLS

A lovely, unusual combination of tastes!

Average

10 Servings
Make Ahead

2 Tbsp. onion, minced
1 egg, beaten
⅔ cup soft bread crumbs
2 6½ oz. cans flaked crab meat, undrained
½ cup celery, minced
2 Tbsp. tomato juice
2 Tbsp. parsley, chopped
½ tsp. salt
½ cup water
1 tsp. Worcestershire sauce
1 lb. bacon, cut into 2 inch lengths

Combine and mix all ingredients, except bacon, and form into small finger-length rolls. Divide rolls into 1 inch sections. Wrap bacon pieces around the crab meat sections and secure with a toothpick. Place on baking tray and broil for about 6 minutes or until bacon is crisp. Turn rolls after 3 minutes so that every part of the bacon is cooked.

CRAB MEAT TIDBITS

Average

2-4 Dozen
Make Ahead
Freeze

1 lb. Velveeta cheese
1 cup butter
2 6½ oz. cans crab meat, drained
1 Tbsp. Worcestershire sauce
1 Tbsp. onion, grated
2 pkgs. English muffins, split into halves

Let cheese and butter stand at room temperature and then mix with hand beater. Add crab meat, Worcestershire sauce and onion. Spread evenly on English muffins; broil. These may be made ahead and frozen, then defrosted and broiled. Recipe is easily halved or doubled. The muffins may also be cut into quarters.

CRAB TRIANGLES

Average

3 Dozen
Make Ahead
Freeze

1 5 oz. jar Old English
    sharp cheese spread
1 Tbsp. Worcestershire
    sauce
1 Tbsp. butter, melted
½ tsp. onion powder
Dash of garlic powder
Dash of paprika
1 6 oz. can King crab meat
    or 6 oz. fresh or frozen
    crab meat
1 egg yolk, slightly beaten
10 slices bread

Stir together cheese, Worcestershire sauce, butter, onion powder, garlic powder and paprika. Heat over low heat until cheese melts. Stir in crab meat and egg yolk. Broil bread slices on one side; spread crab mixture on plain side of bread, being careful to cover edges well so bread doesn't burn. Broil until bubbly. Cut into triangles and serve.

CRAB MELBA

Leftovers (if you have any) are great on toast points!

Average

50 Servings
Make Ahead

4 Tbsp. butter
⅓ cup flour
2 cups half and half
2 Tbsp. tomato paste
½ cup sharp or Gruyere
    cheese, grated
1½ tsp. paprika
½ tsp. garlic powder
⅛ tsp. cayenne pepper
1 Tbsp. lemon juice
¼ lb. mushrooms, finely
    chopped
¼ cup scallions, tops
    included, finely chopped
2 Tbsp. butter
12 oz. *each* flaked crab
    and lobster (or shrimp)
    — frozen may be used
3 Tbsp. pimiento, minced
2 Tbsp. dry sherry

Melt butter until bubbly. Sprinkle with flour, cook and stir 3 minutes. Gradually add half and half. Cook and stir until smooth and thickened. Add tomato paste, cheese, seasonings and lemon juice; cook and stir to melt cheese. Saute mushrooms and onions in butter 5 minutes and add to cream sauce. With fork, stir in crab and lobster (or shrimp) and pimiento. Reheat without boiling; add sherry and adjust seasonings. Serve in chafing dish over low flame with melba rounds or water biscuits. May be made a day before and carefully reheated in double boiler.

DEVILED CRAB IN SHELLS

6-8 Servings
Make Ahead

Easy

2 cups crab meat
1 cup bread crumbs
1 egg, slightly beaten
¼ cup celery, minced
¼ cup green pepper,
  minced
1 Tbsp. Worcestershire
  sauce
Dash of pepper
Dash of tabasco sauce
1 cup heavy cream.

Mix all ingredients thoroughly and stuff into greased shells. Bake at 375° for 12 minutes, or broil. Large shells serve 6-8; small shells serve 20-24.

HOT DEVILED CRAB

The special zip of horseradish makes this a winner!

2 Cups
Make Ahead

Average

4 Tbsp. butter
2 Tbsp. flour
1 Tbsp. parsley
2 Tbsp. lemon juice
1 tsp. mustard
1 Tbsp. horseradish
1 tsp. salt
1 cup milk
1 Tbsp. sherry
⅔ cup crab meat
2 hard-boiled eggs,
  chopped
½ cup bread crumbs
2 Tbsp. butter, melted

Melt butter, add flour and mix. Then add parsley, lemon juice, mustard, horseradish, salt and milk. Stir over medium heat until thickened. Add sherry, crab meat and eggs. Put in baking dish and top with bread crumbs and melted butter. Bake at 350° for 15 minutes. Serve with unsalted crackers.

DEVILED OYSTERS

Once tasted never forgotten!

Average

10-12 Servings
Make Ahead

½ cup butter
½ cup celery, chopped
½ cup green pepper, chopped
1 cup green onion, chopped
1 Tbsp. flour
2 cups milk, warmed
5-6 dozen oysters, depending on size (approximately 2 pints)
Salt and pepper to taste
Lea & Perrins Sauce to taste (use plenty, enough to darken sauce)

Melt butter in heavy iron pot. Saute celery, pepper and onion in butter until tender. Then add flour and warmed milk to mixture to make a cream sauce. Cook for a short while. Cook oysters in own juice in saucepan over medium heat until edges curl. Drain oysters, reserving juice, and add to sauce. Add ½ cup or more strained oyster juice to achieve the right consistency. Season to taste. Serve as dip in a chafing dish or in individual ramekins, or patty shells as a first or main course. This recipe is easily halved.

SCALLOP-BACON ROLLS

Easy

10 Servings
Make Ahead

1 lb. Bay scallops
1 lb. bacon

Cut each bacon strip in half lengthwise and widthwise. Roll one scallop in each quarter strip of bacon; fasten with toothpick. Broil 5 inches from heat, turning frequently to brown evenly. When golden brown, about 7 minutes, drain on paper towels and serve.

SCALLOP BLANKETS

The aroma drives men wild!

Easy   **1 Dozen**

½ lb. scallops, cut into ½
   inch cubes, if large
2 Tbsp. sherry
½ tsp. sugar
½ tsp. salt
6 slices bacon, cut in half
6 water chestnuts, sliced
1 scallion, cut into 1 inch
   pieces

Marinate scallops in sherry and sugar for 30 minutes. Sprinkle with salt. Wrap a piece of bacon around a piece of scallop, a slice of water chestnut and a piece of scallion. Secure with toothpick and broil for 10 minutes, turning once, until golden brown.

ORIENTAL SHRIMP

8 Servings
Make Ahead

Average

2 lbs. raw shrimp shelled
   and deveined

MARINADE:
⅔ cup soy sauce
½ cup peanut oil
2 Tbsp. brown sugar
1½ tsp. ground ginger
6 scallions, minced

Combine all marinade ingredients and marinate shrimp for 4 hours or overnight. When ready to serve, drain shrimp, skewer them and let guests grill their own over cocktail-size hibachi. If desired, shrimp may be grilled in advance and served warm from a chafing dish.

STUFFED CELERY

Easy

12 Servings
Make Ahead

2-4 oz. Bleu cheese
8 oz. cream cheese,
  softened
3 Tbsp. butter or
  margarine, softened
1 tsp. lemon juice
½ tsp. Worcestershire
  sauce
1 large bunch celery
Paprika
1 3 oz. can French-fried
  onions, crumbled

Cream together Bleu cheese, cream cheese, butter, lemon juice and Worcestershire sauce. Cut celery into 4 inch lengths. Fill with cheese mixture. Sprinkle with paprika; press filled stalks into onions. Refrigerate until ready to serve.

MUSHROOMS AURORA

COMPLIMENTS OF WAGNER VINEYARDS, LODI, N.Y.

Easy

Servings As
Desired

Fresh mushrooms
Butter
Wagner's Aurora wine

Simmer fresh mushrooms with butter and Wagner's Aurora. When tender, transfer to a chafing dish, set out toothpicks and enjoy.

MARINATED RAW MUSHROOMS

Easy

8 Servings
Make Ahead

1 lb. small white
   mushrooms

MARINADE:
⅔ cup olive oil
⅓ cup wine vinegar
1 tsp. salt
¼ tsp. pepper
1 Tbsp. fresh parsley,
   minced
1 Tbsp. dill weed
1 shallot, minced
1 clove garlic, minced

Remove stems from mushrooms.

Mix all marinade ingredients. Immerse mushroom caps in marinade. Store in a covered jar. If they are to be used within 24 hours, they can be stored at room temperature. If they are to be kept longer than 24 hours, store in refrigerator.

SPICY MUSHROOMS

A snap to make, a pleasure to serve!

2 Pints
Make Ahead

Easy

⅔ cup tarragon vinegar
½ cup salad oil
4 Tbsp. water
1 clove garlic, minced
Dash of hot sauce
2 tsp. salt
1 Tbsp. sugar
1 onion, sliced
Pinch of Italian seasoning
Pinch of tarragon leaves
2 pints mushrooms,
   capped and cleaned

Mix all ingredients together and refrigerate for at least 8 hours.

MARINATED MUSHROOM ANTIPASTO

Easy

2 4-6 oz. cans mushroom
   crowns, drained, or ½ lb.
   fresh mushrooms
1 14 oz. can artichoke
   hearts (not marinated),
   drained
1 16 oz. can baby carrots,
   drained
1 6 oz. can pitted black
   olives, drained
2 Tbsp. pimiento, chopped
⅔ cup white vinegar
⅔ cup salad oil
¼ cup onion, minced
1 tsp. Italian seasoning
1 tsp. salt
1-2 tsp. sugar
⅛ tsp. ground black
   pepper

Drain vegetables well. Cut large artichokes in half. Place vegetables in small
bowl; add pimiento and set aside. In a
small saucepan, combine remaining
ingredients. Bring to a boil, cool slightly,
pour over vegetables. Cover and refrigerate at least 12 hours. Serve with
toothpicks or on French bread.

ARTICHOKE NIBBLES

Average

2 6 oz. jars marinated
   artichoke hearts
1 small onion, finely
   chopped
1 clove garlic, mashed
4 eggs
¼ cup fine dry bread
   crumbs
¼ tsp. salt
⅛ tsp. pepper
⅛ tsp. oregano
⅛ tsp. tabasco sauce
2 Tbsp. parsley, minced
½ lb. sharp Cheddar
   cheese, grated

Drain both jars of artichokes, placing
marinade from **one** jar of artichokes into
frying pan. Saute onion and garlic in pan
until limp. Chop the thoroughly drained
artichokes. In bowl, beat eggs; add
crumbs and seasonings. Stir in cheese,
artichokes and onion mixture. Bake in
greased 7x11 inch pan at 325° for 30
minutes or until set when lightly
touched. Let cool in pan. Cut into 1 inch
squares. Serve cold or hot.

MUSHROOM CHEESE CANAPES

Easy

4 Dozen
Make Ahead
Freeze

1 cup mushroom caps,
  chopped
1½ cups sharp cheese,
  grated
½ cup green onion,
  chopped
½ cup mayonnaise
1 loaf party rye bread
Butter, softened

Combine mushrooms, cheese, onion and mayonnaise. Spread bread with a thin layer of softened butter. Spread mixture on bread. Place on cookie sheet and broil until cheese melts. Serve immediately. May be assembled in advance and refrigerated or frozen before broiling.

TOASTED MUSHROOM ROUNDS

Easy

2 Dozen
Make Ahead

1 lb. mushrooms, finely
  chopped
1 cup chicken broth
3 Tbsp. flour
3 Tbsp. butter
Bread, cut into rounds

Cover mushrooms with chicken broth and cook until tender. Thicken to a paste with flour and butter. Let cool. Butter small rounds of bread on both sides. Spread with mixture and put together in sandwiches. Toast under broiler.

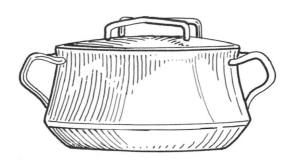

MUSHROOM CRESCENTS

Complicated

**4½ Dozen
Make Ahead
Freeze**

PASTRY:
9 oz. cream cheese
½ cup butter or margarine
1½ cups flour

Soften cream cheese and butter at room temperature. With wooden spoon, stir flour, cream cheese and butter until well combined and smooth. Wrap and chill for at least 30 minutes.

FILLING:
1 medium onion, chopped
2 Tbsp. butter or
  margarine
½ lb. mushrooms, chopped
3 oz. cream cheese
½ tsp. salt
¼ tsp. thyme
⅛ tsp. freshly ground
  pepper

In skillet, saute onion in butter until lightly browned. Add mushrooms and cook over medium-high heat and add cream cheese, a bit at a time, stirring until it has melted. Stir in salt, thyme and pepper. Cool.

CRESCENTS:
1 egg beaten with 1 tsp.
  water

Preheat oven to 450°. Remove ½ dough from refrigerator. Roll on lightly floured board until ⅛ inch thick. Cut into 2½ inch circles. Place ½ tsp. filling on each circle. Fold in half and press edges together with a fork. Use a little egg mixture to seal. Make a small slit in top of each crescent to let steam escape. Repeat with remaining dough and scraps and brush crescents with egg glaze. Bake on ungreased baking sheet for 15 minutes. These may be prepared in advance. Bake, cool, and freeze up to 1 month. Warm at 300° for 20 minutes. Pastries may also be frozen before baking. When ready to serve, glaze with egg and bake at 450° for 15 minutes.

HERB STUFFED MUSHROOMS
Easy   **4 Dozen**

48 medium-large
   mushrooms, (about 2
   pounds)
1¼ cups butter, melted
1 cup green onions, finely
   chopped
1 cup white wine
4 cups herbed seasoned
   stuffing

Wash mushrooms and pat dry. Remove stems and set aside. Arrange caps in a shallow baking dish and generously brush with butter. Chop 1½ cups of mushroom stems and saute with green onions in remaining butter; add more butter, if needed. Add wine. Add stuffing and stir lightly to combine. Spoon mixture into mushroom caps. Bake at 350° for 10 minutes.

CHEESE STUFFED MUSHROOMS
Bet you can't eat just one!

Average

8 Servings
Make Ahead

2 lbs. large mushrooms
½ cup Parmesan cheese,
   grated
¾ cup dry bread crumbs
½ cup onion, chopped
2 cloves garlic, minced
3 Tbsp. parsley, minced
1 tsp. salt
½ tsp. freshly ground
   black pepper
½ tsp. oregano
¾ cup oil

Wash mushrooms, remove stems and chop, reserving caps; mix with cheese, bread crumbs, onion, garlic, parsley, salt, pepper and oregano. Stuff caps. Pour a little oil in baking pan. Arrange mushrooms in pan, pouring a little oil over each one. Bake at 350° for 30 minutes.

SAUSAGE STUFFED MUSHROOMS

Average

12-15 Servings
Make Ahead

1 lb. large mushrooms
3 Tbsp. Parmesan cheese,
  grated
1 clove garlic, chopped
1 small onion, chopped
⅓-½ cup Italian bread
  crumbs
1 Tbsp. parsley
2 Tbsp. butter, melted
4 oz. sausage (Jimmy
  Dean preferred)
Salt and pepper to taste
2 Tbsp. oil

Clean and remove stems from mushrooms. Mix all other ingredients, except oil, together. Fill mushroom caps. Pour oil in bottom of pan and place mushrooms, stuffing side up. Bake at 350° for 20-30 minutes. Tops should be brown.

MUSHROOMS STUFFED WITH CRAB MEAT

A lovely combination of flavors!

12 Servings
Make Ahead

Average

1 cup crab meat, cooked
1 Tbsp. dry bread crumbs
1 Tbsp. onion, finely
  chopped
1 Tbsp. parsley, finely
  chopped
1 Tbsp. chives, finely
  chopped
1 tsp. salt
1 egg, lightly beaten
1½ lbs. large mushrooms
Bread crumbs, buttered
Parmesan cheese, grated

Combine crab meat and bread crumbs. Add onion, parsley, chives and salt. Stir in egg. Trim stems from mushrooms and reserve for another use. Fill caps with crab meat mixture. Sprinkle with buttered bread crumbs and Parmesan cheese. Bake at 350° for 20 minutes.

CLAM STUFFED MUSHROOMS

Average

4 Dozen
Make Ahead
Freeze

2 lbs. fresh mushrooms
1 6½ or 8 oz. can minced clams
½ cup butter
½ cup dry bread crumbs
¾ tsp. salt
½ tsp. pepper
1 clove garlic, minced (optional)

Wash mushrooms and pat dry. Remove stems and mince. Drain clams, reserving liquid. Melt butter; brush mushroom caps with butter. To remaining butter, add clam liquid and minced mushroom stems. Cook for 5 minutes. Add clams, bread crumbs, salt, pepper and garlic and gently mix. Fill mushroom caps with clam mixture and broil for 8 minutes. These are time consuming, but not difficult. They are best when served on a heated tray.

SPECIAL SPINACH SQUARES

Easy

4 Servings
Make Ahead
Freeze

1 10 oz. pkg. frozen chopped spinach
2 eggs
8 oz. sour cream
1 Tbsp. onion, grated
½ cup Parmesan cheese, grated
1 Tbsp. flour
2 Tbsp. butter
½-1 tsp. salt
⅛ tsp. pepper

Cook spinach as directed on package, and drain well. Beat eggs; add to spinach. Blend in other ingredients. Place into a greased 9x9 inch square dish. Bake, uncovered, at 350° for 25-30 minutes. Cool slightly and cut into squares.

ZUCCHINI APPETIZERS

Easy

3 cups unpared zucchini, sliced
1 cup Bisquick baking mix
½ cup onion, finely chopped
½ cup Parmesan cheese, grated
2 Tbsp. parsley, snipped
½ tsp. salt
½ tsp. seasoned salt
½ tsp. dried marjoram or oregano
Dash of pepper
1 clove garlic, finely chopped
½ cup vegetable oil
4 eggs, slightly beaten

Mix all ingredients well. Spread into a greased 13x9x2 inch pan. Bake at 350° for 25 minutes or until golden brown. Cut into 2x1 inch pieces.

HELPFUL HINT

When using glass baking dishes, lower oven temperature by 25 degrees.

STUFFED GRAPE LEAVES

A wonderful start to a Greek meal!

Average

4 Dozen
Make Ahead
Freeze

½ cup long-grain rice
1 small onion, finely
  chopped
3 Tbsp. butter or
  margarine
¼ cup parsley, chopped
¼ cup fresh mint leaves,
  chopped
1 egg, beaten
¾ tsp. salt
Dash of freshly ground
  pepper
1 lb. ground lamb
48 grape leaves (jars of
  grape leaves may be
  found at gourmet food
  stores), rinsed
2 cups water
2 Tbsp. butter
1 tsp. salt
Egg lemon sauce (see
  below)
Cherry tomatoes (optional)

Saute rice and onion in 3 Tbsp. butter until onion is transparent, about 5 minutes. Combine rice, onion, parsley, mint, egg, ¾ tsp. salt and pepper. Add lamb; mix well. Place a rounded tea-spoonful of meat mixture in center of each grape leaf. Fold in sides and roll up. Place in 3 quart saucepan, side by side in layers. Add water, 2 Tbsp. butter and 1 tsp. salt. Press with oven-proof plate that fits inside the saucepan. Cover and simmer for 45 minutes. Drain stuffed leaves, reserving 1 cup broth. Place leaves on platter.

EGG LEMON SAUCE:
2 eggs, separated
3 Tbsp. lemon juice
1 cup reserved broth
Salt and pepper

Beat 2 egg whites until stiff peaks form. Beat 2 egg yolks until light, about 4 minutes. Fold egg whites into yolks. Slowly stir in lemon juice. Gradually add reserved broth to egg mixture. Cook and stir over low heat until slightly thickened and smooth, about 5 minutes. Season to taste with salt and pepper. Serve egg lemon sauce with stuffed grape leaves. Garnish with cherry to-matoes and additional grape leaves, if desired. Serve hot or cold.

HERBED PECANS

A perfect hostess gift!

Easy   **1 Pound**

3 Tbsp. butter or
   margarine
3 Tbsp. Worcestershire
   sauce
1 tsp. salt
½ tsp. cinnamon
¼ tsp. garlic powder
¼ tsp. cayenne pepper
1 lb. pecan halves

Melt butter in skillet; add all other ingredients, except pecans. Add pecans and toss, until coated. Bake on cookie sheet at 300° for 20-25 minutes, stirring often.

SEASONED POPPED CORN

Easy   **1 Quart**

4 Tbsp. butter, melted
¼-½ tsp. curry powder
⅛-¼ tsp. onion powder
⅛ tsp. garlic powder
Dash of cayenne pepper
½ cup popping corn

Combine melted butter with next 4 ingredients. Pop corn and pour seasoned butter over corn, mixing well.

NOTES

VINEYARD
Varietal grapes, harvested by many local vintners to produce fine wines, are grown in the Finger Lakes Region.

SOUPS AND SANDWICHES

SOUPS

Cold

Hot or Cold

Hot

SANDWICHES

GAZPACHO

A wonderful first course on a hot night!

Easy

6 Servings
Make Ahead

1 cup tomatoes, peeled
   and finely chopped
½ cup celery, finely
   chopped
½ cup cucumber, finely
   chopped
½ cup green pepper, finely
   chopped
½ cup green onion, finely
   chopped
2 tsp. parsley, snipped
½ tsp. freshly ground
   pepper
½ tsp. Worcestershire
   sauce
1½ tsp. salt
2 Tbsp. olive oil
1 large clove garlic,
   pressed
3 Tbsp. wine vinegar
2½ cups tomato or V-8
   juice
Croutons for garnish

Combine all ingredients, except croutons, in stainless bowl. Cover and chill overnight. Serve cold with croutons. Can be kept in refrigerator up to 1 week.

VICHYSSOISE

Average

8 Servings
Make Ahead

4 leeks, thinly sliced
3 onions, thinly sliced
4 Tbsp. butter
4 cups chicken stock or
   broth
3 potatoes, peeled and
   thinly sliced
Salt and pepper to taste
2 cups milk
1 cup cream
Chives, snipped

Steam leeks and onions in butter in a large saucepan covered with a buttered round of wax paper and the lid for 20 minutes, or until well softened. Add chicken stock, potatoes, salt and pepper. Simmer until potatoes are very soft. Puree mixture in a food mill or blender, and pour into large bowl. Add milk and cream, and chill for at least 3 hours. When ready to serve, sprinkle with chives.

CHILLED CUCUMBER SOUP

Average

6 Servings
Make Ahead

2 medium cucumbers,
   pared and sliced
1 cup water
¼ cup onion, sliced
¼ tsp. salt
⅛ tsp. white pepper
¼ cup flour (Wondra
   preferred)
2 cups chicken stock
¼ bay leaf
¾ cup sour cream or
   yogurt
1 Tbsp. dill, finely chopped
   (may substitute chives or
   lemon rind)

Place cucumbers, water, onion, salt and pepper in medium saucepan. Cover and cook until soft. Puree in blender; set aside. In saucepan, mix flour and ½ cup chicken stock. Stir until smooth. Add remaining stock, cucumber puree and bay leaf. Cook, stirring, over low heat for about 3 minutes. Chill in covered jar. When ready to serve, stir in sour cream and dill. Correct the seasonings and serve very cold.

HAMBURGER SOUP

Multiply for a hungry crowd!

Easy

4-6 Servings
Make Ahead
Freeze

1 lb. ground chuck
½ cup onion, chopped
1 green pepper, chopped
½ cup celery, chopped
½ cup carrots, chopped
2 cups tomatoes
¼ cup barley
1 Tbsp. salt
1 tsp. pepper
8 cups water
1 envelope Lipton's
   Country Vegetable Soup
   Mix

Brown meat and onions. Put everything, except soup mix, in pan. Bring to boil; let simmer 1 hour; add soup mix and simmer 1 hour more.

HEARTY HODGEPODGE SOUP

Easy

1½ to 2 lbs. ground chuck
¾ cup onion, chopped
1 clove garlic, minced or
   ⅛ tsp. garlic powder
3 10 oz. cans Minestrone
   soup
1 31 oz. can pork and
   beans in tomato sauce
1½ cups celery, chopped
⅛ tsp. garlic powder
1 Tbsp. Worcestershire
   sauce
½ tsp. oregano
3 cups water

In Dutch oven, saute meat, onion and garlic until beef is browned and onion tender. Stir in soup, pork and beans, celery, spices and water. Simmer, covered, for 45 minutes.

BUTTERBALL SOUP

Average

6 Servings

8 slices day old firm white
   bread
3 Tbsp. butter or
   margarine, softened
1 egg
¼ tsp. salt
Dash of pepper
3 13 oz. cans chicken
   broth or homemade
   broth
1 Tbsp. parsley, chopped
Carrots for garnish
Celery for garnish

Remove bread crusts; crumble bread to make fine crumbs. Add butter, egg, salt and pepper. Mix well and knead until mixture can be formed into balls. Shape into approximately 30 balls, ¼ inch in diameter. Heat chicken broth to boiling; drop balls into boiling broth. Simmer 10 minutes or until balls rise to the top. Sprinkle with parsley and serve at once. Add julienne cut carrots and celery, if desired.

CHICKEN SOUP WITH SPINACH DUMPLINGS

Complicated

1 3 lb. broiling-frying
   chicken, cut into pieces
6 cups water
2 sprigs parsley
2 stalks celery, chopped
1 carrot, sliced
1 small onion, chopped
2 tsp. salt
¼ tsp. pepper
1 bay leaf
1 recipe filled dumplings
   (may be doubled for
   heartier soup)

In Dutch oven, combine chicken and water. Add parsley, celery, carrot, onion, salt, pepper and bay leaf. Cover and simmer 1 hour or until chicken is tender. Remove chicken from broth; strain broth and discard vegetables. Skim off excess fat. Remove chicken meat from bones; dice ¼ cup meat and reserve it for filling. Chop remaining chicken; add to broth.

DOUGH:
1 egg
1 Tbsp. water
⅔ cup flour
¼ tsp. salt

Beat egg with water. Add flour and salt. Knead on lightly floured surface for a few minutes. Cover and let rest for 20 minutes. Roll to ⅛ inch thickness. Cut into sixteen 2 inch circles.

FILLING:
¼ cup reserved chicken,
   cooked and diced
¼ cup spinach, cooked
   and finely chopped
1 egg
2 Tbsp. Parmesan cheese,
   grated
2 Tbsp. fine dry bread
   crumbs
⅛ tsp. salt
⅛ tsp. dried thyme,
   crushed
Dash of ground nutmeg
Parsley, snipped for
   garnish

Combine all filling ingredients. Place 1½ tsp. filling on half of each circle of dough. Moisten edges, fold dough over, and seal edges with tines of fork. Bring broth to simmering; drop in filled dumplings. Cook, covered, 10 minutes. Season to taste. Top with parsley.

FAMILY DINNER CHICKEN SOUP

Average

6 Servings
Make Ahead
Freeze

2½ lbs. chicken pieces
1 onion, chopped
2 celery stalks, sliced
3 potatoes, peeled and
 diced
4 carrots, sliced
1 tsp. tabasco sauce
3 Tbsp. soy sauce
Water to cover, about 3½
 cups
1 tsp. salt

Combine all ingredients in large kettle. Cover and cook over low heat 2-3 hours, stirring occasionally. Add water, if necessary. Before serving, remove bones. May chill and remove excess fat; then reheat to serve. Can also make in slow electric cooker; cover and cook on low 10-12 hours.

CURRIED CLAM SOUP

Easy

6 Servings
Make Ahead

Green pepper, chopped
 (as much as you like)
1 medium onion, chopped
4 Tbsp. margarine
1 10 oz. can cream of
 mushroom soup
1 10 oz. can cream of
 celery soup
2 10 oz. soup cans milk
2 6½ oz. cans minced
 clams, not drained
1 2 oz. jar pimiento,
 minced
1 Tbsp. curry

Saute green pepper and onion in margarine. Add remaining ingredients except curry. Mix thoroughly, then add curry. Heat through. This can be made 2 days ahead.

HATTAN CLAM CHOWDER

Average

1½ quarts water
3 medium potatoes, diced
3 medium carrots, sliced
¾ lb. salt pork
2 medium onions, sliced
1 1 lb. can peeled
  tomatoes
4 dozen large cherry-stone
  or chowder clams

Bring water to boil; add potatoes and carrots and cook until tender. Set aside. Slice salt pork and fry in skillet. Remove slices when crisp and reserve for another use. Cook onions in pork fat until browned. Drain fat; add onions to potato and carrot mixture. Add tomatoes and cook mixture over low heat for ½ hour. Open clams; dice and save juice. Add clams and juice; simmer 20 minutes. Place soup in refrigerator or other cold area; skim off excess fat. Reheat and serve.

NEW ENGLAND CLAM CHOWDER

Average

4-6 Servings
Make Ahead

3 cups chicken broth
2 8 oz. cans minced
  clams, undrained
2 medium carrots,
  chopped
2 cups uncooked potatoes,
  chopped
⅓ cup parsley, minced
⅓ cup celery, chopped
1 small onion, chopped
4 Tbsp. butter, melted
2 Tbsp. flour
½ cup evaporated milk
Salt and pepper to taste

Combine chicken broth, clams, carrots, potatoes, parsley, celery and onion in large saucepan. Place over heat and bring to boil. Cover and simmer about 30 minutes. Combine butter and flour in small pan; blend well. Gradually add milk, stirring until well blended. Place over low heat and cook, stirring constantly, until smooth and thickened. Add to vegetable mixture, stirring well. Add salt and pepper to taste. Heat to serve.

CRAB BISQUE

Easy

6 Servings
Make Ahead

2 Tbsp. butter
1½ Tbsp. flour
2½ cups milk
1 tsp. salt
¼ tsp. pepper
⅛ tsp. red pepper
1 cup heavy cream
1 lb. crab meat, picked
  over
2 hard-cooked eggs,
  pressed through a sieve
¼ cup dry sherry
Parsley or chives

Melt butter in saucepan. Blend in flour and cook, stirring, for 1 minute. Remove from heat and gradually stir in milk. Add salt and black and red pepper. Bring to a boil, stirring constantly, until sauce thickens. Cook 2 minutes. Add cream and crab meat, then reheat. Add eggs and sherry. Garnish with parsley or chives.

TOMATO CRAB BISQUE

Easy

4 Servings
Make Ahead

1 6 oz. can crab meat,
  drained
3 Tbsp. sherry
1 10 oz. can cream of
  tomato soup
1 10 oz. can green pea
  soup
1 10 oz. can cream of
  mushroom soup
1½ soup cans of milk
½ tsp. curry powder
1 chicken bouillon cube

Marinate crab meat in 1-2 Tbsp. sherry. Blend soups in blender. Add all ingredients, except crab meat and sherry, and blend a few seconds. Pour into saucepan; add marinated crab meat and simmer 2-3 hours. Add 1-2 Tbsp. sherry while cooking.

OYSTER STEW

Add to your collection of all-time favorites!

Easy   **2-3 Servings**

4 Tbsp. butter
1 pint shelled oysters
2 cups milk and 1 cup
  cream or 3 cups half and
  half
Salt and ground pepper
Dash of Worcestershire
  sauce

Reserve 2 Tbsp. butter. Melt remaining butter; add oysters and their liquor and simmer just until oysters curl. Add remaining ingredients and heat for serving. Float reserved butter on top.

BEAN SPROUT AND SHRIMP SOUP

Average   **4 Servings**

2 cups chicken broth
1 cup fresh bean sprouts
½ cup loosely packed
  watercress leaves and
  stems (may substitute ½
  cup spinach)
1 tsp. butter
½ cup shrimp, cooked and
  chopped or sweetbreads
½-1 tsp. curry powder
½ cup heavy cream

Bring chicken broth to a boil in saucepan. Add bean sprouts and watercress and simmer 5 minutes. Meanwhile, heat butter in a small saucepan and add shrimp. Sprinkle with curry powder and cook briefly until heated through. Add curry-shrimp mixture to broth. Pour mixture into blender and blend until smooth. Return mixture to a saucepan and add cream. Bring to a boil and serve.

QUICKEE COMPANY SOUP

                                                    6 Servings
Easy   **Make Ahead**

1 10 oz. can tomato soup
1 10 oz. can pea or
  asparagus soup
1 10 oz. can cream of
  shrimp soup
1 7 oz. can tiny shrimp,
  drained
1½ soup cans half and
  half or milk
Sherry to taste
Curry powder (optional)

Place all ingredients in saucepan. Heat thoroughly and serve.

78

CREAM OF ARTICHOKE SOUP

Easy

4-6 Servings
Make Ahead

2 8 oz. cans artichoke
   hearts, drained
1½ cups chicken bouillon
   (add more for thinner
    soup)
Lemon juice to taste
2 cups light cream

Combine all ingredients in blender and blend thoroughly. When ready to serve, heat gently and garnish with lemon slices, croutons or watercress. This can be made well in advance.

CREAM OF CARROT AND TOMATO SOUP

Complicated

8-12 Servings
Make Ahead

4 cups fresh tomatoes,
   peeled or equivalent
   canned
2 lbs. medium-size carrots
6 Tbsp. butter
Salt and freshly ground
   pepper
¼ cup water
3 Tbsp. flour
1¾ cups chicken broth
3 cups milk
1 cup heavy cream
Tabasco sauce to taste
¼ cup dill, chopped
1 cup sour cream

Put tomatoes in saucepan and cook, uncovered, for 30 minutes. Trim carrots, scrape and cut into ¼ inch rounds. Heat half the butter in heavy saucepan and add carrots, salt and pepper to taste and water. Cover and cook 30 minutes. Melt remaining 3 Tbsp. butter in another saucepan and add flour, stirring with a wire whisk. Add chicken broth, stirring rapidly with whisk. When thickened and smooth, continue cooking an additional 30 minutes. Combine carrots, tomatoes and sauce. Puree mixture in an electric blender or food processor. Pour into large saucepan and bring to a boil. Stir in milk and cream. Add salt and pepper to taste. Add tabasco sauce and half the dill. Beat sour cream, adding a little salt to taste. Stir in remaining dill. Serve soup hot or cold with a dollop of sour cream.

CREAM OF BROCCOLI SOUP

To warm up those taste buds on a cold winter night!

Easy

6 Servings
Make Ahead

2 10 oz. pkgs. frozen
chopped broccoli
2 10 oz. cans cream of
mushroom soup
2 soup cans of milk
½ cup dry white wine
2 Tbsp. butter
1 tsp. garlic powder
½ tsp. dried tarragon,
crushed
Dash of white pepper

In large saucepan cook broccoli until tender; drain. Add soup and all other ingredients. Let simmer for ½ hour and serve.

GOLDEN GARTER CREAM OF BROCCOLI SOUP

COMPLIMENTS OF
GOLDEN GARTER RESTAURANT, ITHACA, N.Y.

Average

8-10 Servings
Make Ahead

2 quarts chicken stock
1 lb. fresh or frozen
broccoli, diced
1 small white onion, diced
1½ cups butter
1 cup flour
Salt and pepper

Bring chicken stock to a boil in stock pot. Add broccoli and onion and boil until tender, but do not over cook. In separate pot, melt butter; add flour and simmer for 5 minutes; add this mixture slowly to stock pot. Stir well until soup thickens; salt and pepper to taste and remove from heat. Let stand 1 hour; reheat in double boiler before serving. Very good if served the next day.

HELPFUL HINT

To remove taste of excess salt, add 1 tsp. each of vinegar and sugar.

BEAN SOUP

Easy

6 Servings
Make Ahead
Freeze

1 lb. navy beans
1 meaty ham bone
2 medium onions, diced
1½ cups carrots, sliced
1 2 lb. can tomatoes
1 tsp. salt
¼ tsp. pepper
1 tsp. Worcestershire
   sauce
2 stalks celery, sliced

Wash and pick over beans. Cover beans with 6 cups of water. Bring to a boil. Boil gently for 2 minutes. Remove from heat, then cover and let stand 1 hour. Do not drain. Add remaining ingredients and simmer, covered, for at least 3 to 3½ hours. Remove bone and cut up ham. Add ham pieces to soup. Slightly mash vegetables. Serve hot.

CREAM OF CELERY SOUP

Average

4 Servings
Make Ahead

2 cups celery, diced
3 Tbsp. butter
2 Tbsp. flour
2 cups chicken stock (or
   substitute bouillon cubes
   dissolved in 2 cups
   water)
1 cup heavy cream
Salt and white pepper
1 Tbsp. sherry (optional)

Saute celery in butter until tender. Carefully stir in flour and cook until bubbly to eliminate floury taste. Add chicken stock and heavy cream. Season gently with salt and pepper. Cook, stirring, until thickened; add sherry. More celery may be added, if desired.

CORN CHOWDER

Easy

6-8 Servings
Make Ahead
Freeze

3½ cups milk
3 Tbsp. butter
1 small onion, sliced
2 cups water
3 medium potatoes, finely
   diced
1 1 lb. can creamed corn
Salt and pepper

Scald milk and set aside. In large pan, melt butter, add onion and cook until lightly browned. Add water and potatoes and cook until potatoes are soft. Add mixture to milk, along with corn and salt and pepper to taste. Heat and serve.

MINESTRONE SOUP

Average

6-8 Servings
Make Ahead
Freeze

1 onion
1-2 potatoes
Celery
Carrots
5½ oz. salt pork
1 Tbsp. tomato puree
  (more if needed)
Freshly ground pepper
2 garlic cloves
1½ quarts chicken stock
1 10 oz. pkg. frozen green
  peas, thawed
1 cup spaghetti, cooked al
  dente and chopped
1½ tsp. basil
Parsley, chopped
Parmesan cheese, grated

Cut all vegetables, except peas, and salt pork into strips. Saute pork without allowing it to brown. Add puree and pepper. Press juices from garlic cloves into pork mixture. Add sliced vegetables and chicken stock and let soup boil, uncovered, for about 10 minutes. Add peas and cooked spaghetti; season with basil, pepper and parsley. Add salt only if needed. Serve soup with crusty bread and plenty of Parmesan cheese.

CREAM OF MUSHROOM SOUP

At last — a delicious soup low in calories!

6 Servings
Make Ahead

Average

½ lb. mushrooms
½ lemon
2 Tbsp. corn oil margarine
1 cup onion, chopped
2 Tbsp. flour
4 cups chicken stock
2 cups water
Salt and pepper
3 Tbsp. nondairy creamer

Chop mushrooms and sprinkle with juice of ½ lemon. Melt margarine and add mushrooms and onion. Cook slowly until onion is soft. Add flour and cook 2 minutes, stirring constantly. Add chicken stock and water; season with salt and pepper and cook at **slow** boil for 20 minutes. Whirl soup in blender and strain if lumpy. Season to taste. More lemon juice may be added. Reheat and add nondairy creamer.

82

MUSHROOM BARLEY SOUP

Average

1 lb. fresh mushrooms,
  rinsed and drained
6 Tbsp. butter
1 cup onion, finely
  chopped
1 clove garlic, finely
  chopped
2 10 oz. cans condensed
  beef broth
5 10 oz. soup cans of
  water
3 Tbsp. tomato paste
¾ tsp. salt
Dash of freshly ground
  black pepper
1 bay leaf
½ cup barley
¼ cup parsley, chopped
1½ cups celery, chopped
  including some leaves
1½ cups carrots, sliced
4 Tbsp. dry sherry
2 cups sour cream
  (optional)

Chop ½ lb. mushrooms. Slice remaining ½ lb. mushrooms and set aside. In large saucepan, melt 4 Tbsp. butter, add the chopped mushrooms along with onion and garlic; saute 5 minutes. Stir in broth, water, tomato paste, salt, black pepper and bay leaf. Heat to boiling. Stir in barley. Reduce heat; cover and simmer for 1 hour. Add parsley, celery and carrots; cook, covered, about 30 minutes, or until vegetables and barley are tender. In medium skillet, melt remaining 2 Tbsp. butter. Add the reserved sliced mushrooms and saute 5 minutes. Add to soup along with sherry. Ladle into large soup bowls and serve with a dollop of sour cream.

SPLIT PEA SOUP

Easy

1 lb. split peas, well
  washed
3 quarts cold water
1 large onion, chopped
1 cup celery, chopped
  (optional)
1 ham bone
Salt and pepper to taste
Ham, diced (optional)
Croutons

Put split peas in a large kettle. Add cold water, onion, celery, ham bone, salt and pepper and cook slowly for about 3 hours, until soup is thickened and peas are very soft. Strain through coarse sieve, pushing solids through as much as possible. Reheat, adding ham, if desired. Serve with croutons.

MUSHROOM BISQUE

The subtle sherry flavor makes this special!

Average

8 Servings
Make Ahead
Freeze

1 lb. mushrooms
4 cups chicken broth
1 medium onion, chopped
7 Tbsp. butter
6 Tbsp. flour
3 cups milk
1 cup heavy cream
1 tsp. salt
White pepper
Tabasco sauce
2 Tbsp. sherry

Wash mushrooms, cut stems. Slice 6 caps and reserve. Grind and chop remaining caps very fine. Simmer, covered, in broth with onion for 30 minutes; saute reserved caps in 1 Tbsp. butter and reserve for garnish. Melt remaining butter in saucepan; add flour and stir with wire whisk. Meanwhile, bring milk to boil and add all at once to butter-flour mixture, stirring vigorously with whisk until sauce is thick and smooth; then add cream. Combine mushroom broth mixture with sauce and season to taste with salt, pepper and tabasco. Reheat and add sherry before serving. Garnish with sauteed sliced mushrooms.

FRENCH ONION SOUP

Average

6 Servings
Make Ahead

4 Tbsp. butter
1 lb. onions, peeled and
   finely sliced
Salt and black pepper
½ tsp. mustard
2 tsp. flour
4 cups beef stock
1 cup white wine
French bread, sliced and
   lightly toasted
Parmesan cheese, grated

Melt butter in large saucepan and add onions, salt, pepper and mustard. Cook over low heat, stirring occasionally, until onions are browned, about 20-30 minutes. Add flour and stir until smooth. Add stock and wine, stirring constantly until mixture boils. Turn down heat and simmer for 30 minutes. Soup can also be made in crock pot and simmered all day after ingredients are browned. To serve, place French bread slices in oven-proof crocks, sprinkle cheese over bread, pour soup into crocks and place under broiler until cheese melts.

SOUP A L'OIGNON GRATINEE

Easy

6-8 Servings
Make Ahead

½ cup butter
6 large onions, sliced
2 quarts hot water
5-6 beef bouillon cubes
Salt, pepper and parsley to
   taste
½ loaf French bread,
   sliced
½ lb. Swiss cheese,
   grated

Place butter in large saucepan. Add onions. Saute slowly until onions are transparent, very tender and auburn in color. Add hot water, bouillon cubes and seasonings. Bring to a boil, reduce to simmer, cover, and cook for 15-20 minutes. Line a large casserole or soup tureen with bread slices. Place in 350° oven for a few minutes to toast. Sprinkle cheese over bread; ladle soup over all, but do not disturb bread. Place in oven for about 1 hour.

MEATBALL SOUP

Average

8 Servings
Make Ahead
Freeze

1½ lbs. ground chuck
3 Tbsp. butter or
   margarine
1 1 lb. 12 oz. can
   tomatoes
2 10 oz. cans beef
   consomme
1 pkg. dry onion soup mix
   or 1 10 oz. can clear
   onion soup
4 pared carrots, sliced 1/4
   inch thick
¼ cup celery tops,
   chopped
¼ cup parsley, chopped
1 bay leaf
¼ tsp. dried oregano
   leaves
½ tsp. salt
10 peppercorns
¼ tsp. dried basil leaves
1 cup water

With hands, lightly shape ground chuck into 1 inch balls. In hot butter, in 6 quart saucepan, saute meatballs, turning until browned all over. Drain fat. Add remaining ingredients. Bring just to boiling, reduce heat and simmer, covered, for 45 minutes, stirring occasionally to break up tomatoes. Serve very hot.

CREAM OF SPINACH SOUP

Average

4 Servings
Make Ahead

¼ cup boiling water
2 10 oz. pkgs. frozen
  spinach, thawed
¼ cup onion, finely
  chopped
4 Tbsp. butter
¼ cup flour
4 cups milk
1 tsp. salt
Dash of MSG
Provolone cheese,
  coarsely grated

Add boiling water to thawed spinach and let stand until spinach is heated through (or heat frozen spinach with water until thawed and warmed through). Put into blender and blend thoroughly. Brown onion in butter, then stir in flour, cooking until bubbly. Slowly add milk and cook, stirring constantly, until thickened. Add spinach, salt and MSG. Set over low heat ½ hour longer to develop flavor. When serving, top with Provolone cheese.

SUMMER SQUASH SOUP

A savory treat from your summer garden!

Average

2½ Quarts
Make Ahead
Freeze

4 Tbsp. butter
1 large onion, thinly sliced
½-1 tsp. garlic powder or
  2 garlic cloves, minced
3 lbs. yellow summer
  squash, sliced or cubed
3½ to 4 cups chicken
  stock (homemade is
  best)
1 cup half and half
1½ tsp. salt
½ tsp. ground white
  pepper
Fresh parsley, minced
8 thin slices squash

Heat butter in large pan over medium-high heat. Add onion and garlic and saute until transparent and soft. Add squash and chicken stock. Simmer until squash is tender. Transfer in batches to blender, adding a little half and half to each batch. Blend until smooth. Stir in salt and pepper. Serve hot or chilled; garnish with parsley and squash slices.

ENGLISH WINTER SOUP

A real treat for turnip fanciers!

Average

4-6 Servings
Make Ahead
Freeze

½ lb. potatoes
½ lb. carrots
½ lb. onions
½ lb. turnips
1 parsnip
1 rutabaga
2 Tbsp. butter
4 cups water
2-3 tsp. seasoned salt
Pepper
2 Tbsp. flour
2½ cups milk
Parsley, minced

Clean and prepare vegetables; cut into small pieces. Melt butter in large saucepan. Add vegetables and cook for 2-3 minutes. Add 3½ cups water and seasonings. Bring to a boil and simmer until vegetables are tender. Mix flour to smooth paste with remaining ½ cup water and add to soup. Cook for 2-5 minutes. Process in blender or food processor and return to pan. Add milk and adjust seasoning, if necessary. Sprinkle with parsley before serving.

HEARTY TOMATO MUSHROOM BISQUE

Leftovers never had it so good!

Average

6 Servings
Make Ahead
Freeze

1 lb. leftover steak or roast beef
1 lb. leftover pork (chops or roast)
3 10 oz. cans tomato soup
¾ cup water
2 celery stalks with leaves
1 cup carrots, sliced ¼ inch thick
2 lbs. fresh mushrooms, sliced

Trim all fat from meat. Cut into ½ inch cubes and put into bottom of Dutch oven. Pour tomato soup over meat and add water; stir well. Add celery stalks and cover. Simmer over low heat, 1½ hours, stirring occasionally to make sure mixture doesn't stick to bottom of pan and burn. Add carrots and mushrooms and simmer, **uncovered,** for 1 hour. If gravy seems too thin, turn up heat slightly and stir. Serve in bowls with hot, crunchy Italian bread or over the crusty bread. This recipe may be doubled.

TOMATO BOUILLON SOUP

Easy

4 Servings
Make Ahead

1 10 oz. can beef bouillon
1 12 oz. can tomato or V-8
   juice
Salt and pepper
Dash of lemon juice
¼ cup raw instant rice

Combine all ingredients; heat and serve.

TOMATO CHEESE BISQUE

6-8 Servings
Make Ahead

Easy

1 10 oz. can tomato soup
1 10 oz. can potato soup
1 10 oz. can cheese soup
1 cup half and half
½ cup sauterne
1 13 oz. can evaporated
   milk
¼ cup sharp Cheddar
   cheese, shredded
1-2 Tbsp. onion, minced

Combine all ingredients and cook until cheese melts. Serve hot.

DON'T THROW OUT THE BONES
VEGETABLE SOUP

10 Servings
Make Ahead
Freeze

Average

Bones and meat bits from
   beef, veal or lamb roast
Salt and pepper
2 bay leaves
3 onions, 1 whole, 2
   chopped
4 carrots, 1 whole, 3
   chopped
2 stalks celery with tops
1 16 oz. can tomatoes
¼-½ cup barley

Place bones and meat bits in large pot or Dutch oven and cover with 3 quarts of water. Add salt, pepper, bay leaves, 1 whole onion and 1 whole carrot. Cover and simmer several hours. Let cool and skim fat. Remove bones and meat and discard carrot, onion and bay leaves. Put good meat pieces back in pot. Add remaining ingredients and cook 1 hour or until vegetables are done.

CREAM OF ZUCCHINI SOUP

Easy

10-12 Servings
Make Ahead
Freeze

½ cup shallots or onions,
  minced
3 Tbsp. butter or
  margarine
3 lbs. zucchini, cut into ½
  inch chunks
6 cups chicken broth
1½ tsp. wine vinegar
4 Tbsp. farina (cream of
  wheat)
Salt and white pepper
½ cup sour cream
Dill, tarragon, chives or
  parsley for garnish

Saute onions in butter until tender, but not browned. Add zucchini, broth and vinegar. Bring to a boil; stir in farina. Simmer, partially covered, for ½ hour. Puree in blender and return to pot. Thin with more liquid, if necessary. Season carefully with salt and pepper. Just before serving, beat in sour cream and heat through (don't boil). Garnish with dill, tarragon, chives or parsley. This soup is equally good served hot or cold.

ZUCCHINI SOUP

A way to enjoy your garden all year long!

Average

3 Pints Base
Make Ahead
Freeze

SOUP BASE:
3 lbs. zucchini
1½ cups canned beef
  broth
2 cups boiling water
1½ tsp. salt
½ cup onion, chopped
⅛ tsp. garlic powder

Remove stem and quarter zucchini lengthwise. Combine remaining ingredients and zucchini. Cook until zucchini is tender. Strain and reserve liquid. Put zucchini into food mill or blender, until pureed. Return to saucepan with reserved liquid. This can be frozen or canned.

To make soup for 4:
2 cups zucchini base
1 cup half and half
Parmesan cheese, grated
Bacon bits
Parsley, snipped

Combine soup base and half and half and heat in double boiler. Garnish with rest of ingredients.

TURKEY OPEN-FACED SANDWICHES

Easy   **4 Sandwiches**

Curly lettuce leaves
Turkey breast, sliced
Fresh tomato, peeled and
  thickly sliced
4 slices bacon, crisply
  cooked
4 slices bread, toasted

Place lettuce, turkey, tomato and then bacon on toasted bread.

SANDWICH DRESSING:
1 cup mayonnaise
¼ cup chili sauce
2 Tbsp. sweet pickle,
  chopped
1 hard-boiled egg, finely
  chopped

Mix dressng ingredients and then generously top sandwiches.

BARBECUED BEEF BUNDLES

Can be doubled or tripled for a crowd!

Easy

**6 Servings
Make Ahead
Freeze**

1 lb. ground chuck
1 large onion, chopped
¾ cup catsup
1 Tbsp. prepared mustard
1 Tbsp. Worcestershire
  sauce
1 Tbsp. cider vinegar
1 Tbsp. sugar
Hamburg rolls

Brown meat and onion. Mix together remaining ingredients and add to browned meat and onion. Cover and simmer for 20 minutes. Serve in warmed hamburg rolls. This recipe may be made in advance and refrigerated; when ready to serve, just reheat.

MICROWAVED SLOPPY JOES

Easy

4-6 Servings
Make Ahead
Freeze

1 lb. ground beef
2 Tbsp. onion, minced
½ cup canned tomato
   sauce or paste
2 Tbsp. brown sugar
2 Tbsp. vinegar
2 tsp. prepared mustard
1 tsp. chili powder
1 tsp. Worcestershire
   sauce
½ tsp. salt
¼ tsp. pepper
4 hamburg rolls

Place ground beef in 1½ quart glass casserole. Cook, covered, in microwave oven on high for 5 minutes, stirring once. Drain fat. Add onion, tomato sauce, brown sugar, vinegar, mustard, chili powder, Worcestershire sauce, salt and pepper; mix thoroughly. Cook 3 minutes, stirring once. Let stand for 10 minutes to blend flavors. Cook for 3 minutes longer, stirring once. Serve hot mixture over split hamburg rolls.

DIET REUBEN SANDWICH

Easy

1 Sandwich

1 slice rye bread
1 tsp. Dijon mustard
2 oz. white turkey meat,
   sliced
¼ cup sauerkraut, drained
1 slice Swiss cheese

Toast bread lightly. Spread with mustard. Top with turkey and sauerkraut. Bake at 325° for 4-5 minutes. Place cheese on top and broil until cheese melts.

BAGELOVER'S IMPERIAL CRAB

COMPLIMENTS OF

GOLDEN GARTER RESTAURANT, ITHACA, N.Y.

Average   **2-4 Servings**

Butter
2 Bagelover's bagels,
   sliced
½ lb. crab meat
2 Tbsp. fresh green
   pepper, finely chopped
1 canned pimiento, diced
3 Tbsp. mayonnaise
½ tsp. dry English mustard
1 Tbsp. prepared mustard
1 egg yolk
½ tsp. salt
Dash of pepper
2 Tbsp. bread crumbs
Salad oil
Paprika

Butter outside of bagels. Place on shallow baking pan, sliced side up. Mix crab meat, green pepper, pimiento, mayonnaise, dry mustard, prepared mustard, egg yolk, salt and pepper. Mix thoroughly and spread mixture on bagel. Sprinkle bread crumbs on crab meat mixture. Sprinkle salad oil on bread crumbs and sprinkle on paprika. Bake at 400° for approximately 12-15 minutes or until top is lightly browned.

 ## BUMSTEADS

4 Servings
Make Ahead
Freeze

Easy

¼ cup sharp Cheddar
   cheese, cubed
2 hard-boiled eggs,
   chopped
1 6½ oz. can tuna, flaked
1 Tbsp. green pepper,
   chopped
1 Tbsp. onion, chopped
1 Tbsp. green olives,
   chopped
1 Tbsp. sweet pickle,
   chopped
½ cup mayonnaise (more
   if desired)
4 hamburg rolls

Mix all ingredients, except rolls, together. Add enough mayonnaise to wet thoroughly. Fill rolls generously. Wrap each roll in foil. Bake at 300° for 30 minutes.

IROQUOIS INDIANS

The Iroquois Indians were the first to live on the banks of the Finger Lakes. They formed a federation of tribes. The Five Nations, which included the Mohawk, Oneida, Onondaga, Cayuga and Seneca.

BREADS, PICKLES AND PRESERVES

BREADS

Yeast

Quick

Muffins

Coffee Cakes

Other

PICKLES

RELISHES

JAMS AND JELLIES

OLD-FASHIONED WHITE BREAD

A traditional bread for today's woman!

Average

2 Loaves
Make Ahead
Freeze

2 yeast cakes
¼ tsp. sugar
½ cup warm water
2 Tbsp. shortening (Crisco
  preferred) or margarine
1 Tbsp. salt
6 Tbsp. sugar
¼ cup powdered milk
2 cups *hot* water
7-8 cups flour

Dissolve yeast and ¼ tsp. sugar in warm water; set aside. Add shortening, salt, sugar and powdered milk to **hot** water. Add yeast mixture to hot water mixture and combine. Add flour, 1 cup at a time, stirring until smooth after each cup. After adding 4 cups flour, when dough cleans bowl, turn onto board and start kneading in flour. Fold in quarters, punch like a pillow and keep folding, kneading and turning until dough is elastic and satiny, about 15 minutes. Place in greased bowl, cover with cloth and place in warm, draft free place. When doubled in bulk, punch down and let rise again, about 45 minutes. Grease loaf pans; shape into oval loaves and place in pans and let rise. Bake at 375° about 40-45 minutes, or until browned. Test for doneness by tapping. It should sound hollow. Let cool in pans 5 minutes, then turn out of pans.

CINNAMON ROLLS

Average

3 Dozen
Make Ahead
Freeze

Old-Fashioned White
  Bread dough
½ cup butter or margarine,
  melted
½ cup nut meats, chopped
1 cup sugar
3 Tbsp. cinnamon

Using Old-Fashioned White Bread as base, after second rising, roll into long, fat rectangle. With pastry brush, paint inside of dough with melted butter. Spread nut meats over all and then cover with cinnamon and sugar. Don't use up all the sugar. Roll up dough jelly roll fashion across width, not length. When finished rolling, paint with butter to make it stick. With knife cut into 1 inch sections. Cut only 1 or 2 sections at a time. Dip into butter and then into sugar. Place into buttered pans at least 1½ inches apart. Cover and let rise until doubled. Bake at 350° for 30-40 minutes.

CHERRY VANOCKA

COMPLIMENTS OF KELLE BLIEK AND
THE WAYNE COUNTY HISTORICAL SOCIETY

1½ cups butter
⅓ cup flour
2 pkgs. dry yeast
½ cup water
¾ cup milk, scalded
¼ cup sugar
1 tsp. salt
1 egg, beaten
4 cups flour

Cream butter with ⅓ cup flour. Roll butter mixture between 2 sheets of wax paper to form a 12x6 inch rectangle. Chill thoroughly. Dissolve yeast in lukewarm water. Combine scalded milk, sugar and salt. Cool mixture to lukewarm. Add yeast and egg. Mix well. Add 4 cups flour. Turn out and knead on lightly floured surface until smooth and glossy, about 5 minutes. Roll dough into a 14 inch square on a lightly floured surface. Place chilled butter mixture on half the dough. Fold over other half of dough, sealing edges well with heel of hand. Roll dough on lightly floured surface into a 20x12 inch rectangle. Fold in thirds, so that you have three layers. Roll again into a 20x12 inch rectangle. Repeat the folding and rolling 2 more times. Chill ½ hour after last rolling. Roll into a 15x14 inch rectangle; lightly make two lines dividing dough into three equal sections. On the two outside sections make 7-9 diagonal cuts. They must be the same on each side.

FILLING:
1 20 oz. can cherry pie
  filling
½ tsp. almond extract
½ tsp. orange rind
2 tsp. wheat germ
1½ Tbsp. coconut
2 Tbsp. almonds, crushed

Mix first five ingredients together. Spread filling down the center section; sprinkle with crushed almonds. Fold the dough strips over filling to make a braid-like bread. Tuck the last strips under the vanocka. Place on a cookie sheet and bake in preheated 350° oven for 50-60 minutes. Remove from oven when golden brown.

GLAZE:
½ cup confectioners'
  sugar
Milk

Mix sugar and enough milk to desired consistency. Spread on warm vanocka.

PORTUGUESE SWEET BREAD

Average

2 Loaves
Make Ahead
Freeze

2 pkgs. active dry yeast
1 cup plus 1 tsp. sugar
1 cup lukewarm water
   (approximately
      100°-115°)
½ cup butter
4 eggs
1 Tbsp. salt
5-6 cups flour
   (approximately)

Combine yeast, 1 tsp. sugar and water in a large bowl and allow to proof. Melt butter in saucepan and stir in 1 cup sugar. Add to yeast mixture and stir to combine. Add 3 eggs and salt and mix well. Then add 5 cups flour, 2 cups at a time, until dough leaves side of bowl and can be kneaded onto floured board. Knead about 10 minutes, until dough is smooth and elastic, adding additional flour, as necessary. Place dough in buttered bowl, cover with plastic wrap, and let rise until double in bulk, about 1½ to 2 hours. Punch down dough and divide into 2 equal pieces. Shape into round loaves and place into 2 buttered pans or onto cookie sheet. Cover and let rise again until doubled in bulk. Brush tops with remaining egg, lightly beaten. Bake at 350° for 30 minutes or until bread is a rich, dark, shiny color and sounds hollow when tapped on top and bottom. Cool on racks.

WHOLE WHEAT BREAD

It's even better toasted!

Average

2 Loaves
Make Ahead
Freeze

¾ cup milk
3 Tbsp. sugar
4 tsp. salt
⅓ cup butter or margarine
⅓ cup molasses
1½ cups warm milk
2 pkgs. active dry yeast
  (or cakes)
About 3½ cups whole
  wheat flour, unsifted
About 3½ cups all-purpose
  flour, sifted

Scald milk; stir in sugar, salt, butter and molasses; cool to lukewarm. Measure warm milk into large bowl. Sprinkle or crumble in yeast; stir until dissolved. Stir into lukewarm milk mixture, 2 cups whole wheat flour, and 2 cups all-purpose flour; beat until smooth. Add enough remaining whole wheat and white flour to make soft dough. Turn out onto lightly floured board and knead until smooth and elastic, about 8-10 minutes. Place in greased bowl, turning to grease top. Cover; let rise in warm place (80-85°) free from draft, until doubled in bulk, about 1 hour. Punch down. (Push fist into center of dough and pull edges into center; turn over.) Then divide dough in half; shape into loaves. Place into two greased 9x5x3 inch bread pans. Cover; let rise in warm place until doubled in bulk, about 1 hour. Bake at 400° for 25-30 minutes. Remove from pans and cool on wire racks.

HELPFUL HINT

To proof yeast, add 1 Tbsp. sugar to yeast and dissolve in ¼ cup warm water in a 1 cup measure. Set aside for 10 minutes. If it doubles in volume, it's active.

96

WHOLE WHEAT RAISIN BREAD

Average

4 Loaves
Make Ahead
Freeze

¼-½ cup brown sugar or
   honey
1 Tbsp. salt
5 cups lukewarm water
3 Tbsp. or 3 pkgs. yeast
½ cup lukewarm water
8 cups whole wheat flour
½ cup butter, melted and
   cooled to lukewarm
4½ plus cups white flour
   (as needed for
    kneading)
½ cup raisins
Cinnamon

Dissolve sugar and salt in 5 cups water. Sprinkle yeast on top of ½ cup water. Combine both mixtures with flour and butter and mix thoroughly. Add white flour, 1 cup at a time until dough leaves sides of bowl and looks smooth. Let sit 15 minutes. Knead until elastic, about 5 minutes. Let rise until double in size. Divide into 4 portions on floured surface. Let sit 15 minutes. Roll out on floured surface, sprinkle with a handful of raisins and some cinnamon, and shape into loaves. Set in greased bread pans and let rise in warm place until double. Bake at 375° for 40 minutes. The amount of whole wheat flour can be increased for a courser bread. The amount of white flour would be decreased accordingly.

DILLY BREAD

Average

6 Servings
Make Ahead
Freeze

1½ cups cottage cheese
¼ cup water
2 Tbsp. sugar
2 Tbsp. onion, minced
1 Tbsp. butter
3 tsp. dill seed
1 tsp. salt
¼ tsp. baking soda
1 egg
2¼ to 2½ cups flour
1 pkg. yeast dissolved in
   ¼ cup warm water
Butter, softened

Heat cottage cheese to lukewarm in pan and then add ¼ cup water. Pour remaining ingredients, except flour and softened yeast mixture, into large bowl. Add softened yeast mixture. Then add flour to form a stiff dough, beating as flour is added. Cover dough. Let rise in warm place (85-90°) until light and doubled in size, about 50-60 minutes. Stir down dough. Turn into greased 8 inch round (1½ to 2 qt.) casserole. Let rise in warm place until light, about 40 minutes. Bake at 350° for 40-50 minutes or until golden brown. Brush with soft butter. It is excellent warm.

POCKET BREAD

Look at Herb Pita Toasts for a nice variation!

Average

6 Servings
Make Ahead
Freeze

¾ cup warm water
1 pkg. yeast
½ tsp. salt
1 tsp. sugar
2 cups flour
Cornmeal

Mix all ingredients, except cornmeal, together in medium-size bowl. Knead mixture, adding small amount of flour if mixture is unworkable. Divide into 6 balls. On floured surface roll into 4 inch circles. Sprinkle cookie sheet with cornmeal and place dough circles on cookie sheet. Let rise 10 minutes. Bake at 500° for 7-10 minutes. Watch carefully. To serve, cut in half and pull apart pocket. Spread with seasoned butter or fill with sandwich goodies.

HERB PITA TOASTS

Easy

1-2 dozen
Make Ahead

6 pita bread rounds
¾ cup butter, softened
2 Tbsp. parsley, minced
1 Tbsp. chives, snipped
1 Tbsp. lemon juice
1 large garlic clove,
   crushed and minced *or*
   ½ tsp. garlic powder
Salt and pepper

Cut pita bread rounds into halves or quarters. Cream remaining ingredients together. Cover and let stand at least 1 hour. Spread over pita bread and bake at 450° for 5 minutes.

APPLE-DATE TEA BREAD

Average

2 Loaves
Make Ahead
Freeze

3 cups flour
2 tsp. baking soda
½ tsp. salt
½ tsp. ground cloves
½ tsp. nutmeg
1 tsp. cinnamon
2 cups sugar
¾ cup margarine
2 eggs
1 cup cold coffee
1 cup dates, chopped
2 cups apples, unpeeled
   and cut into small pieces
1 cup raisins
1 cup walnuts, chopped

Sift dry ingredients together and set aside. Cream margarine and sugar. Add eggs. Alternately add the sifted dry ingredients and coffee. Add rest of ingredients. Place in greased loaf pans and bake at 375° for 50-60 minutes.

APRICOT NUT BREAD

Average

1 Loaf
Make Ahead
Freeze

2½ cups flour
1 cup sugar
3½ tsp. baking powder
1 tsp. salt
3 Tbsp. salad oil
½ cup milk
1 egg
1 cup nuts, finely chopped
¾ cup orange juice
4 tsp. orange peel, grated
1 cup dried apricots, finely
   chopped

Combine all ingredients and beat with mixer on medium speed or in food processor for 30 seconds, scraping sides of bowl. Pour into 2 small or 1 large greased and floured loaf pan. Bake at 350° for 1 hour or until fork inserted in center comes out clean.

99

SPECIAL BANANA BREAD

A child's delight!

Average

1 Loaf
Make Ahead
Freeze

1½ cups flour
1 tsp. baking soda
4 Tbsp. sour cream
½ cup butter or margarine,
  softened
1¼ cups sugar
2 eggs
1 cup bananas, mashed
  (2-3 bananas)
6 oz. chocolate chips
½ cup walnuts, chopped
1 tsp. vanilla
Pinch of salt

Sift flour 2 times and set aside. Mix baking soda and sour cream and set aside. Cream butter with sugar until light and fluffy; add eggs one at a time, beating well after each addition. Add flour and sour cream mixtures alternately with butter mixture. Stir in bananas, chocolate chips and walnuts. Add vanilla and salt. Place in greased and floured loaf pan and bake at 350° for 45-60 minutes. May also bake in 2 small loaf pans using same temperature and time.

BLUEBERRY BREAD

A nice welcome for a new neighbor!

Easy

8-10 Servings
Make Ahead
Freeze

2 cups flour
4 tsp. baking powder
½ tsp. salt
1½ Tbsp. butter or
  margarine, softened
¾ cup sugar
1 egg
¾ cup milk
  (approximately)
1 cup blueberries
3 Tbsp. sugar
1 tsp. cinnamon

Into a bowl put flour, baking powder and salt. Blend in butter and sugar. In a measuring cup, beat egg lightly with a fork; add enough milk to measure ¾ cup plus 2 Tbsp. Beat milk mixture into flour mixture. Stir in blueberries and put batter in greased 8 inch square pan, spreading evenly. In small dish, combine sugar and cinnamon. Sprinkle mixture over batter. Bake at 350° for 40 minutes, or until well browned and pulled away from sides of pan. Serve warm. This is yummy for breakfast, lunch or dinner.

BLUEBERRY ORANGE BREAD

Average

1 Loaf
Make Ahead
Freeze

2 Tbsp. butter
¼ cup boiling water
½ cup orange juice
3 tsp. orange rind
1 egg
1 cup sugar
2 cups flour
1 tsp. baking powder
¼ tsp. salt
½ tsp. baking soda
1 cup blueberries

Melt butter in boiling water; add orange juice and rind. Beat egg and sugar together and mix with orange mixture. Add dry ingredients. Fold in blueberries. Bake at 350° for 60-70 minutes.

CRANBERRY-BANANA BREAD

Fill your freezer for the holidays!

Average

1 Loaf
Make Ahead
Freeze

4 Tbsp. butter
1¼ cups sugar
1 egg, beaten until smooth
2 cups flour
1½ tsp. baking powder
½ tsp. baking soda
1 tsp. salt
⅔ cup banana, mashed
1¼ cups fresh or frozen
  cranberries, coarsely
  chopped
½ cup walnuts, chopped

Blend butter and sugar; add egg. Sift together dry ingredients. With a spoon, add dry ingredients to creamed mixture until all flour is moistened. Fold in banana, cranberries and nuts. Pour into greased loaf pan. Bake at 350° for 65-70 minutes. Cool 10 minutes before removing from pan.

CRANBERRY-ORANGE NUT BREAD

Average

**2 Loaves
Make Ahead
Freeze**

4 cups flour, sifted
1½ cups sugar
1 Tbsp. baking powder
1 tsp. salt
1 tsp. baking soda
2 cups cranberries, cut in halves
1 cup walnuts or pecans, chopped
2 tsp. orange rind, grated
2 eggs, beaten
1½ cups orange juice
½ cup salad oil

Sift together dry ingredients. Stir in cranberries, nuts and orange rind. Combine eggs, orange juice and salad oil. Add to dry ingredients, stirring until just moistened. Put in two 8½x4½x2½ inch lightly greased and floured loaf pans. Bake at 375° for 50-60 minutes or until done. Cool thoroughly.

ORANGE NUT BREAD

Average

**2 Loaves
Make Ahead
Freeze**

2 eggs
2 cups sugar
4 Tbsp. shortening, melted
1 6 oz. can concentrated orange juice and water to make 1 cup
4 cups flour
2 tsp. baking powder
1 cup boiling water with 2 tsp. baking soda (use 2 cup measure as this bubbles)
1 cup walnuts, chopped (black preferred)
1 tsp. vanilla
1 cup dates, chopped (optional)

Mix all ingredients well and place into two well greased 9x5 inch loaf pans. Bake at 350° for 1 hour or until toothpick comes out clean. Cool 10 minutes before removing from pan. May also make 4 smaller loaves and bake for 45 minutes.

RHUBARB NUT BREAD

Freeze and enjoy the taste of rhubarb all year long!

Easy

2 Loaves
Make Ahead
Freeze

1½ cups brown sugar
⅔ cup salad oil
1 egg
1 tsp. baking soda
1 tsp. salt
1 tsp. vanilla
1 cup sour milk
2½ cups flour
2½ cups rhubarb, diced
½ cup nuts, chopped
½ cup sugar
1 Tbsp. butter, softened

Beat together brown sugar, oil and egg. Mix baking soda, salt, vanilla and sour milk. Add to first mixture. Add flour, rhubarb and nuts. Pour batter into 2 greased loaf pans. Sprinkle top with mixture of sugar and butter. Bake at 325° for 60 minutes.

BOSTON BROWN BREAD

Better than Mother used to make!

Average

2 Loaves
Make Ahead
Freeze

2 cups buttermilk
⅔ cup molasses
1 cup rye flour
1 cup whole wheat flour
1 cup yellow cornmeal
2 tsp. baking soda
1 tsp. salt
2 Tbsp. brown sugar
1 cup raisins
2 Tbsp. butter or
    margarine, melted

Lightly grease insides of two 1 lb. size coffee cans. In large bowl, combine buttermilk and molasses. Sift both kinds of flour, cornmeal, baking soda, salt and sugar over buttermilk mixture. Add raisins. Stir well. Stir in butter. Pour into coffee cans, no more than ⅔ full. Cover each can loosely (so the batter can rise) with foil; secure with elastic bands. Place cans in kettle or Dutch oven half filled with water. Bring to a boil, cover, and steam for 2 hours, adding more water as necessary. Remove from heat; let cans cool completely in water, then remove to wire rack to stand for 10 minutes. Remove bread from cans; let cool completely, then wrap in foil; refrigerate until ready to use. To serve, preheat oven to 350°. Unwrap bread; heat for 20 minutes or until hot.

GOODIE BREAD

You won't be satisifed with potato chips once you've tasted these!

Average

8 Servings
Make Ahead

¾ cup butter, softened
¾ tsp. oregano
¾ tsp. garlic salt
¾ tsp. onion salt
¾ tsp. parsley flakes
¾ tsp. seasoned salt
   (Jane's Crazy Mixed-Up
   Salt preferred)
Paprika
1 loaf Veri-Thin
   Pepperidge Farm Bread
   or Arnold's Melba Bread

Mix butter and spices, except paprika. Spread on bread and cut into halves or quarters. Sprinkle with paprika. Place on cookie sheet. Bake at 250° for 1 hour, then turn off oven and leave bread in closed oven overnight. Serve with soups, salads or snacks.

HOT HERB BREAD

Easy

1 Loaf
Make Ahead
Freeze

½ cup butter, softened
¼ tsp. dried dill weed
1 tsp. parsley flakes
¼ tsp. oregano, crumbled
1 clove garlic, minced
1 loaf white bread (Italian,
   sliced preferred)
Parmesan cheese, grated
Parsley for topping

Blend all ingredients except bread and cheese. Spread on each slice of bread. Put loaf back together and place in aluminum foil, leaving top exposed. Sprinkle top with cheese and additional parsley. Bake at 400° for 10 minutes.

BEER BREAD

Easy

1 Loaf
Make Ahead
Freeze

3 cups self-rising flour
1 12 oz. can beer
1 Tbsp. sugar
Butter, softened

Mix ingredients in oiled loaf pan. Butter top and bake at 350° for 1 hour and 15 minutes.

GRUYERE BREAD

Complicated

2 Rings
Make Ahead
Freeze

2 cups milk
½ cup butter, cut into
  pieces
2 tsp. salt
Dash of pepper
2 cups flour, sifted
8 eggs
½ lb. natural Gruyere
  cheese, grated
4 Tbsp. Swiss cheese,
  grated
Milk

Scald milk and cool. Strain milk into a large saucepan and add butter, salt and pepper. Bring mixture to a rolling boil and add flour all at once. Cook paste over low heat, beating it briskly with wooden spoon, until mixture forms a ball and leaves the sides of the pan clean. Remove pan from heat and beat in eggs, one at a time, incorporating each egg thoroughly before adding the next. When the paste is shiny and smooth, mix Gruyere cheese into mixture. Let dough cool. Divide dough in half. With an oval spoon, scoop out from one half of the dough pieces the size of an egg. With a rubber spatula push them off the spoon onto a buttered baking sheet in a ring, leaving a space in the middle about 2½ inches in diameter. Use a teaspoon to make smaller ovals on top of the first layer. Repeat the procedure with remaining dough to make 2 rings. Brush dough with milk and sprinkle each ring with 2 Tbsp. Swiss cheese. Bake at 375° for 45 minutes, or until they are well puffed and golden brown.

MEXICAN CORN BREAD

Average

6-8 Servings
Make Ahead

1 cup yellow cornmeal
1 8.5 oz. can cream style
  corn
¾ cup milk
⅓ cup oil
1 tsp. salt
½ tsp. baking soda
2 eggs
1 4 oz. can green chili
  peppers (optional)
1 cup or more sharp
  cheese, grated

Mix all ingredients together except cheese. Bake in slightly greased casserole or 8 inch square pan at 350-375° for 30-40 minutes. Sprinkle cheese on top during last few minutes — just long enough to melt. This is a very moist corn bread.

RAISED JOHNNY CAKE

COMPLIMENTS OF
CORNING/PAINTED POST HISTORICAL SOCIETY

1 cup flour
1 cup yellow corn meal
1 Tbsp. sugar
2 tsp. baking powder
1 tsp. salt
½ tsp. baking soda
¾ cup sour milk
1 large egg
¼ cup margarine, melted
  or salad oil

Combine all ingredients. Bake for 30 minutes in a pre-heated, well greased, cast iron skillet. We use this recipe regularly, using our footed skillet and serve it to visiting school children. Source unknown. Bake at 425° for 20 minutes.

ONION KUCHEN

Easy

8 Servings
Make Ahead

2 medium onions, peeled,
  sliced and separated
  into rings
3 Tbsp. butter or
  margarine
1 pkg. refrigerated
  homestyle or buttermilk
  biscuits (10)
1 egg
1 cup sour cream
½ tsp. salt
1 tsp. poppy seeds

Saute onion in butter or margarine just until soft. Separate the 10 biscuits; place in a single layer in an ungreased 8 inch layer-cake or spring-form pan, pressing together to cover bottom completely. Spoon onion mixture on top. Beat egg slightly in a small bowl; blend in sour cream and salt. Spoon over onion mixture; sprinkle with poppy seeds. Bake at 375° for 30 minutes or until topping is set. Slice in wedges; serve warm.

SAVORY TOMATO QUICK BREAD

Average

1 Loaf
Make Ahead
Freeze

2½ cups flour
1 Tbsp. baking powder
1 tsp. salt
1 tsp. garlic powder
1 tsp. oregano, crushed
1 Tbsp. sugar
½ cup Mozzarella cheese, shredded
¼ cup Parmesan cheese, grated
⅓-⅔ cup milk
1½ cups tomatoes, peeled, chopped and drained, reserving liquid
2 eggs
¼ cup salad or olive oil

Stir together flour, baking powder, salt, garlic powder, oregano, sugar and cheeses. Add enough milk to drained tomato liquid to make ⅔ cup. Blend liquid with eggs and oil. Stir liquid and tomatoes into flour mixture until thoroughly moistened. Pour batter into 8½x4½ inch greased loaf pan. Bake in preheated 350° oven for 75-80 minutes. If bread browns before baking time is complete, cover with foil tent. Cool 10 minutes in pan and turn onto wire rack and cool thoroughly. Best served warm.

ZUCCHINI BREAD

Average

1 Bundt Loaf
Make Ahead
Freeze

3 eggs
1 cup salad oil
2½ cups sugar
2 cups unpeeled raw zucchini, grated
2 tsp. cinnamon
1 tsp. salt
1 tsp. baking soda
¼ tsp. baking powder
3 cups flour
1 cup walnuts, chopped

Preheat oven to 350°. Beat eggs until foamy; gradually beat in oil and sugar. Add zucchini, cinnamon, salt, baking soda and baking powder and mix well. Blend in flour. Fold in walnuts. Pour into greased bundt pan and bake for 1 hour or until bread tests done. Cool 10 minutes before removing from pan.

BROWN SUGAR MUFFINS

Easy

1 Dozen
Make Ahead
Freeze

TOPPING:
¼ cup light brown sugar
¼ cup flour
2 Tbsp. butter
2 tsp. cinnamon

Mix topping ingredients until crumbly. Preheat oven to 375°. Lightly grease bottoms of 12 muffin pan cups.

BATTER:
4 Tbsp. butter, softened
½ cup brown sugar, packed firmly
1 egg
½ cup milk
1⅓ cups flour
½ tsp. salt
1½ tsp. baking powder

At medium speed, beat butter until fluffy; beat in brown sugar, then egg until very light and fluffy. At low speed, blend in milk, flour, salt and baking powder until just combined. Divide into muffin cups. Sprinkle topping over muffins and bake for 20 minutes.

CINNAMON MUFFINS

Average

1 Dozen
Make Ahead
Freeze

5 Tbsp. shortening
¾ cup sugar
2 eggs, separated
1 cup flour
¼ tsp. salt
¾ tsp. baking powder
1 tsp. nutmeg
½ cup milk
1 tsp. vanilla
Cinnamon
Sugar

Cream shortening and sugar together. Add egg yolks. Sift together dry ingredients. Add milk and vanilla alternately with dry ingredients. Fold in 2 stiffly beaten egg whites. Grease muffin pans well and fill ⅔ full. Bake at 375° for 20 minutes. Shake muffins in cinnamon-sugar while warm.

108

BEST BLUEBERRY MUFFINS

Let the children make this one!

Easy

1 Dozen
Make Ahead
Freeze

1½ cups flour, sifted
10 Tbsp. sugar
2½ tsp. baking powder
½ tsp. salt
1 egg
½ cup milk
1 cup fresh blueberries

Sift dry ingredients together; add egg and milk. Fold in blueberries. Put into greased muffin tins and bake at 400° for 20-25 minutes.

BLUEBERRY MUFFINS

Average

1 Dozen
Make Ahead
Freeze

½ cup margarine, softened
¾-1 cup sugar
2 eggs
1 tsp. vanilla
2 cups flour
2 tsp. baking powder
½ tsp. salt
½ cup milk
2½ cups blueberries (may
use frozen blueberries)
2 tsp. sugar (topping)

Cream margarine and sugar; add eggs and vanilla. Add dry ingredients and milk alternately. Mash ½ cup blueberries and add to above. Add rest of whole blueberries. Grease cups and **tops** of muffin tins. Fill muffin cups ½ full. Sprinkle sugar on muffin batter. Bake at 375° for 30 minutes. Let cool in pan for 30 minutes before removing.

CINNAMON POPOVERS

Easy

8 Popovers

3 eggs
1 cup milk
1 cup flour
3 Tbsp. butter, melted
1 tsp. cinnamon
¼ tsp. salt

In blender, combine eggs, milk, flour, butter, cinnamon and salt. Cover and blend 30 seconds or until combined. Fill 8 **well greased** custard cups or muffin tins half full. Bake at 400° for 40 minutes. Remove from custard cups. Serve hot with butter or margarine, if desired.

109

BUTTERMILK BRAN MUFFINS

Batter keeps for weeks!

Average

**3½ Dozen
Make Ahead
Freeze**

1 cup boiling water
2 cups All-Bran (Kellogg's
  preferred)
1 cup butter or margarine
2 eggs
1½ cups sugar
2 cups buttermilk
1 tsp. salt
2½ cups flour
2½ tsp. baking soda
1 cup whole bran buds,
  (Nabisco or Kellogg's
  preferred)
1 cup raisins or dates

Pour boiling water over All-Bran and let stand; cream butter, eggs, sugar and then add buttermilk. Add salt, flour and baking soda. Add bran buds, raisins or dates, and All-Bran and water mixture. Store overnight in a sealed jar. This may be kept up to 6 weeks in refrigerator. As wanted, place in greased muffin cups and bake at 375° for 15-20 minutes.

CHEDDAR BRAN MUFFINS

Average

**1½ Dozen
Make Ahead
Freeze**

1¼ cups buttermilk or sour
  milk
1 cup whole bran
4 Tbsp. shortening
⅓ cup sugar
1 egg
1½ cups flour, sifted
1½ tsp. baking powder
½ tsp. salt
¼ tsp. baking soda
1 cup Cheddar cheese,
  shredded

Pour buttermilk or sour milk over bran in small bowl; let stand until softened. Cream shortening and sugar until light and fluffy. Beat in egg. Sift together flour, baking powder, salt and baking soda. Add to creamed mixture alternately with milk-bran mixture. Stir in cheese. Fill greased muffin pans ⅔ full. Bake at 400° for 20-25 minutes. Serve warm.

APPLE-SOUR CREAM COFFEE CAKE

Average

10 Servings
Make Ahead

CAKE:
½ cup margarine, softened
1 cup sugar
2 eggs
2 cups flour
1 tsp. baking powder
1 tsp. baking soda
¼ tsp. salt
1 cup sour cream
1 tsp. vanilla

Cream margarine and sugar. Add eggs and beat at medium speed until well blended. Sift dry ingredients; add gradually to margarine mixture, beating at slow speed until well blended. Add sour cream and vanilla and blend well at medium speed. Grease bundt-tube pan **well**.

TOPPING:
½ cup sugar
1 heaping Tbsp. cinnamon
3 small apples, thinly sliced
3 Tbsp. walnuts, chopped (optional)

Combine sugar and cinnamon and dust greased pan with approximately 1 Tbsp. of this mixture. Reserve another Tbsp. cinnamon-sugar mixture. Pour ½ cake batter into pan. Spread apples and nuts evenly over batter and sprinkle cinnamon-sugar mixture evenly over apples. Pour remaining batter over this. Sprinkle reserved Tbsp. cinnamon-sugar mixture over top. Bake at 350° for 50-60 minutes. Cool 20 minutes and turn out onto plate. **Do not** let cool completely in pan. It will never come out in one piece.

CINNAMON APPLE COFFEE CAKE

Average

14-16 Servings
Make Ahead
Freeze

6-8 medium apples
2¼ cups sugar
4 tsp. cinnamon
4 eggs
½ cup orange juice (any fruit juice may be used)
1 cup oil
2½ tsp. vanilla
3 tsp. baking powder
3 cups flour

Grease and flour tube pan. Peel apples and cut into thin slices. Add ½ cup sugar and cinnamon; set aside. Beat eggs and orange juice by hand. Continue to beat by hand while adding oil and 1¾ cups sugar. Add vanilla, baking powder and flour, mixing well. Layer batter, apples, batter and remaining apples in tube pan. Bake at 350° for 1¼ to 1½ hours.

BLITZ COFFEE CAKE

Too simple to be as good as it is!

Easy

CAKE:
1 scant cup sugar
4 Tbsp. margarine
1 egg
1¾ cups flour
3 tsp. bakng powder
Pinch of salt
1 cup milk

Combine sugar and margarine; add egg and mix. Combine dry ingredients and add to sugar mixture alternately with milk. Spoon mixture into greased 9x9 inch pan.

TOPPING:
¼ cup brown sugar
1 tsp. cinnamon
¼ cup nuts, chopped

Combine topping ingredients and sprinkle evenly on top of batter. Bake at 350° for 30 minutes.

SOUR CREAM COFFEE CAKE

Average

1 cup unsalted butter,
    softened
1 cup sugar
1 cup sour cream
3 eggs, separated
1¾ cups flour, sifted
1 tsp. baking powder
1 tsp. baking soda

Cream butter and sugar. Add sour cream and egg yolks and beat until fluffy. Add flour, baking powder and baking soda. Beat egg whites until stiff; fold into batter. Pour ½ batter into greased tube pan.

TOPPING:
½ cup sugar
½ cup nuts, chopped
1½ tsp. cinnamon
2 Tbsp. butter

Combine all ingredients, except butter. Divide topping in ½ and sprinkle on ½ batter. Add rest of batter and top with rest of topping. Dot with butter. Bake at 325° for 1 hour. Cool in pan for 20 minutes.

PANCAKES
Average   **4-6 Servings**

1¼ cups flour
¼ tsp. salt
1 Tbsp. baking powder
1 Tbsp. sugar
3 eggs, separated
2 cups milk
4 Tbsp. butter, melted

Sift flour, salt, baking powder and sugar into bowl. Beat egg yolks into dry ingredients. Add milk and butter and mix well. Beat egg whites until stiff and fold into batter. Batter will be thin and lumpy. Fry on medium-high heat in **well greased** heavy frying pan or griddle.

BIRKETT MILLS ORIGINAL BUCKWHEAT PANCAKE RECIPE

COMPLIMENTS OF
YATES COUNTY GENEALOGICAL AND HISTORICAL SOCIETY, PENN YAN, N.Y.

Average   **4 Servings**
                                     Make Ahead

2 cups sour milk or
  buttermilk
1 tsp. salt
½ cake compound yeast
1 Tbsp. molasses
A sufficient amount of light
  buckwheat flour to make
  a thick batter
½ tsp. baking soda

Put first five ingredients in an earthen crock. Set in a warm place to rise overnight. In the morning add baking soda, dissolved in warm water. If batter is too thick, thin with water. Save a little of this batter as a starter for the next day's cakes and no more yeast need be added. Buckwheat cakes, to be light and crisp, must be served immediately from a hot greased griddle.

GERMAN PANCAKES
Average   **6 Servings**

6 eggs, separated
2 Tbsp. sugar
3⅓ cups milk
⅓ cup salad oil
3 cups flour
4 tsp. baking powder
1 tsp. salt

Beat egg whites until stiff. Beat together yolks, sugar, milk and oil. Sift together flour, baking powder and salt; add to milk mixture and fold in egg whites. Prepare as regular pancakes.

 # WAFFLES

This is no ordinary waffle!

6 Servings
Freeze

Easy

1¾ cups flour
¼ cup cornmeal
1 tsp. salt
1 tsp. baking soda
2 cups buttermilk
1 egg, slightly beaten
5 Tbsp. shortening, melted
Cheese, grated (optional)

Mix all dry ingredients together. Stir in buttermilk, egg, shortening and cheese. Put in pitcher and pour onto hot greased griddle. Good with creamed ham or chicken or the traditional maple syrup.

OVERNIGHT FRENCH TOAST DELUXE

4 Servings
Make Ahead

Easy

8 slices French bread (¾ inch thick)
4 eggs
1 cup milk
1 Tbsp. sugar
⅛ tsp. salt
2 Tbsp. orange juice
½ tsp. vanilla extract
4 Tbsp. butter
Confectioners' sugar mixed with a little cinnamon

Place bread in a 13x9 inch baking dish. Combine eggs, milk, sugar, salt, orange juice and vanilla and beat well. Pour mixture over bread slices; turn slices over to coat evenly. Cover and refrigerate overnight. Melt butter in a large skillet. Remove bread from dish and saute in butter for 4 minutes on each side or until browned. Sprinkle toast with confectioners' sugar and serve immediately.

TEA SCONES

Average

1½ Dozen
Make Ahead
Freeze

2 cups all-purpose flour
½ cup sugar
2 tsp. cream of tartar
1 tsp. baking soda
¾ tsp. salt
½ cup shortening
½ cup raisins, currants, figs or prunes
2 eggs, slightly beaten
¼ cup milk

Sift dry ingredients together. Blend in shortening with pastry blender until mixture resembles fine bread crumbs. Add remaining ingredients. Mix with fork, divide into 2 parts and turn each part out onto floured board. Do not handle. Flatten with rolling pin into circles ½ inch or more thick. Cut into triangles (optional) and place on greased and floured baking sheet. Bake at 400° for 15 minutes, or until golden brown. Serve warm and lightly buttered.

BREAD AND BUTTER PICKLES

Average

3 Pints
Make Ahead

2 lbs. cucumbers, sliced
and unpeeled
2 large onions, sliced
1 large green pepper,
shredded
2 oz. salt
15 fluid oz. wine vinegar
12 oz. soft brown sugar
½ tsp. ground tumeric
¼ tsp. ground cloves
1½ tsp. mustard seed
½ tsp. celery seed

Place cucumbers, onions, pepper and salt in large mixing bowl. Mix well, cover and leave for 3 hours. Rinse vegetables very thoroughly in cold water. Drain well and put in saucepan. Add vinegar. Bring to boil; then simmer gently until vegetables are soft. Add sugar and spices; stir over low heat to dissolve sugar. Bring to boil and take off heat. Turn into bowl and leave to become cold. Pour into jars and process.

CANDIED DILL PICKLES

Easy

1 Quart
Make Ahead

1 quart dill pickles, cut
into chunks or slices
1½ cups sugar
½ cup white vinegar
1 Tbsp. pickling spices
1 stick cinnamon

Drain and rinse pickles. Boil together sugar, vinegar and spices. Pack pickles in a jar. Add stick cinnamon in the center of pickles. Pour hot syrup over pickles. Let stand overnight. Drain syrup off pickles into saucepan. Bring to a boil and then pour over pickles. Repeat process for 3 more days. Chill before serving. After pickles are gone, pour syrup over raw cauliflower and marinate 1 week for delicious pickled cauliflower.

REFRIGERATOR PICKLES

Easy

1 Gallon
Make Ahead

2-3 dozen medium
cucumbers, thinly sliced
1 quart cider vinegar
3 cups sugar
½ cup salt
1 bay leaf
1 tsp. black pepper
8 cloves garlic
Dill crushed (lots of it)

Slice cucumbers and reserve. Mix together vinegar, sugar, salt, bay leaf and pepper. Bring to a boil. Add garlic and dill to cucumbers. Pour syrup over cucumbers, garlic and dill. Let cool. Refrigerate for 4 weeks before eating.

116

APPLE AND DATE CHUTNEY

Easy

3 Pints
Make Ahead

2 cups cooking apples,
    diced
1 cup cooking dates,
    chopped
1 cup brown sugar
2½ cups vinegar
1 large onion, chopped
1 Tbsp. salt
1 tsp. allspice
1 tsp. ground ginger

Boil all ingredients together for 1 hour or until it is a good dark color. Put into sterilized jars.

CORN RELISH

Average

12 Pints
Make Ahead

24 ears of corn, corn
    stripped from ears
1 large head cabbage,
    chopped
12 green peppers,
    chopped
1 2.87 oz. can mustard
    seed
1 quart vinegar
2 cups water
1 tsp. tumeric
1 Tbsp. salt
1½ lbs. sugar
2 Tbsp. celery seed
6 onions, chopped

Combine all ingredients and cook in large pot for ½ hour. Pour into pint jars and process.

HOT CHILI SAUCE

Average

4 Quarts
Make Ahead
Freeze

6 medium onions
12 red hot peppers
20 large ripe tomatoes
4 cups white vinegar
5½ cups sugar
3 Tbsp. salt

Be very careful working with hot peppers. Wear rubber gloves and do not get juice near your eyes. Grind peeled onions and unseeded peppers in food processor or meat grinder. Peel tomatoes and cut into chunks. Place all ingredients in an enamelware pot and simmer, stirring often, about 1 hour or until thickened. Can according to standard canning procedures. Use it on hamburgers, hot dogs, meat loaf or as an hors d'oeuvre on top of cream cheese with crackers.

HOT DOG RELISH

Average

10 Pints
Make Ahead

12 green tomatoes
5 green peppers
3 red peppers
3 large onions
3 cups cider vinegar
1 9 oz. jar mustard
5 cups sugar
1 cup flour
2 Tbsp. salt
2 Tbsp. celery seed
2 Tbsp. tumeric

Finely grind tomatoes, peppers and onions in food grinder and drain. Add remaining ingredients and cook until mixture thickens. Pour hot into hot canning jars. Turn jars up-side down until cooled.

118

INDIA RELISH

Average

6 large onions
4 quarts green tomatoes
3 red sweet peppers
3 cups vinegar
½ oz. celery seed
2 oz. white mustard seed
3 cups sugar
⅓ cup salt
1 tsp. dry mustard

Put onions, tomatoes and peppers through food grinder or food processor. Add vinegar and scald for 20 minutes. Drain. Add all seasonings and heat thoroughly. Pack in hot sterile jars and seal.

PEPPER HASH

Average

12 red sweet peppers, seeded
12 green sweet peppers, seeded
2-3 large onions
3 cups brown or white vinegar
1½ cups white sugar
3 tsp. canning (Kosher) salt

Put peppers and onions through medium blade of food processor or in meat grinder. Place in non-metallic cooking pot and cover with boiling water. Let stand for 10 minutes. Drain. Add vinegar, sugar and salt. Bring to a boil, reduce heat and simmer for 15-20 minutes. Do **not** overcook or color is lost. Can in sterile glass jars according to routine procedures.

HOT MUSTARD SAUCE

Too many uses to list!

Easy

½ cup dry mustard
½ cup vinegar
1 egg
¼ cup sugar
⅛ tsp. salt
1 cup mayonnaise

Mix dry mustard and vinegar in glass jar. Cover and let stand overnight. In top of double boiler, beat egg, sugar and salt and add mustard mixture. Cook over hot, not boiling, water. Stir constantly, about 10 minutes, until mixture thickens slightly and coats spoon. When cool, add mayonnaise and beat until smooth. Put in jar(s) and store in refrigerator.

PIQUANT MUSTARD

Average

1⅓ Cups
Make Ahead

5 Tbsp. dry mustard
⅓ cup sugar
1 Tbsp. all-purpose flour
½ tsp. salt
Dash of red pepper
2 eggs, beaten
½ cup vinegar
1 Tbsp. butter or
   margarine

Combine mustard, sugar, flour, salt and pepper in top of double boiler. Add eggs and vinegar, blending thoroughly until thickened. Add butter; stir until melted. Cool mixture. Store in a jar in refrigerator.

SWEET MUSTARD SAUCE

Easy

1 Cup
Make Ahead

4 Tbsp. dry mustard
½ cup sugar
Salt and pepper to taste
2 eggs
½ cup light cream
¼ cup wine vinegar

Combine all ingredients, except vinegar, in top of double boiler. Beat with electric beater or wire whisk while slowly adding wine vinegar. Cook about 10 minutes or until thickened, stirring frequently. Serve with sliced kielbasa, ham or as a dip for Chinese egg rolls.

HOT PEPPER JELLY

Delicious served over cream cheese and spread on crackers!

Average

6 Cups
Make Ahead

¼ cup hot peppers,
   chopped
1½ cups sweet bell
   peppers, chopped
6½ cups sugar
1½ cups vinegar
1 bottle or 2 pouches
   Certo
Few drops green food
   coloring

Grind peppers. Mix peppers, sugar, vinegar and food coloring together in 6-8 quart saucepan and bring to a boil. Boil 3 minutes. Add Certo, bring to a full rolling boil and boil hard 1 minute, stirring constantly. Let stand 5 minutes. Skim off foam with large metal spoon and pour into sterile jars. Wipe away any drips from edge of jars with damp cloth. Seal jars by spooning ⅛ inch hot paraffin onto hot jelly surface. Make sure paraffin touches all sides and prick any air bubbles. Cool and store.

120

PEACH RUM JAM

Average

8 ½-Pints
Make Ahead

3¾ cups prepared
   peaches (3½ lbs. ripe
   peaches)
5½ cups sugar
1 box Sure-Jell fruit pectin
2¼ Tbsp. lemon juice
¼ cup rum

Chop or grind peaches. Measure sugar and set aside. Add Sure-Jell fruit pectin to fruit and mix well. Stir lemon juice and rum into prepared fruit. Place over high heat and stir until mixture comes to a hard boil. Stir in sugar at once. Bring to a full rolling boil and boil hard for 1 minute, stirring constantly. Remove from heat and skim off foam with metal spoon. Pack into hot sterile jars.

WINE JELLY

Easy

6 ½-Pints
Make Ahead

3¾ cups sugar
3 cups red wine
¾ cup water
1 box Sure-Jell or 1 pkg.
   Certo

Measure sugar and set aside. Combine wine, water and Sure-Jell and mix well. Place over high heat and stir until mixture comes to a hard boil. Be careful not to burn bottom of pan. Stir in sugar at once. Bring to a full rolling boil and boil hard for 1 minute, stirring constantly. Remove from heat and skim off foam with metal spoon. Pack into hot sterile jars. Good served with pork, lamb or even peanut butter!

NOTES

EThorborg 82

COWLES HALL — ELMIRA COLLEGE
Founded in 1855 as one of the first women's colleges, Elmira College
today is an independent, co-educational, liberal arts institution. Cowles
Hall was the original College building.

EGGS, CHEESE, PASTA AND RICE

SCOTCH EGGS

Average

4 Servings
Make Ahead

4 hard-boiled eggs
2 Tbsp. flour
8 oz. ground sausage
1 oz. fresh bread crumbs
   (1 slice white bread)

COATING:
1 egg
¼ cup milk
Bread crumbs

Shell cooked eggs, then lightly roll in flour. Mix sausage and fresh bread crumbs. Divide sausage mixture into fourths and place evenly and smoothly around the lightly floured eggs.

Mix egg and milk together. Coat hard-boiled eggs, then firmly roll each egg in bread crumbs. Deep fry in fat for about 4-5 minutes or until sausage is cooked and golden brown. Halve each egg with sharp knife dipped in hot water. Serve hot or cold.

BIRDS NESTS

Easy

4 Servings

4 slices bread, buttered
4 slices ham
4 slices American cheese
   or 4 oz. Cheddar
   cheese, shredded
4 eggs, separated
Salt and pepper

Place slices of buttered bread on baking sheet, and then place ham and cheese on top of bread. Whip egg whites until firm and divide evenly on top of cheese. Place egg yolks in small hole made in center of egg whites. Season to taste and bake at 350° for 15-20 minutes or until lightly golden.

SAUSAGE BRUNCH EGGS

8-10 Servings
Make Ahead

Average

2 lbs. bulk breakfast
   sausage
1 6 oz. box
   cheese-flavored
   croutons
6 eggs
2½ cups milk
2 cups Cheddar cheese,
   shredded
1 10 oz. can cream of
   mushroom soup
½ cup milk

Brown sausage and drain well. Spread in bottom of 13x9x2 inch dish. Sprinkle with croutons. Beat eggs with 2½ cups milk and pour over all. Sprinkle with cheese, cover, and refrigerate overnight. Before baking, blend soup with ½ cup milk and pour over all. Bake, uncovered at 350° for 1 to 1½ hours. Let sit before cutting.

EASIEST CHEESE SOUFFLE
Easy   **2 Servings**

2 eggs
⅔ cup heavy cream
¾ cup Cheddar cheese,
    grated (Swiss cheese
    may be substituted)
¾ cup Parmesan cheese,
    grated
Dash of pepper

Add eggs to cream and beat slightly. Add cheeses and pepper and beat again for a minute. Pour into greased 1 quart baking dish and bake in a preheated 450° oven for 25 minutes or until golden brown.

ASPARAGUS CHEESE PUFF
Average   **6 Servings**

4 slices white bread
2 Tbsp. butter, softened
1 onion, chopped
1 14 oz. can asparagus,
    cut up and drained *or* 1
    lb. fresh or frozen
    asparagus, cooked,
    drained and cut up
4 slices American cheese
3 eggs
¼ tsp. salt
¼ tsp. pepper
½ tsp. curry
1 cup milk
½ cup light cream

Stack bread and trim crusts; cut in half. Arrange bread in buttered 8x8 inch dish and sprinkle with onion. Place asparagus over bread and onion. Top with cheese. Beat eggs with salt, pepper and curry. Add milk and cream; beat well. Pour evenly over bread and asparagus. Bake at 450° for 20 minutes. This will be puffed and golden brown.

MONTEREY CHEESE ENCHILADAS

Esta delicioso!

Average

6 Servings
Make Ahead

2 large onions, chopped
2 large green peppers, chopped
3 Tbsp. salad oil
Salt
2 10 oz. cans enchilada sauce, (El Paso mild preferred)
1 cup sour cream
12 corn tortillas
1 lb. Monterey Jack cheese, cut into thick strips
½ lb. cooked ground beef or cooked chicken (optional)
2 cups Cheddar cheese, shredded

Cook onions and green peppers in oil until soft. Salt to taste. In skillet, blend enchilada sauce and sour cream; heat to simmer. Dip tortillas in enchilada sauce and let stand to soften. Place tortillas in baking dish. Put 1/12th of onion, pepper, Monterey Jack cheese and ground beef or chicken, if desired, in each and roll. Pour remaining sauce over all and top with shredded cheese. Bake at 375°, uncovered, for 20-25 minutes. If tortillas become too soft to roll, or to save time, layer as a casserole.

SOUR CREAM ENCHILADAS

Easy

6 Servings

2 10 oz. cans cream of chicken soup
½ cup sour cream
1 4 oz. can green chilies chopped
½ tsp. salt
12 corn tortillas
2 cups Longhorn cheese, grated
½ cup green onions, chopped

Heat soup, sour cream, green chilies and salt. Fry each tortilla about 10 seconds (should remain pliable). Put a handful of cheese and onion on each tortilla. Add 1 Tbsp. heated sauce. Roll tortilla and place in shallow casserole. Pour remaining sauce over enchiladas. Sprinkle with additional cheese. Bake at 350° for 20-30 minutes.

125

ARTICHOKE QUICHE

Complicated   **6 Servings**

FILLING:
2 8½ oz. cans artichoke
   hearts
½ cup ricotta cheese
3 eggs, beaten
2 slices bread
½ cup whole milk
2 Tbsp. butter
1 shallot or green onion,
   minced
½ lb. fresh mushrooms,
   sliced or chopped
½ tsp. parsley
¼ tsp. salt
¼ tsp. freshly ground
   pepper
1 tsp. oregano

Drain and mash or quarter artichokes. Add cheese and eggs. Soak bread in milk and add to mixture. Saute shallots and mushrooms in butter. Blend in parsley and seasonings. Pour into shell and cover with top crust.

PASTRY:
½ cup sweet butter
2 cups flour
8 oz. cream cheese,
   softened

Cream butter with cheese. Add flour and blend with fork. Wrap in wax paper and chill 1 hour. Divide dough and roll 2 crusts between wax paper. Just before baking, assemble quiche with filling in a 9 or 10 inch pie plate. Cover edge of pie crust with a cuff of foil to prevent burning. Remove foil after 25 minutes. Bake at 425° for 35 minutes. Cool for 10 minutes before serving.

HELPFUL HINT

For easier removal of shells from hard-boiled eggs, pour off hot water, then shake pan to thoroughly crack egg shells. Place eggs under cold water and slip off shells.

MUSHROOM AND SWISS CHEESE QUICHE

8 Large Servings
16 Small Servings
Make Ahead
Freeze

Average

,1 cup mushrooms, thinly
    sliced
1½ Tbsp. butter
2 slices bacon, diced
1 cup Swiss cheese,
    cubed
1 onion, minced
1 10 inch pie shell, baked
2 cups heavy cream
½ tsp. nutmeg
½ tsp. pepper
4 eggs, lightly beaten

Saute mushrooms in butter 3 minutes. In another pan, saute bacon until crisp and drain on absorbent paper. Combine mushrooms and bacon; add cheese and onion. Turn mixture into pie shell. Stir cream, nutmeg, and pepper into eggs. Pour mixture into pie shell. Bake at 400° for 10 minutes; reduce heat to 300° and bake 30 minutes longer.

SALMON QUICHE

6 Servings
Make Ahead

Average

CRUST:
1 cup whole wheat flour
⅔ cup sharp Cheddar
    cheese, shredded
¼ cup almonds, chopped
½ tsp. salt
¼ tsp. paprika
6 Tbsp. cooking oil

Combine ingredients in order. Set aside ½ cup crust mixture. Press remaining mixture into bottom and up sides of 9 inch pie pan or quiche pan. Bake at 400° for 10 minutes. Remove and lower oven temperature to 325°. Crust may be prepared ahead and refrigerated.

FILLING:
1 15½ oz. can salmon
¼ cup mayonnaise
3 eggs, beaten
½ cup sharp Cheddar
    cheese, shredded
1 Tbsp. onion, grated
¼ tsp. dried dill weed
1 cup sour cream
3-5 drops bottled hot
    pepper sauce

Drain salmon, reserving liquid. Add water to liquid to equal ½ cup. Flake salmon, removing bones and skin; set aside. Blend mayonnaise and salmon liquid. Stir in salmon, eggs, cheese, onion, dill weed, sour cream and hot pepper sauce. Spoon filling into crust; sprinkle with reserved crust mixture and bake at 325° for 45 minutes or until firm in center.

127

VEGETABLE QUICHE

A different dish with a terrific taste!

Average   **6 Servings**

1 20 oz. pkg. frozen
   cauliflower, broccoli and
   carrot mixture
OR FRESH:
1 cup broccoli florets
1 cup cauliflower florets
1 cup carrots, cut into ½
   inch slices
1 cup heavy cream
½ cup milk
3 eggs, beaten with pinch
   of salt
½ tsp. dry mustard
Dash of cayenne pepper
¼ cup Parmesan cheese
1 9 inch frozen deep dish
   pie shell
1½ cups sharp cheese
   (New York State
   Cheddar preferred)
Sweet Hungarian paprika
   for garnish

Steam vegetables (frozen or fresh) until almost done. Remove to colander to drain **dry**. Beat cream, milk, eggs, salt, mustard and cayenne pepper together until smooth. Sprinkle Parmesan cheese in bottom of pie crust. Arrange half of the dry vegetables in one layer, cover with half of the sharp cheese, then remaining vegetables and cheese. Carefully pour the custard mixture over vegetables and cheese using a fork or spoon handle to make sure the custard mixture has no air holes and fills in all the space. Sprinkle top with paprika. Bake at 375°, on a tray to catch all spills, for 1 to 1¼ hours or until a knife blade comes out clean when inserted.

RICOTTA CHEESE PIE

Easy   **6-8 Servings
                                   Make Ahead**

4 eggs
1 lb. ricotta cheese
1 lb. bag frozen
   international vegetables,
   cooked or equal amount
   of fresh cooked
   vegetables, drained
2 Tbsp. soy sauce (more,
   if desired)
1 garlic clove, minced
   (more, if desired)
3 oz. pepperoni, sliced
   (optional)

In large bowl beat eggs slightly; add cheese and mix until blended (a whisk does nicely). Add cooked vegetables and mix. Add soy sauce and garlic. This can be bland without spices, so test for yourself. Pour mixture into a greased 8 inch pie plate. Cook at 400° for 10 minutes; turn down oven to 375° and continue to cook for another 20-30 minutes, or until toothpick comes out clean.

128

MANICOTTI

You don't have to be Italian to like this one!

Average

6-8 Servings
Make Ahead
Freeze

1 lb. manicotti
3 slices bread, broken into
  small pieces
¾ cup milk
1 lb. ground beef
½ lb. ground pork
  (optional)
1 egg
½ lb. Mozzarella cheese,
  grated
1 Tbsp. parsley
½ tsp. salt
½ tsp. pepper
4-5 cups spaghetti sauce
½ cup Parmesan cheese,
  grated

Parboil manicotti in boiling, salted water, 10 minutes. Drain. Soak bread in milk. Brown meat; blend milk, bread, egg, Mozzarella, parsley, salt and pepper. Fill partially cooked manicotti and arrange in baking dish which has a layer of sauce in the bottom. Cover with sauce and sprinkle with Parmesan cheese. Bake at 350° for 20 minutes.

SPINACH MANICOTTI

Average

6-8 Servings
Make Ahead
Freeze

2 lbs. ground sausage
1 onion, chopped
2 10 oz. pkgs. frozen
  spinach, cooked and
  drained
1½ cups bread crumbs
3 eggs
½ cup ricotta cheese
1-2 pkgs. manicotti,
  cooked to pkg.
  directions
32 oz. spaghetti sauce

Brown meat and onion. Add spinach, bread crumbs, eggs and cheese. Cover bottom of 9x13 inch baking dish with sauce. Stuff manicotti with mixture. Place in baking dish and pour more spaghetti sauce over all. Bake at 325° for 30-40 minutes or until bubbly.

LASAGNE

Average

SAUCE:
- 1 3 lb. 3 oz. can chopped tomatoes and juice
- 1 1 lb. 12 oz. can tomato paste
- 2 tsp. salt
- 1 tsp. garlic salt
- 2 Tbsp. basil

Put all ingredients into saucepan. Bring to a light boil and then simmer 30 minutes.

FILLING:
- 18 lasagne noodles
- 4 lbs. ricotta cheese
- ¼ cup parsley flakes
- 4 eggs
- 1 cup Parmesan cheese, grated
- 1 tsp. salt
- 1 tsp. pepper
- 2 lbs. Mozzarella cheese, sliced

Cook noodles according to package directions. Put a layer of noodles on bottom of a greased 3-4 inch deep pan. Mix ricotta cheese, parsley, eggs, Parmesan cheese, salt and pepper. Spread filling like icing on cake. Put a layer of Mozzarella cheese on top of filling; add a generous amount of sauce. Repeat layers, making a total of 3 layers. Bake at 375° for 30-45 minutes. Let cool and then place in refrigerator until cold. When ready to serve, cover with foil and bake at 425° until heated through.

HELPFUL HINT

Add 2 tsp. oil to water when boiling pasta to prevent sticking.

SPINACH LASAGNE WITH RED WINE SAUCE

Average

¾ lb. lasagne
¼ cup oil
1 onion, chopped
2 cloves garlic, crushed
1 lb. ground sirloin
1 cup mushrooms, sliced
1 cup tomatoes, pureed
1 6 oz. can tomato paste
¾ cup red wine
1 egg
1 10 oz. pkg. spinach, chopped (if frozen, thaw and drain well)
1 cup cottage cheese
1 cup Parmesan cheese, grated
½ lb. Mozzarella cheese, cut into strips

Cook lasagne according to package directions. Heat 1 Tbsp. oil in skillet and saute onion, garlic and meat until browned. Add mushrooms, tomatoes, tomato paste and red wine to skillet. Simmer 20 minutes. Meanwhile, blend together egg, spinach, cottage and Parmesan cheeses and remaining oil. Pour ½ meat sauce into 13x9 inch dish. Cover with layer of lasagne. Spread spinach mixture over lasagne. Cover with another layer of lasagne and meat sauce. Bake, covered, at 350° for 40 minutes. Remove cover and place strips of Mozzarella cheese on top of lasagne. Bake until bubbly. Serve hot.

CHEESY NOODLES

Average

1 8 oz. pkg. thin noodles
1 cup creamed cottage cheese
1½ cups sour cream
1 clove garlic, minced
¾ cup onion, chopped
1 7 oz. can boned chicken or 1 cup cooked chicken, diced
1 tsp. salt
Dash of tabasco sauce
½ cup Parmesan cheese, grated
Paprika

Cook noodles, drain. Mix all other ingredients, except Parmesan and paprika, and combine with noodles. Bake at 350° for 50 minutes. Add Parmesan cheese and bake 10 minutes more. Sprinkle with paprika.

SPINACH NOODLE CASSEROLE

Average

1 lb. pkg. noodles
2 10 oz. pkgs. frozen
   chopped spinach
1 lb. fresh mushrooms,
   sliced
½ onion, grated
2-4 Tbsp. butter or
   margarine
1 10 oz. can cream of
   chicken soup
1 10 oz. can cream of
   mushroom soup
1 cup sour cream
2 Tbsp. Worcestershire
   sauce
Salt and pepper to taste
2 Tbsp. butter or
   margarine

Cook noodles and drain. Cook spinach and drain well. Saute mushrooms and onion in butter. Mix all ingredients, except 2 Tbsp. butter, together. Place in large greased casserole. Dot with butter. Bake at 350° for 30 minutes or until bubbly.

VARIATION:
1 7 oz. can tuna fish or 1
   lb. ground beef, cooked
   and drained

Add tuna or cooked ground beef before baking.

NOODLES ROMANOFF A LA NEW YORK

Easy

8 Servings
Make Ahead

1 12 oz. pkg. curly egg
  noodles
1 cup small curd cottage
  cheese
1 cup New York State
  sharp Cheddar cheese,
  grated
1 small onion, finely
  chopped
2 cloves fresh garlic,
  minced
Dash of tabasco sauce
2 tsp. Worcestershire
  sauce
1 cup sour cream
Sweet Hungarian paprika

While noodles are boiling (with a dash of oil added to water), mix cottage cheese and ½ cup Cheddar cheese, onion, garlic, sauces and sour cream. Drain cooked noodles; add to cheese mixture. Pour into buttered shallow serving dish and sprinkle with remaining ½ cup Cheddar cheese. Sprinkle with paprika and bake at 350° for 30 minutes. These noodles perk up a simple meat dish and the recipe may be easily halved for family meals.

FETTUCCINE A LA CARBONARA

A must for a late night supper!

Easy

6 Servings

1 lb. fettuccine
½ lb. bacon, thickly sliced
  and cut into ¼ inch
  strips
4 eggs, well beaten
Pinch of salt
1 cup Parmesan cheese,
  freshly grated
Generous dash black
  pepper, freshly grated
Fresh parsley, chopped

In a large pot, with a dollop of oil added to water, boil fettuccine. Fry bacon until crispy; drain on paper towels. In serving bowl, beat eggs with pinch of salt; stir in cheese. When pasta is cooked, drain and add to egg-cheese mixture. The heat of the pasta will cook the egg and melt the cheese. Toss pasta mixture until there is a rich creamy sauce. Toss in bacon, black pepper and sprinkle with parsley.

SEAFOOD WITH GREEN FETTUCCINE

Easy   **4 Servings**

1 clove garlic
2 Tbsp. olive oil
1 shallot, minced
1 cup heavy cream
½ cup dry white wine
1 pint scallops, chopped
1 6½ oz. can minced
　clams, drained
Pepper
1 lb. shrimp, cooked
⅔-1 lb. green fettuccine,
　cooked

Saute garlic in olive oil; discard garlic. Add shallot and cook 5 minutes. Add cream and wine and simmer several minutes. Reserve ½ cup cream sauce. Add scallops, clams and pepper and cook until scallops are tender, about 4 minutes. Add shrimp and warm thoroughly. Toss fettuccine with reserved ½ cup sauce and serve with seafood sauce.

PASTA PIQUANT

Average   **4 Servings**

2-4 oz. Roquefort or Bleu
　cheese (vary amount
　according to taste)
1½ Tbsp. butter
½ cup heavy cream
½ lb. fettuccine
5 marinated artichokes, cut
　into pieces
2 Tbsp. Parmesan cheese,
　grated
Parsley, chopped

Combine cheese, butter and cream in enamel saucepan; heat over low heat and stir until blended. Cook pasta in salted water until al dente; drain thoroughly. Keep warm, but do not let it sit. Add cheese mixture to fettuccine, then artichoke pieces and Parmesan cheese. Toss lightly until pasta is coated. Garnish with parsley and serve immediately.

RIGATONI WITH ARTICHOKES

Average

4 Servings

2 Tbsp. oil (olive
  preferred)
¼ cup onion, finely
  chopped
1 clove garlic, minced
Salt and pepper to taste
4-6 cooked artichoke
  hearts, chopped or 1 8½
  oz. can, drained and
  chopped
1 pint heavy cream
1 lb. rigatoni, fettuccine or
  linquine
4 Tbsp. Parmesan cheese,
  grated
4 Tbsp. butter or
  margarine, diced
Parsley

Warm oil; saute onion and garlic with salt and pepper. Add artichoke hearts and continue to cook for a few minutes. Pour cream into onion mixture and cook over medium heat until sauce has thickened. Cook rigatoni in boiling water until al dente; drain. Toss rigatoni in serving bowl with cheese, butter and parsley. Add cream sauce and stir thoroughly.

PARTY PASTA WITH PROSCIUTTO

A dressy and delicious pasta variation!

Average

6-8 Servings

2 cups imported
  prosciutto, shaved
½ cup plus 2 Tbsp. butter
  (not margarine)
1 lb. pasta (spinach pasta
  may be used)
1½ cups heavy cream
½ cup Parmesan cheese,
  freshly grated
½ cup chives, chopped
1 8 oz. can artichoke
  hearts packed in water,
  drained and cut in
  halves or quarters

Saute prosciutto in ¼ cup butter until golden brown. Cook and drain pasta. In large skillet or Dutch oven, melt 6 Tbsp. butter over low heat; add pasta and toss with melted butter. Add cream, cheese, ¼ cup chives and artichoke hearts. Toss well with fork, lifting gently. Turn pasta mixture onto heated platter; arrange prosciutto over top and sprinkle with remaining chives.

135

PASTA ASPARAGUS

Average   **4-6 Servings**

4 Tbsp. butter or
  margarine
2 Tbsp. onion, chopped
½ lb. asparagus, cut into 2
  inch pieces
½ cup water
1 chicken bouillon cube, or
  1 tsp. chicken stock
  base
⅛ tsp. salt
½ lb. thin spaghetti or
  vermicelli
⅓ cup half & half or milk
¼ cup Parmesan cheese,
  grated
Dash of pepper

Heat butter over medium-high heat in saucepan. Add onion and saute until golden; do not brown. Add asparagus, water, bouillon cube and salt. Reduce heat and simmer about 15 minutes. Add spaghetti to large pot of rapidly boiling, salted water and cook until al dente, about 5-6 minutes. Drain well. Return spaghetti to pot. Add asparagus mixture and half and half and cook over medium-low heat until warmed through. Top with Parmesan cheese and pepper before serving.

PASTA CON BROCCOLI

Easy   **8 Servings**

1 lb. ditalini or any small
  macaroni
1 lb. broccoli, chopped or
  1-2 10 oz. pkgs. frozen
  chopped broccoli
2 cloves garlic, pressed
¼ cup olive oil
⅓ cup pine nuts
1 tsp. salt
⅛ tsp. pepper
3 Tbsp. water
⅓ cup dried currants or
  raisins (optional)
Cheese, grated for garnish.

Cook ditalini according to package directions. Drain. Steam broccoli until tender or cook frozen broccoli according to package directions. Drain. In large saucepan, saute garlic in oil. Add pine nuts and brown. Add macaroni, broccoli, salt, pepper and water and raisins or currants, if desired. Simmer for 10 minutes. Top with grated cheese.

BOLOGNESE MEAT SAUCE

A lovely taste of Northern Italy!

Average

4 Servings
Make Ahead
Freeze

4 Tbsp. butter
2 Tbsp. olive oil
1 medium onion, chopped
1 carrot, finely chopped
1 stalk celery, finely
chopped
1 tsp. parsley, chopped
¼ lb. pancetta or
prosciutto, finely
chopped
1½ lbs. ground veal
Salt and freshly ground
pepper
1 cup dry white wine
1 28 oz. can crushed
Italian-style tomatoes
½ cup milk or half and half

Melt butter with oil in saucepan. When butter foams, add onion, carrot, celery, parsley and pancetta. Saute over medium heat until lightly browned. Add veal. Cook and stir until meat is no longer pink. Season with salt and pepper. Increase heat and stir in wine, cooking until wine has evaporated. Press tomatoes through food mill and sieve to remove seeds, if desired. Stir tomato pulp into veal mixture. Cover and reduce heat. Simmer, stirring occasionally, 1 to 1½ hours, or until sauce reaches a medium thick consistency. Add milk and cook 5 minutes longer. Makes 2½ to 3 cups of sauce. This is delicious with homemade pasta.

VEGETARIAN PASTA SAUCE

Average

5 Cups
Make Ahead
Freeze

4 cloves garlic, minced
2 Tbsp. olive oil
2 16 oz. cans stewed
tomatoes, chopped
1 16 oz. can tomato sauce
1 Tbsp. light brown sugar
1 tsp. sweet basil
½-1 tsp. leaf thyme
1 tsp. Italian seasoning
1 tsp. red peppers,
crushed
Black pepper, freshly
ground
1 lb. pasta, cooked al
dente

Saute garlic in oil. Do not brown, as this makes garlic bitter. Add tomatoes, tomato sauce, sugar and herbs. Simmer gently 15 minutes. Serve over pasta. For a sweet pepper sauce, 2 red or 2 green peppers may be added to the oil when sauteing garlic.

ZESTY SPAGHETTI SAUCE

Average

4 Servings
Make Ahead
Freeze

1 onion, finely chopped
½ cup *olive* oil
1¼ cups prosciutto,
   chopped
⅓ cup white wine
1 3 lb. can tomatoes
Salt and pepper to taste
2 tsp. crushed basil
4 Tbsp. butter
Spaghetti

Cook onion in oil until tender. Add prosciutto and brown a little. Add wine, tomatoes, salt and pepper. Simmer 45 minutes and then add basil and butter. Serve over spaghetti.

BARLEY CASSEROLE

A pleasant change from potatoes!

Easy

6 Servings
Make Ahead

1 large onion, chopped
½ lb. mushrooms, sliced
4-5 Tbsp. butter
1 cup Pearl barley
Salt
Pepper
2 cups consomme

Saute onion and mushrooms in butter until soft. Add barley and saute until lightly browned. Add salt and pepper to taste. Put in buttered casserole dish and add 1 cup consomme. Cover and cook at 350° for 25-30 minutes. Uncover, add second cup of consomme and cook until liquid is absorbed, about 15-20 minutes.

GOURMET RICE

Easy

6-8 Servings
Make Ahead

1 cup onion, chopped
6 Tbsp. butter
1½ cups converted rice
2 10 oz. cans beef bouillon
¼ tsp. pepper
½ cup slivered almonds
1½ cups mushrooms,
   sliced

Saute onion in 3 Tbsp. butter until tender. Add rice and stir until golden brown. Add bouillon and pepper and stir well. Heat to boiling, cover pan, reduce heat and simmer for 15-20 minutes or until liquid is absorbed. Saute almonds and mushrooms in 3 Tbsp. butter. When rice is tender, add almonds and mushrooms and toss together.

138

HERB RICE RING

Easy

1½ cups rice (use regular or Chinese rice, not instant)
3 cups cold water
¼ cup fresh parsley, minced
½ tsp. leaf thyme
2 Tbsp. butter
1 tsp. salt

Place rice and water in saucepan, bring to a boil, reduce heat to medium-low, cover pan. After 12-14 minutes, lift cover. If rice has made its own vent halves, like moon craters, it is done. If not, cover and cook another 2-3 minutes. Stir remaining ingredients into cooked rice. Place in buttered ring-mold and let mold set in a flat pan of hot water until ready to serve. Tip out of mold and fill center with creamed chicken, turkey and gravy mixture or a sauced vegetable mixture. Rice can also be served in individual custard molds. This makes leftover chicken or turkey a party dish.

RICE DELIGHT

Easy

6-8 Servings

2 cups white rice
1 onion, minced
4 Tbsp. margarine
4 cups water
2 tsp. salt
2 beef bouillon cubes
¾ cup seedless raisins
Slivered almonds
Ginger
Cinnamon

Saute rice with onion in margarine 3-5 minutes. Add water, salt and bouillon cubes. Cover, bring to a boil, reduce heat and cook 20 minutes. Add raisins, almonds, ginger and cinnamon to taste. A great side dish with pork or ham!

HELPFUL HINT

For white fluffy rice, add 1 tsp. lemon juice to 1 qt. water.

RICE WITH ASPARAGUS

Average   **6-8 Servings**

1 lb. fresh asparagus (may
    substitute equivalent
    frozen or canned)
1 quart chicken or beef
    broth
½ cup butter
1 small onion, thinly sliced
1 cup long-grain rice
½ cup dry white wine
2 Tbsp. heavy cream
½ cup Parmesan cheese,
    grated
Dash of pepper

Clean asparagus and discard the hard parts; cut tender parts of stems into 1 inch pieces. Keep tips separate. Bring broth to a boil. Heat 4 Tbsp. butter in a saucepan; add onion and cook until transparent. Add asparagus stem pieces. Add rice and stir rapidly. When rice is coated, add wine and allow to evaporate. Add broth, one ladle at a time. Rice should never get too dry, but should not be drowned, just barely covered with liquid. After about 10 minutes, add asparagus tips and continue to stir while adding broth. When rice is almost done, about 25 minutes, add cream, cheese, pepper and at the very end, the last 4 Tbsp. butter. Mix well and serve very hot. Eat immediately. Fresh peas may be substituted when fresh asparagus is not available.

WILD RICE WITH WINE CASSEROLE

6-8 Servings
Make Ahead

Average

1 6 oz. box long-grain wild
    rice (Uncle Ben's
    Original preferred)
⅓ cup butter or margarine
2-3 onions, chopped
2 Tbsp. flour
1 cup white wine
1 cup chicken broth
Salt and pepper
1 cup bread crumbs,
    buttered (Pepperidge
    Farm preferred)

Cook rice according to directions on box. Do not overcook. Melt butter in skillet; add onions and cook until browned. Keeping heat low, add flour, wine, chicken broth, salt and pepper to taste. After it has thickened, pour sauce over cooked rice in a greased casserole and mix together well. Top with buttered bread crumbs. Bake at 375° for ½ hour or until browned on top. Let stand about 10 minutes before serving.

BLUFF POINT

Bluff Point offers a panoramic view of Keuka Lake, one of the largest
Finger Lakes.

SALADS AND SALAD DRESSINGS

BLUEBERRY SALAD MOLD

Easy

8 Servings
Make Ahead

1 3 oz. pkg. blackberry or
  black raspberry gelatin
1 cup boiling water
1 15 oz. can blueberries
  packed in light syrup,
  (Wyman's preferred)
1 8 oz. can crushed
  pineapple
1 pkg. Dream Whip
Sour cream

Dissolve gelatin in water; add blueberries and pineapple, juice and all. Chill
until partially set. Whip Dream Whip
according to directions on package.
Fold Dream Whip into partially set
gelatin. Pour into 1 quart mold and chill
until set. Top with sour cream.

HOLIDAY FRUIT SALAD

Easy

12 Servings
Make Ahead

1 6 oz. pkg. raspberry
  gelatin
2 cups boiling water
½ cup Burgundy wine
2 16 oz. cans *whole*
  cranberry sauce
1 20 oz. can crushed
  pineapple, *not* drained
⅔ cup pecans or walnuts,
  chopped

Dissolve gelatin in water, then add
remaining ingredients in order given.
Place into a 2 quart mold or bundt pan
and refrigerate overnight.

BURGUNDY CHERRY MOLD

Average

8 Servings
Make Ahead

1 6 oz. pkg. cherry gelatin
Sherry or Burgundy (red
  wine)
1 16 oz. can pitted red
  sweet Bing cherries
  (reserve juice)
Walnuts or cream cheese

Dissolve gelatin in 2 cups boiling water.
Add wine to remaining juice from can to
make 1½ cups. Stuff each cherry with
a walnut or with cream cheese. Add
cherries to slightly cooled gelatin and
pour into 1 quart mold. Refrigerate at
least 4 hours or overnight.

141

CHERRIES JUBILEE FRUIT SALAD

Perfect with poultry!

Average

8 Servings
Make Ahead

1 16 oz. can pitted dark
  sweet cherries
1 3 oz. pkg. cherry gelatin
½ cup sherry
1 16 oz. can sliced pears,
  drained
3 oz. cream cheese, cut
  into small cubes
¼ cup pecans, chopped
Lettuce leaves

Drain cherries, reserving syrup. Cut cherries in half. Add water to syrup to total 1½ cups liquid. In medium saucepan, combine gelatin and syrup mixture. Heat and stir until gelatin is dissolved. Remove from heat; stir in sherry. Chill until partially set. Reserve 4 pear slices for garnish; fold remaining pears into gelatin mixture with cherries, cheese, and pecans. Turn into 4½ cup mold. Garnish with pear slices and lettuce.

CRANBERRY CHICKEN SALAD

Average

10-12 Servings
Make Ahead

1 frying chicken, cooked
  and chopped
1 cup celery, chopped
½ cup stuffed olives,
  chopped
1 cup mayonnaise
2 hard-boiled eggs, diced
1 tsp. onion, minced
Salt to taste
1 pkg. unflavored gelatin
1 32 oz. can jellied
  cranberry sauce
1 3 oz. pkg. lemon gelatin
½ cup orange juice

Mix chicken, celery, olives, mayonnaise, eggs, onion and salt together. Set aside. Soften unflavored gelatin in ½ cup cold water, then after 5 minutes add ½ cup boiling water. Combine with chicken mixture, then pour into a 2 quart mold or an attractive bowl, lightly rubbed with oil. Set in refrigerator for 20-30 minutes. Beat cranberry sauce until mushy. Add lemon gelatin dissolved in ¾ cup hot water, then add orange juice. Pour this mixture over the top of chilled chicken mixture and chill until set. Do not invert this salad.

HELPFUL HINT

Add extra zip to gelatin salads by substituting ginger ale for water.

CRANBERRY SALAD MOLD

Average

6-8 Servings
Make Ahead

1 lb. can whole cranberries
1 cup boiling water
1 3 oz. pkg. strawberry
   gelatin
1 Tbsp. lemon juice
¼ tsp. salt
½ cup mayonnaise
1 apple, diced
¼ cup nuts, chopped

Drain cranberries; strain and save liquid. Mix liquid with boiling water and gelatin. Stir until dissolved; add lemon juice and salt. Chill until thickened. Add mayonnaise and beat until fluffy. Add cranberries, apples and nuts. Pour into 1½ quart mold. Chill at least 4 hours.

MANDARIN ORANGE SALAD

Use as a refreshing summer dessert!

Easy

4-6 Servings
Make Ahead

1 6 oz. pkg. orange gelatin
3 cups boiling water
1 pint orange sherbet
2 11 oz. cans Mandarin
   oranges, drained

Dissolve gelatin in boiling water. Add orange sherbet immediately; dissolve completely. Add drained Mandarin oranges. Chill and serve.

LEMON-LIME GELATIN SALAD

Easy

12 Servings
Make Ahead

1 3 oz. pkg. lime gelatin
1 3 oz. pkg. lemon gelatin
2 cups cottage cheese
1 20 oz. can crushed
   pineapple, drained
½ cup nutmeats, chopped
½ cup sweetened
   condensed milk
1 tsp. horseradish

Dissolve gelatins in water as directed on packages. When gelatin is partially set, add remaining ingredients and put into 9x13 inch pan. Chill several hours before serving.

PINEAPPLE LAYER SALAD

A church supper favorite!

Average

8-10 Servings
Make Ahead

1 3 oz. pkg. lemon gelatin
2 cups boiling water
1 8 oz. can crushed
   pineapple, drained
   (reserving juice)
2 large bananas, sliced
8 marshmallows, quartered
   or 16 mini marshmallows

Dissolve gelatin in water; cool until slightly thickened. Add remaining ingredients and pour into 9x9 inch pan. Chill until firm.

DRESSING:
1 cup pineapple juice (use
   water to make full cup)
½ cup sugar
2 Tbsp. butter
1 Tbsp. lemon juice
2 Tbsp. flour
1 egg
1 cup heavy cream
1 cup (or more) Cheddar
   cheese, grated (use
   orange for color)

Mix all ingredients except cream and cheese. Cook slowly until thickened, stirring constantly. Cool. Whip cream and fold in dressing mixture. Spread over firm salad and cover thickly with a layer of grated cheese. Chill several hours.

RED RASPBERRY SALAD

At last — a gelatin salad even men like!

Average

10-12 Servings
Make Ahead

1 pint fresh or 2 16 oz.
   cans or 2 10 oz. boxes
   frozen raspberries
1 20 oz. can crushed
   pineapple
1 6 oz. can frozen orange
   juice, thawed
1 6 oz. pkg. raspberry
   gelatin
1 cup boiling water

Thaw raspberries. Drain raspberries and pineapple reserving both juices. Add thawed orange juice to drained juices. This should measure 2 to 2½ cups. Add water to make 2 cups, if juices measure less. Dissolve gelatin in boiling water. Add juices and chill until partially set. Add raspberries and pineapple. Place mixture into 1½ to 2 quart mold and chill until set.

144

STRAWBERRY SALAD MOLD

A favorite family recipe!

12 Servings
Make Ahead

Easy

1 6 oz. pkg. strawberry
  gelatin
1 cup boiling water
2 10 oz. pkgs. frozen
  strawberries
1 20 oz. can crushed
  pineapple, drained
3 bananas, diced
1 cup nuts, chopped
2 cups sour cream

Combine first 6 ingredients and pour into 1½ to 2 quart mold. Serve with sour cream. You may also jell ½, then spread sour cream on top and add remaining gelatin.

GINGER ALE FRUIT SALAD

10-12 Servings
Make Ahead

Average

SALAD:
1 6 oz. pkg. lemon gelatin
3 cups hot water
1 cup ginger ale
1 16 oz. can fruit cocktail,
  drained, reserving juice
1 8 oz. can crushed
  pineapple, drained,
  reserving juice

Combine gelatin and hot water; stir until dissolved. Add ginger ale. Refrigerate until gelatin is firm, then whip with electric beaters until light and spongy. Fold in fruit cocktail and pineapple. Pour into 2 quart mold or 9 inch square pan and refrigerate until set.

DRESSING:
2 Tbsp. cornstarch
1 cup sugar
1 tsp. butter
1 cup reserved fruit juice
1 medium apple, chopped
  (optional)
Juice of 1 lemon
½ cup whipped cream or
  Cool Whip

Put all ingredients, except whipped cream or Cool Whip, in saucepan. Cook until thickened; let chill. Stir in whipped cream or Cool Whip and mix well. Serve with salad. Dressing may be frozen.

MOLDED CUCUMBER SALAD

Easy

1 3 oz. pkg. lemon gelatin
½ cup boiling water
1 lb. cream cheese, softened
1 cup cucumbers, diced
1 small onion, grated
2 Tbsp. salad dressing
3 hard-boiled eggs, diced
Salt to taste

Dissolve gelatin in water and pour over cream cheese. Blend until smooth. Add remaining ingredients and pour into 2½ cup mold. Chill until set.

SUMMER DREAM SALAD

Average

**6-8 Servings
Make Ahead**

1 3 oz. pkg. lime gelatin
1¼ cups hot water
1 cup cucumber, grated
1 Tbsp. vinegar
¾ tsp. onion, grated
½ tsp. salt
Dash of pepper
¼ tsp. oregano

Dissolve gelatin in water. Add cucumbers, vinegar, onion, salt, pepper and oregano. Pour into 1 quart mold. Chill until firm.

DRESSING:
½ cup mayonnaise
½ cup sour cream
Horseradish to taste

Mix all ingredients. Serve with salad.

146

NO FUSS FRUIT SALAD

Easy

6 Servings
Make Ahead

2 cups fruit juice of your
choice
2 Tbsp. sugar
1 envelope unflavored
gelatin
Fresh fruit of your choice
(apple juice and green
seedless grapes or
orange juice and mixed
fruit)

Mix ½ cup fruit juice, sugar and gelatin
and heat until dissolved or put in
microwave for 30 seconds. Add additional 1½ cups fruit juice. Chill until
thickness of unbeaten egg whites. Add
fresh fruit of your choice (except
pineapple as enzymes will destroy the
gelatin). Pour into 2 quart mold and chill
until firm. Let your imagination soar with
the fresh fruit of your choice.

BLUEBERRY RICE SALAD

Easy

6 Servings
Make Ahead

2 cups brown rice, cooked
and chilled
2 cups fresh blueberries
½ cup unsweetened
coconut, shredded
½ cup pecans or almonds,
chopped
Honey to taste
(approximately ¼ cup)
Heavy cream
(approximately ⅓ cup)

Combine all ingredients except heavy
cream. Add heavy cream to moisten.
Serve.

FROZEN FRUIT COCKTAIL SALAD

Easy

10-18 Servings
Make Ahead
Freeze

1 13 oz. can fruit cocktail,
drained
2 cups miniature
marshmallows
1 8 oz. can crushed
pineapple, not drained
Few grains of salt
2 cups sour cream

Mix all together and pour into 9 inch
square pan or 18 paper-lined muffin
cups. Freeze, covered with foil or plastic
wrap. Remove from freezer about an
hour before serving.

147

FROZEN PINEAPPLE-BANANA SALAD

Average

4-6 Servings
Make Ahead
Freeze

1 cup sour cream
½ of a 4½ oz. container
  Cool Whip
½ cup sugar
2 Tbsp. lemon juice
1 tsp. vanilla
1 13 oz. can crushed
  pineapple, drained
2 bananas, diced
½ cup nuts, chopped
Cherries

Mix all ingredients, except fruit and nuts. Fold in fruit and nuts. Place in 1 quart mold. Freeze overnight. Remove from freezer about 1 hour before serving. Garnish with cherries.

FRUIT SALAD WITH PECAN-YOGURT DRESSING

Easy

6 Servings
Make Ahead

DRESSING:
1 cup plain yogurt
1 Tbsp. honey
2 tsp. lemon juice
¼ cup pecans, finely
  chopped

Mix together until well blended. Chill and pour over fruit.

FRUIT:
1 cup fresh pineapple,
  cubed or equivalent
  canned, drained
2 bananas, sliced
1 cup seedless grapes
2 pears, peeled and diced
2 apples, diced

Mix all together.

ORANGE SALAD

Easy

6 Servings
Make Ahead

3 oranges
1 11 oz. can Mandarin
    oranges
½ 6 oz. can pitted ripe
    olives
¼ cup olive oil
¼ cup vinegar
1 tsp. black pepper
½ tsp. garlic powder

Peel oranges and cut each section in half. Drain Mandarin oranges. Slice olives in half. Mix all ingredients together in bowl.

TACO DINNER SALAD

Average

8 Servings
Make Ahead

1 lb. ground beef
1 small onion, chopped
1 pkg. taco seasoning
1 15½ oz. can kidney
    beans, drained
1 4 oz. bag tortilla chips,
    slightly crushed
1 large head lettuce, torn
    into pieces
2 tomatoes, sliced
1 avocado, sliced
1 cup Cheddar cheese,
    grated
1 8 oz. bottle Thousand
    Island dressing

Brown beef and onion; drain. Add taco seasoning and beans. Cool. Add remaining ingredients. Toss. All but meat mixture and dressing may be combined ahead and refrigerated until serving. Serve with corn muffins or bread.

WALDORF CHICKEN SALAD

Easy

8-10 Servings
Make Ahead

4 Cortland or red tart
  apples
Mayonnaise thinned with
  New York State wine
  (Wagner's Seyval Blanc
  preferred)
4 whole chicken breasts,
  cooked, chilled and
  boned
1 cup walnuts, coarsely
  chopped
½-1 cup celery, chopped
  (optional)
Leaf lettuce

Cut apples into eighths and then cut each piece into 5-6 pieces. Drop apples into mayonnaise-wine mixture. (Wine will prevent discoloration of apples.) Cut chicken into chunks and add with walnuts and celery to apple-mayonnaise mixture. Chill overnight. Serve on leaf lettuce.

HOT CHICKEN SALAD

Average

6 Servings
Make Ahead

4 cups cooked chicken,
  diced
1 cup mayonnaise
¾ cup cream of chicken
  soup
2 cups celery, chopped
4 hard-boiled eggs,
  chopped
1 tsp. salt
1 tsp. onion, minced
2 Tbsp. lemon juice
2 Tbsp. pimientos,
  chopped
1 cup potato chips,
  crushed
⅔ cup sharp Cheddar
  cheese, shredded
½ cup slivered almonds
  (optional)

Mix chicken, mayonnaise, soup, celery, eggs, salt, onion, lemon juice and pimientos. Place in large greased shallow casserole; refrigerate overnight. Add potato chips, cheese and almonds. Bake at 400° for 25 minutes.

150

TUNA PINEAPPLE SALAD

Easy

8 Servings
Make Ahead

3 bananas, diced
1 9 oz. can crushed
  pineapple, *drained well*
¼ cup celery, diced
Dash of salt
¾ cup mayonnaise
2 Tbsp. lemon juice
2 7 oz. cans tuna fish
Lettuce leaves
Watercress

Mix bananas with pineapple. Mix celery, salt, mayonnaise and lemon juice; fold in banana mixture. Add tuna. Do not mix too much. Serve over lettuce leaves. Use watercress sprigs for garnish.

SHRIMP AND CRAB MEAT SALAD WITH SAUCE LAMAZE

Average

4-6 Servings

SALAD:
15 medium shrimp, cooked
  (may substitute
  equivalent amount of
  lobster)
1 7 oz. can lump crab
  meat
1 hard-boiled egg,
  chopped
1 medium white radish or 4
  red radishes, finely
  chopped
1 cup celery, finely
  chopped
1 medium carrot, finely
  chopped
Juice of 2 lemons
½ tsp. salt
Dash of mace
Dash of savory
Lettuce leaves for garnish
8-12 whole red radishes
  for garnish
1 tomato, cut into wedges
  for garnish

Combine shrimp, crab meat, egg, radish, celery and carrot. Sprinkle with lemon juice. Add salt, mace and savory and gently mix.

(Continued)

151

COLD SAUCE LAMAZE:

1½ cups mayonnaise
1 Tbsp. prepared mustard
1 Tbsp. catsup
½ Tbsp. chili sauce
½ tsp. A-1 sauce
1 Tbsp. pimiento, finely chopped
1 Tbsp. celery, finely chopped
½ Tbsp. chives, finely chopped
½ Tbsp. green pepper, finely chopped
½ Tbsp. parsley, finely chopped
1 hard-boiled egg, finely chopped
½-1 Tbsp. horseradish

Blend mayonnaise, mustard, catsup, chili sauce and A-1 sauce. Add all remaining ingredients. Mix Sauce LaMaze with salad ingredients, except garnishes. Arrange lettuce leaves on plate; put salad on leaves and garnish with radishes and tomato. This can be done on individual plates or on a large serving platter. The sauce is excellent on seafood, eggs or poultry. It is also good as a salad dressing on any cold salad.

CRAB MEAT AND SHRIMP SALAD

Easy

6-8 Servings
Make Ahead

Butter, softened
6 slices thin bread, crust removed (Pepperidge Farm preferred)
1 7 oz. can crab meat or equivalent fresh
1 7 oz. can tiny shrimp or equivalent fresh
1 cup scallions, finely chopped
1½ stalks celery, diced
2 hard-boiled eggs, diced
1 cup mayonnaise
1 Tbsp. lemon juice

Butter bread and break into small cubes. Drain crab meat and shrimp. Add all ingredients together and mix well. Refrigerate overnight. Serve over lettuce or use to stuff tomatoes.

ASPARAGUS VINAIGRETTE

A sophisticated, yet simple salad!

Easy

**4 Servings
Make Ahead**

6 Tbsp. salad oil
3 Tbsp. lemon juice
1 tsp. parsley, minced
½ tsp. dry mustard
¼ tsp. salt
¼ tsp. pepper
⅛ tsp. garlic powder
1 14½ oz. can asparagus,
   drained, or *better*, use
   fresh asparagus, cooked
Lettuce, cut up
Deviled eggs
Cherry tomatoes

Combine first seven ingredients in small bowl; beat with whisk until blended. Pour over asparagus. (If using fresh, cook first.) Chill several hours. Serve on bed of lettuce and garnish with eggs and tomatoes.

BROCCOLI SALAD

Unusual and sweet!

Average

**6 Servings
Make Ahead**

SALAD:
1 large head broccoli,
   broken into bite-size
   pieces (about 4 cups)
¼ cup raisins
6-8 green onions, sliced *or*
   1 medium onion,
   chopped
1 cup Cheddar cheese,
   cubed
8 slices bacon, cooked
   and crumbled

Place all ingredients, except bacon, in glass bowl. Reserve bacon.

DRESSING:
1 14 oz. can sweetened
   condensed milk
½ milk can cider vinegar
1 egg
3 Tbsp. prepared mustard

Combine dressing ingredients with wire whisk or in blender. Pour over salad and mix well. (Make sure broccoli is dry or else dressing will not cling!) Refrigerate for 6 hours or overnight. Garnish with bacon before serving.

153

BEAN SPROUT SALAD

Average

⅓ cup vinegar
3 Tbsp. water
3 Tbsp. sugar
1 tsp. garlic salt
Dash pepper
1 Tbsp. soy sauce
2 Tbsp. green pepper, chopped
2 Tbsp. onion, minced
1 16 oz. can bean sprouts, rinsed and drained or the equivalent of fresh bean sprouts
3 Tbsp. oil

Combine vinegar, water, sugar, garlic salt, pepper and soy sauce in small saucepan. Heat over medium heat until sugar dissolves and the mixture is warmed through. Combine peppers, onions and bean sprouts in covered container. Pour heated mixture on vegetable mixture. Mix lightly and cool. Stir in oil. Chill until serving time. Serve as a salad itself; or over salad greens.

COPPER PENNIES SALAD

This keeps for weeks!

Average

4½ cups (2 lbs.) fresh carrots, sliced ¼ inch thick
2 medium onions, thinly sliced
1 medium green pepper, cut into thin strips
1 10 oz. can tomato soup
¾ cup vinegar
½ cup cooking oil
1 tsp. Worcestershire sauce
1 tsp. prepared mustard
½ tsp. salt
⅔ cup sugar

Cook carrots in small amount of boiling, salted water until just tender, about 8-10 minutes; drain. Combine with onions and green pepper in large bowl. Stir together remaining ingredients; pour over vegetables in bowl. Cover and marinate in refrigerator several hours or overnight. Drain, reserving marinade. Serve in lettuce-lined bowl, if desired. Return any leftover vegetables to marinade and keep refrigerated.

CAULIFLOWER AND PEA SALAD

8 Servings
Make Ahead

Average

SALAD:
2 10 oz. pkgs. frozen
  peas, cooked, drained
  and chilled
4-6 green onions, thinly
  sliced
1 cup celery, sliced
2 cups fresh raw
  cauliflower, broken into
  pieces

Mix all vegetables and chill.

DRESSING:
1 5 oz. can evaporated
  milk
2/3 cup salad oil
1/2 tsp. salt
Dash of pepper
1 tsp. dry mustard
1 tsp. dill
4 1/2 Tbsp. vinegar

Mix dressing in mixer, or put ingredients in jar and shake. Add to chilled vegetables.

MAKE AHEAD CAULIFLOWER SALAD

8 Servings
Make Ahead

Average

1/2 lb. bacon
1 head cauliflower, broken
  into pieces
1 head lettuce, broken into
  pieces
3/4 cup mayonnaise
1 tsp. dried minced onion
1/4 cup sugar
1/2 cup Parmesan cheese,
  grated

Cook bacon until crisp; drain fat and break into pieces. Combine all ingredients, including bacon. Mixture may look dry; however, after standing it creates more juice. Refrigerate at least 8 hours or overnight. More mayonnaise may be added before serving, if too dry.

155

COLD CAULIFLOWER SALAD
WITH MUSTARD DRESSING

Also doubles as a tasty hors d'oeuvre!

Easy

8 Servings
Make Ahead

1 large head cauliflower
Salt to taste
4 slices lemon

Day ahead, wash cauliflower and break into florets. In 1 inch salted, boiling water, covered with lemon slices, cook cauliflower until tender but not soft, about 10 minutes. Drain. Place cauliflower in ice water and cool completely. Drain cauliflower, cover, and place in refrigerator.

MUSTARD DRESSING:
½ cup mayonnaise
⅓ cup brown mustard
2 Tbsp. sour cream
2 Tbsp. lemon juice
½ tsp. salt
Pepper to taste

Combine all dressing ingredients.

Romaine lettuce
2 large tomatoes, sliced
2 Tbsp. parsley

To assemble: put lettuce on serving platter with tomato slices. Mound cauliflower in center and spoon mustard dressing over cauliflower. Sprinkle with parsley.

CUCUMBER SALAD

COMPLIMENTS OF

SCHUYLER COUNTY HISTORICAL SOCIETY, MONTOUR FALLS, N.Y.

Easy

2 Servings

1 cucumber, peeled and
   thinly sliced
1½ tsp. salt
1 cup heavy sour cream
2 Tbsp. lemon juice
3 Tbsp. onion, chopped
¼ tsp. sugar
¼ tsp. white pepper
2 Tbsp. parsley, chopped

Toss cucumber with salt. Chill 1 hour. Combine rest of ingredients. Fold in cucumber and chill 2 hours or more.

156

MARINATED CUCUMBERS

Easy

4 Servings
Make Ahead

1-2 firm cucumbers,
   washed and trimmed
¼ cup cider vinegar
¼ tsp. salt
2 Tbsp. sugar
Dash pepper

VARIATION:
Above ingredients plus 1
   cup sour cream

Score cucumber skins with fork; slice. Make sauce of remaining ingredients by shaking all together in a small jar or blending in bowl. Pour over and mix well with cucumbers. Refrigerate for at least 1 hour. Drain cucumbers before serving. For a nice variation, after draining cucumbers, add sour cream for delicious sour cream cucumbers.

CAESAR SALAD

Average

10-12 Servings

3 heads romaine lettuce
¼ tsp. salt
¼ tsp. freshly ground
   pepper
3 garlic cloves, peeled and
   pressed
3 flat anchovies
2 sprigs watercress
   (optional)
1 Tbsp. Parmesan cheese,
   grated
½ tsp. dry mustard
½ tsp. Worcestershire
   sauce
Juice of ½ lemon
3 Tbsp. wine vinegar
8 Tbsp. olive oil
3 egg yolks
3 slices Italian bread,
   crumbled into croutons,
   or ½ pkg. commercial
   croutons
Ground pepper
Parmesan cheese, grated

Tear heads of romaine lettuce, rinse under cold water, drain and wrap in towel. Set aside. Using a large salad bowl, blend salt, pepper and garlic. Crush anchovies into mixture doing same with watercress, if desired. Sprinkle cheese over the above. Add mustard and Worcestershire sauce and blend. Wrap half of one lemon in cloth and add by squeezing into above ingredients. Blend as before. Add vinegar and oil and blend. Blend egg yolks into ingredients. Add croutons 20 minutes before serving. Break lettuce into bowl. Serve, adding ground pepper and Parmesan cheese.

MEXICAN SALAD

Easy   **12 Servings**

SALAD:
1 head lettuce, broken into   Toss all ingredients.
  pieces
1 cup kidney beans
1 red onion, chopped
1 6 oz. can pitted black
  olives, sliced
2 tomatoes, diced
1 pkg. regular Doritos

DRESSING:
1 12 oz. jar creamy Italian   Mix together Italian dressing and sour
  dressing or Marie's   cream. Toss with salad.
  Garlic Italian Dressing
8 oz. sour cream

VEGETABLE SALAD

A salad that keeps and keeps!

Easy   **12-15 Servings**
                                      Make Ahead

1 large head lettuce,   Layer or mix lettuce, onion, water
  washed, drained and   chestnuts, celery and peas in 9x13x2
  torn into pieces   inch pan or glass casserole. Sprinkle
2 bunches green onions,   with sugar; frost with mayonnaise.
  sliced, tops included   Cover with Romano cheese. Cover with
2 8 oz. cans water   plastic and refrigerate overnight.
  chestnuts, drained and
  sliced
8 ribs celery, sliced
  diagonally
1 10 oz. pkg. frozen peas,
  thawed
3 Tbsp. sugar
2 cups mayonnaise
1-2 cups Romano cheese,
  grated

24 HOUR SALAD

Average

1 head lettuce
1 10 oz. pkg. frozen green peas, thawed, but not cooked
1½ cups celery, chopped
1½ cups green pepper, chopped
¾ cup onion, chopped
1 cup Cheddar cheese, shredded
½ lb. bacon, cooked and crumbled
2 cups mayonnaise
2 Tbsp. sugar

Break lettuce into a deep **clear** bowl. Add peas in a layer, then add chopped vegetables, cheese and bacon in layers. Whip mayonnaise and sugar to be sure sugar is dissolved. Put mayonnaise across entire salad to "seal". Cover with plastic wrap and refrigerate 24 hours.

MUSHROOM-BEET AND BEAN SALAD

Even better made with fresh or frozen vegetables!

Easy

SALAD:
1 16 oz. can cut wax beans, drained
1 16 oz. can cut green beans, drained
1 8 oz. can mushrooms, drained
1 16 oz. can small whole beets, drained
½ cup celery, diced
1 onion, sliced
1 green pepper, cut into rings

DRESSING:
½ cup vinegar
¾ cup sugar
½ cup salad oil
1 tsp. salt
½ tsp. pepper

Mix all dressing ingredients. Pour dressing over vegetables. Stir vegetables and marinate for 6-8 hours or overnight. Serve cold.

BILL WAGNER'S FAVORITE SALAD

COMPLIMENTS OF WAGNER VINEYARDS, LODI, N.Y.

Easy

**Servings As
Desired**

Fresh Spinach
Sliced mushrooms
Sliced shallots or small
  onions
Topped with a dressing of
  Wagner's Aurora and
  yogurt

Simply mix plain yogurt and Wagner's Aurora to a smooth consistency and pour over salad. Superb!

SPINACH SALAD

So good you can make a meal of it!

Easy

**6-8 Servings
Make Ahead**

1 10 oz. bag fresh
  spinach, washed and
  drained
5-10 slices bacon, fried
  crisp and crumbled
3-5 hard-boiled eggs,
  chopped
Sliced mushrooms
Seasoned croutons
Parmesan cheese, grated
Swiss or Cheddar cheese,
  cut into chunks

Combine all ingredients and toss with dressing.

DRESSING:
2 Tbsp. catsup or chili
  sauce
1½ cups mayonnaise
  (Hellmann's preferred)
3 Tbsp. salad oil
¼ cup milk
½ cup sugar
2 Tbsp. red wine vinegar
Salt and pepper to taste

Combine all ingredients and shake in jar until blended. Toss with salad ingredients.

160

7 LAYER SALAD

Average

8 Servings
Make Ahead

½ of 10 oz. bag fresh
  spinach, washed, patted
  dry, and broken into
  pieces
3-4 hard-boiled eggs,
  sliced
Salt and pepper
2-3 green onions or ¼ cup
  sweet onion, sliced
4 slices bacon, crisply
  fried and crumbled
½ large head of lettuce,
  broken into pieces
1 10 oz. pkg. frozen peas,
  thawed, not cooked
Mayonnaise
Sour cream
2 cups Cheddar cheese,
  grated

In a clear glass bowl, if available, place
a layer of spinach. Place eggs on top of
spinach; sprinkle with salt and pepper.
Follow with green onions, bacon, lettuce, peas, and more salt and pepper.
Mix equal parts of mayonnaise and sour
cream and spread over **top** of salad; do
not stir. Completely cover salad.
Sprinkle with grated cheese. Cover with
plastic wrap and refrigerate at least 8
hours or overnight. When serving, dig to
the bottom!

CREAMY SPINACH SALAD

Easy

4-6 Servings
Make Ahead

½ cup sour cream
¼-⅓ cup creamy French
  dressing
1 10 oz. bag fresh
  spinach, torn into
  bite-size pieces
1 11 oz. can Mandarin
  oranges, chilled and
  drained
1 small cucumber, sliced
1 cup sharp Cheddar
  cheese, shredded
½ cup walnuts, chopped
  (optional)
1 medium red onion, sliced
  (optional)

Blend sour cream and French dressing.
In large bowl, combine spinach, or-
anges, cucumber, cheese, walnuts and
onion. May be made ahead to this point.
Pour sour cream mixture over greens.
Toss lightly.

GLEN IRIS SPINACH SALAD

COMPLIMENTS OF GLEN IRIS INN, CASTILE, N.Y.

Easy   **6 Servings**

½ cup mayonnaise
2 Tbsp. wine vinegar
¼ cup sugar
¼ cup light cream
2 10 oz. bags spinach,
    cleaned
½ sweet red onion, thinly
    sliced
1 hard-boiled egg, sliced
Mushrooms, sliced
Bacon, cooked and
    crumbled

Mix together with a French whip mayonnaise, vinegar, sugar and cream. Pour on spinach and onion just before serving. Garnish with egg, mushrooms and bacon. Dressing will keep in refrigerator several days.

KOREAN SALAD

                                        6-8 Servings
Average   **Make Ahead**

SALAD:
½ 10 oz. bag spinach, torn
    in pieces
½ of a 1 lb. can of bean
    sprouts, drained
1 5 oz. can water
    chestnuts, drained and
    thinly sliced
5-6 slices bacon,
    crisp-cooked, drained of
    fat and crumbled
2 hard-boiled eggs, sliced
Salt and pepper

In a salad bowl, combine spinach, bean sprouts, water chestnuts, bacon and eggs. Sprinkle lightly with salt and pepper.

DRESSING:
1 cup salad oil
½ cup sugar
⅓ cup catsup
¼ cup vinegar
2 Tbsp. onion, grated
2 tsp. Worcestershire
    sauce

Combine dressing ingredients. Blend in blender or shake in jar until well mixed. Add to salad and toss lightly.

162

UNTOSSED SALAD

Glass bowl is a must!

Average

1 8 oz. bottle sweet French dressing (Casino preferred)
1 10 oz. bag fresh spinach, broken into pieces
Salt and pepper
7-8 slices bacon, cooked crisp and crumbled
5 hard-boiled eggs, sliced
1 head iceberg lettuce, broken into pieces
½ 10 oz. pkg. frozen peas
Red onion, cut into rings
Sugar
2 cups mayonnaise (Hellman's preferred)
3 cups Swiss cheese, grated

Cover bottom of a 4 quart deep bowl with ¾ of a bottle of French dressing. Pack down ¾ of spinach. (Be sure spinach is very dry.) Sprinkle with salt and pepper. Cover with bacon and eggs. Layer lettuce on top; sprinkle with salt and pepper. Add layer of uncooked peas; add layer of onion rings. Sprinkle with sugar. Add mayonnaise in a layer ¾ inch thick. Add Swiss cheese. Add rest of spinach and remains of dressing. Cover and refrigerate overnight.

SAUERKRAUT SALAD

Average

1-2 cups sugar (depending on taste)
⅓ cup vinegar
3 Tbsp. oil
1 27 oz. can sauerkraut, drained
1 cup celery, chopped
½ cup green pepper, chopped
1 small onion, chopped
1 3 oz. can pimiento, chopped
Dash of salt

Combine all ingredients and chill overnight.

NEW YORK DELI POTATO SALAD

Average

6 Servings
Make Ahead

6-8 medium new potatoes
1 cup mayonnaise
  (Hellmann's preferred)
9 Tbsp. whole milk
5 Tbsp. dehydrated
  parsley flakes
2 Tbsp. vinegar
2 Tbsp. sugar
3 Tbsp. onion, finely
  chopped
Salt and pepper

Boil potatoes with jackets on. While potatoes are boiling and then slightly cooled, make sauce. Thin mayonnaise with milk, adding 1 Tbsp. at a time, and beating after each addition. It will be very thin. Add parsley, vinegar, sugar, onion and pepper. As the strength of vinegars vary, taste often to obtain the correct sugar-vinegar blend. Remove jackets from cooked potatoes. Slice potatoes into thin slices while still warm. Salt generously, add sauce and combine carefully. Leave out on counter for 1 hour to mellow. Refrigerate until cold.

INCREDIBLE MACARONI SALAD

Definitely not your ordinary macaroni salad!

Average

8-10 Servings
Make Ahead

1 7¼ oz. pkg. macaroni
  and cheese dinner
1 10 oz. pkg. frozen peas
1 medium tomato, chopped
¾ cup salad dressing or
  mayonnaise
½ cup celery, sliced
¼ cup onion, chopped
½ tsp. salt
Dash pepper
6 hard-boiled eggs

Prepare macaroni and cheese as directed on package. Add peas, tomato, salad dressing, celery, onion and seasonings. Chop 5 eggs and add to mixture. Mix lightly. Chill. Stir in additional dressing before serving, if desired. Garnish with remaining egg.

HELPFUL HINT

Prick eggs before boiling to prevent cracking.

FANCY OLIVE ANTIPASTO

Average

2 lbs. bulk green olives
    with pits, drained
3 cups celery, cut into
    chunks
1½ cups carrots, cut into
    chunks (optional)
1 large red onion, sliced
½ 2 oz. jar capers, with a
    little juice
⅛ tsp. cayenne pepper
1½ tsp. oregano
¼ cup vinegar
½ cup oil
Dash of salt and pepper
Lettuce leaves (optional)
Tomato slices (optional)

Toss all ingredients, except lettuce and tomatoes, together. Marinate at least 10 hours. Serve on lettuce leaves with tomato slices. May be kept refrigerated for weeks. Recipe may be halved easily.

BLEU CHEESE DRESSING

Easy

1 Quart
Make Ahead

2 cups mayonnaise
(Hellman's preferred)
4-8 oz. Bleu cheese to
taste
1 cup buttermilk
1 tsp. garlic salt
⅛ tsp. garlic powder
1 small onion, grated
(optional)

Blend all ingredients in blender. Recipe may be halved.

ELEGANT BLEU CHEESE DRESSING

Easy

1½ Cups
Make Ahead

½ cup mayonnaise
5 Tbsp. buttermilk
½ tsp. garlic salt
¼ tsp. seasoned salt
and/or pepper
¼ tsp. orange extract
3 oz. cream cheese
3-4 oz. Bleu cheese

Combine all ingredients except Bleu cheese; crumble in Bleu cheese. Refrigerate.

CREAMY FRENCH DRESSING

Easy

1 Pint
Make Ahead

1 10 oz. can tomato soup
1 tsp. salt
½ cup sugar
½ tsp. pepper
¾ cup vinegar
1 Tbsp. Worcestershire
sauce
1 tsp. dry mustard
1 tsp. onion juice
1 clove garlic, minced
½ tsp. paprika
1 Tbsp. celery seed
(optional)

Place all ingredients in large covered jar. Chill and shake well before serving.

TANGY FRENCH DRESSING

Easy

1½ Cups
Make Ahead

½ cup sugar
1½ tsp. paprika
1½ tsp. salt
1 tsp. dry mustard
½ cup vinegar
1 cup salad oil

Blend sugar, paprika, salt and dry mustard. Slowly add vinegar and salad oil, and beat 3 minutes. If desired, put clove of garlic in dressing.

FRUIT SALAD FRENCH DRESSING

Average

1½ Cups
Make Ahead

⅓ cup sugar
1 tsp. celery seed
1 tsp. salt
1 tsp. paprika
1 tsp. dry mustard
½ tsp. onion juice
4 Tbsp. vinegar
1 cup oil, chilled in
   refrigerator

Mix dry ingredients. Add onion juice, 2 Tbsp. vinegar and ½ cup oil. Beat well with mixer. Add remaining 2 Tbsp. vinegar and ½ cup oil and beat again. Let stand several hours in refrigerator before using. This dressing should be very thick.

GARLIC SALAD DRESSING

Will last for weeks!

Easy

2 Cups
Make Ahead

1 cup vegetable oil
½ cup vinegar
3 tsp. salt
1 tsp. sugar
1 tsp. dry mustard
Dash of pepper
3 cloves garlic, grated
1 small onion, grated

Combine ingredients in tightly covered jar. Shake well and refrigerate.

ITALIAN SALAD DRESSING

Easy

2 Cups
Make Ahead

1½ cups oil
½ cup wine vinegar
2 Tbsp. water
1 tsp. sugar
2 tsp. salt
1 tsp. paprika
½ tsp. oregano
¼ tsp. garlic powder

Mix in blender or shake in jar. Store in refrigerator.

LIGHT ITALIAN SALAD DRESSING

Easy

1 Cup
Make Ahead

1 cup oil
Juice of 1 lemon
1 tsp. sugar
1 tsp. salt
1 Tbsp. cider vinegar
1 Tbsp. garlic vinegar

Mix all ingredients. Store in refrigerator.

 ## SPINACH SALAD DRESSING

At last, a dressing that's really different!

Easy

¾-1 Cup
Make Ahead

½ cup mayonnaise
2 tsp. red wine vinegar
Dash salt
Cayenne pepper
2 hard-boiled eggs, grated
Onion, grated (to taste)
1 tsp. sugar

Mix together all ingredients. This can be stored in refrigerator several days. Mix lightly with fresh crisp spinach.

CREAMY DRESSING WITH BACON

Equally good as a sauce for meat or poultry!

Average

4 slices bacon
4 eggs
1 tsp. prepared mustard
2½ cups sugar
1 Tbsp. cornstarch
½ tsp. salt
1 tsp. paprika
⅛ tsp. cayenne pepper
1 cup hot water
1 cup distilled white
  vinegar
1 Tbsp. butter
Hard-boiled eggs

Fry bacon until crisp and break into small bits. Place in preheated quart jar. Beat eggs with mustard until thick. Mix sugar with cornstarch and seasonings and stir into eggs. Add water and vinegar. Place over very low heat or use double boiler and cook, stirring constantly, until mixture thickens. DO NOT BOIL. Add butter and pour over bacon in jar. Use on salads or cooked green vegetables. Garnish with hard-boiled eggs. This dressing keeps indefinitely in refrigerator.

NOTES

GLEN IRIS INN

The Glen Iris Inn is located within Letchworth State Park. This Park, known as "The Grand Canyon of the East", contains the 17 mile long, 600 feet deep Genesee Gorge.

MEATS AND MEAT MARINADES

CHEDDAR CHIPPED BEEF

Perfect for a Sunday brunch!

Average   **4 Servings**

¼ lb. chipped beef
2 Tbsp. onion, minced
½ cup butter
3 Tbsp. flour
1 cup milk
¼ lb. mushrooms, sliced
    and sauteed
1 cup sour cream
1 cup Cheddar cheese,
    grated
Parsley, chopped

In a heavy skillet, saute chipped beef and onion in butter until onion is translucent. Blend in flour and milk and cook sauce, stirring constantly, until thickened and smooth. Add mushrooms, sour cream and cheese. Stir mixture until ingredients are well blended, but do not boil. Garnish with chopped parsley. Serve over toast points.

REUBEN CASSEROLE

6-8 Servings
Make Ahead

Easy

1 16 oz. can sauerkraut
⅓ cup Thousand Island
    dressing
12 oz. corned beef,
    shredded (beef in pkg.
    may be used)
8 oz. Swiss or Muenster
    cheese slices
Approximately ½ of 8 oz.
    loaf party rye bread
1 Tbsp. butter or
    margarine, melted

Preheat oven to 400°. In 13x9 inch baking dish, with fork, stir sauerkraut with its liquid and dressing; top with a layer of meat. Bake for 15 minutes, or until bubbly. Remove dish from oven. Place cheese on top of meat in a single layer; top with a layer of bread. Lightly brush bread with butter. Bake 10 minutes longer, or until bread is crisp.

E-Z SHEPHERD'S PIE
Easy   **6 Servings**

1 lb. ground beef, browned
   and drained (seasoned
   to taste)
1 10 oz. can cream of
   celery or cream of
   mushroom soup
½ cup milk
1 8 oz. can or 10 oz. pkg.
   frozen peas and onions
Mashed potatoes to serve
   6 (instant potatoes may
      be substituted)
Butter

In large baking dish, combine all ingredients, except potatoes. Mix thoroughly. Top with mashed potatoes. Dot with butter. Bake at 375° for 30 minutes.

CABBAGE ROLLS

Average

8-12 Servings
Make Ahead
Freeze

2 medium cabbages
1½ lbs. ground chuck
½ lb. ground veal
½ lb. ground pork
2 eggs
1 cup converted rice,
   cooked as directed
   (Uncle Ben's preferred)
2 Tbsp. butter
Salt and pepper to taste
4 garlic cloves, crushed
1 large onion, diced
2-3 16 oz. cans tomato
   sauce

Core cabbages. Parboil in salted water until semi-hard, not cooked. Separate large leaves. Drain well. Combine all remaining ingredients, except tomato sauce. Place small amount of meat mixture in center of each cabbage leaf and roll cabbage, covering meat and tucking in edges of leaf. Place cabbage rolls in large pot with lid. Pour tomato sauce over rolls to cover. Cover and simmer or bake at 325° for 2½ hours. Serve with fresh fruit salad and crusty French or Italian bread.

172

MAFIA CHILI

Mama Mia it's good!

Average

8 Servings
Make Ahead
Freeze

½ lb. ground beef
6 green tomatoes,
   chopped
1 large onion, chopped
1 green pepper, chopped
½ cup mushrooms,
   chopped
2 cloves garlic, minced
2-3 Tbsp. oil
1 15 oz. can tomato sauce
1 15 oz. can stewed
   tomatoes
1 16 oz. can kidney beans,
   drained
1 10 oz. can condensed
   bean soup with bacon
2 Tbsp. chili sauce
2 Tbsp. catsup
½ cup Chianti (can
   substitute any red wine)
3 beef franks, cooked and
   sliced thin
1 tsp. cumin
Chili powder to taste
Salt and pepper to taste
Seasoned salt to taste

Brown beef; drain off fat and set aside. In large pan, saute green tomatoes, onion, green pepper, mushrooms and garlic in oil. Add remaining ingredients and simmer 1½ to 2 hours.

HELPFUL HINT

Dry bread placed in the broiler pan, under the rack, will soak up fat and reduce smoking.

FANTASTIC CHILI

Average

1 lb. ground beef
Pinch oregano
⅓ cup cooking wine, red
  or white
1 lb. can stewed tomatoes
1 6 oz. can tomato sauce
1 6 oz. can tomato paste
  and ½ can water
1 or 2 16 oz. cans red
  kidney beans
2 tsp. chili powder
Salt and pepper to taste
1 Tbsp. sugar

Brown beef and drain off fat. Add oregano and wine and simmer 5 minutes. Cook all tomato ingredients and water on medium heat for 15 minutes. Add undrained beans to tomato mixture and cook over medium heat for 15 minutes. Add meat mixture to tomato mixture. Add chili powder, salt, pepper and sugar. Cook another 20 minutes on low heat.

MEATBALLS IN BEER SAUCE

Average

2 lbs. ground beef
1 lb. bulk hot or sweet
  Italian sausage
2 eggs
1 cup seasoned bread
  crumbs
2 tsp. sage
1 tsp. salt
½ tsp. pepper

Mix all ingredients together. Make 1 inch balls and brown on all sides.

SAUCE:
½ bottle family-size catsup
1 cup brown sugar
1 12 oz. can beer

Mix all ingredients together and add meatballs. Bake, covered, at 350° for 1 hour, stirring occasionally. Meatballs may be frozen before adding to sauce.

PIZZA MEATLOAF

Easy

4-6 Servings
Make Ahead
Freeze

1½ lbs. ground beef or
   ground round
¾ cup cracker or bread
   crumbs
½ cup onion, finely
   chopped
1 egg
1 16 oz. can tomato sauce
1 Tbsp. oregano
Salt and pepper to taste
2 cups Mozzarella cheese,
   grated

Mix all ingredients except cheese. Flatten mixture to ½-1 inch thickness. Put cheese on top and roll up jelly roll style. Bake at 350°-375° for 1 hour.

SUMMER MEAT LOAF

Just as tasty in the winter — served hot!

Average

8 Servings
Make Ahead
Freeze

2 lbs. ground chuck
1 cup sour cream
1 envelope dried onion
   soup mix
1 egg
3 stale hot dog rolls,
   crushed
½ cup tomato or V-8 juice
1 tsp. leaf thyme
1 tsp. leaf tarragon
2 tsp. black pepper,
   coarsely ground

Mix all ingredients. Place in loaf pan and bake at 325° for 1½ hours. Remove from oven and let sit for 30 minutes. Drain off fat. Place in larger baking pan, top side up.

GLAZE:
½ cup brown sugar
¼-⅓ cup catsup

Mix ingredients and glaze top and sides of meat loaf. Bake at 350° for ½ hour. Cool. Remove to platter and chill overnight in refrigerator.

BAKED STUFFED FLANK STEAK

Tastes like you worked for hours!

Average

6 Servings
Make Ahead

RICE STUFFING:
1 8 oz. pkg. long-grain and wild rice (Uncle Ben's preferred)
½ cup Parmesan cheese, grated

Cook rice according to directions. Stir in cheese.

FLANK STEAK:
1¾-2 lbs. flank steak
1 clove garlic, crushed
2 Tbsp. soy sauce
½ tsp. pepper
2 Tbsp. butter or margarine
½ cup condensed beef broth
½ cup water
1 Tbsp. crystallized ginger, crushed or ¾ tsp. powdered ginger

Wipe flank steak with damp paper towel. Score both sides lightly into diamonds with sharp knife. Rub both sides of steak with garlic. Brush each side with soy sauce and pepper. Lay steak flat; spread with 1 Tbsp. butter. Place rice stuffing over steak, keeping about 1½ inches from edges. Roll up, from end to end, around stuffing. Fasten with skewers. Tie roll in 2-3 places with twine. Spread remaining Tbsp. butter over surface. Place in roasting pan. Dilute beef broth with water. Pour over roll. Sprinkle with ginger. Roast at 350° for 45-60 minutes, basting occasionally with pan liquid. Serve juices as gravy.

FLANK STEAK TERIYAKI

Perfect for summer cookouts!

Easy

6-8 Servings
Make Ahead

2-4 lbs. flank steak
½ cup soy sauce
¼ cup bottled barbecue sauce
2 Tbsp. oil
¼ cup honey
1 clove garlic, crushed
6 drops of tabasco sauce or hot chili pepper

Marinate steak 3-8 hours or overnight, turning meat occasionally. Broil steak on each side 5-10 minutes. Carve diagonally. Serve with rice and pineapple or noodles.

CONTINENTAL STEAK ROLLS WITH SOUR CREAM SAUCE

Average

4 Servings
Make Ahead

MEAT AND PASTRY
RECTANGLES:
1 lb. round steak or 4 4 oz.
minute steaks
¼ cup flour
¼ tsp. salt
⅛ tsp. pepper
2 Tbsp. shortening
3 Tbsp. onion, finely
chopped
3 Tbsp. mushrooms, finely
chopped
1 8 oz. can crescent rolls,
(Pillsbury preferred)

If using round steak, pound with mallet to ½ inch thickness. Cut steak into 4 rectangles. Coat with flour, salt and pepper. Brown in shortening. Saute onion and mushrooms until tender. Place 1½ Tbsp. mixture on one end of browned meat; fold over end, covering the mushroom mixture. Unroll dough, leaving 2 triangles joined to form 4 rectangles. Press to seal. Place folded meat on dough rectangles and fold ends. Place seam-side down on cookie sheet. Bake at 400° for 10-12 minutes. Serve with sour cream sauce.

SOUR CREAM SAUCE:
1 cup sour cream
1 Tbsp. butter or
margarine
½ tsp. parsley
¼ tsp. salt

Combine all ingredients in saucepan. Heat thoroughly, but do not boil. Serve over steak rolls.

GRILLED ROUND STEAK

Easy

4 Servings
Make Ahead

2 lbs. top round steak
2 small onions, chopped
½ cup wine vinegar
¼ cup lemon juice
¼ cup soy sauce
1 Tbsp. Worcestershire
sauce
1 clove garlic, minced
1 tsp. salt

Combine all ingredients, except meat, to make marinade. Shake together in jar. Allow to stand 2-3 hours. Place meat in shallow dish; pour marinade over it. Refrigerate 2-3 hours, turning meat occasionally. Broil or grill meat 5 inches from heat. Brush with marinade. Cut diagonally.

PEPPER STEAK

Average

6 Servings
Make Ahead

1 3 lb. chuck roast or
   round steak
2 tsp. meat tenderizer
3 Tbsp. onion, minced
2 tsp. thyme
1 tsp. marjoram
¾ cup wine vinegar
½ cup olive or salad oil
3 Tbsp. lemon juice
1 tsp. garlic salt
¼ cup peppercorns,
   coarsely chopped

Sprinkle meat on both sides with tenderizer; pierce deeply with fork. Place in shallow pan. Combine all ingredients except peppercorns; pour over and around meat. Let stand at room temperature for 1-2 hours turning meat every 30 minutes. Remove meat from marinade; pound half peppercorns into each side with wooden mallet. Grill over coals until desired doneness.

BOEUF BOURGUIGNONNE

Average

6 Servings
Make Ahead
Freeze

20 small onions, peeled
3 Tbsp. butter, clarified
6 oz. bacon, cut into ½
   inch pieces
3 lbs. beef chuck, cut into
   2 inch cubes
3 Tbsp. brandy, warmed
3 Tbsp. flour
2 cups red wine
2 cups beef stock
1¼ tsp. tomato paste
2 cloves garlic, crushed
1 large carrot, peeled and
   diced
Bouquet garni (parsley,
   thyme and bay leaf tied
   together)
Salt
Pepper, freshly ground
8 oz. small mushrooms,
   lightly sauteed in butter
Parsley, chopped

Brown onions in butter, then brown bacon. Remove bacon and onions and reserve. Add meat and brown on all sides. Flame with brandy. Stir in flour and cook for 1 minute; then stir in red wine, stock, tomato paste, garlic, carrot and bouquet garni. Season with salt and pepper. Cover and simmer for 1½ hours. Add onions and bacon and cook for 45 minutes longer. Add mushrooms and cook for an additional 15 minutes. Garnish with chopped parsley.

178

BEER BEEF STEW

Equally delicious made with venison!

Average

6-8 Servings
Make Ahead
Freeze

6 medium onions, sliced
1-2 cloves garlic, minced
¼ cup salad oil
2 lbs. beef for stewing, cut into 1 inch cubes
Flour for dredging
Salt and pepper
½ cup canned beef bouillon
12 oz. beer, at room temperature
1 Tbsp. parsley, chopped
1 bay leaf
¼ tsp. thyme
2 Tbsp. light brown sugar

Saute onion and garlic in oil until tender. Dredge meat in seasoned flour. Brown meat in the same pan after removing vegetables. Put meat and vegetables in a heavy casserole or Dutch oven. Heat bouillon in skillet, stirring up pieces of meat remaining. Pour over meat and vegetables. Add beer to cover meat. Stir in remaining seasonings and sugar. Cover and place in lower ⅓ of oven. Bake at 350° for 2½ hours. More beer may be added, if liquid evaporates. Serve in soup bowls over noodles.

FRENCH STEW

Easy

6-8 Servings
Make Ahead
Freeze

1 cup Burgundy
1 10 oz. can cream of mushroom soup
1 pkg. dried onion soup mix
2 lbs. chuck roast, cubed
1 2 oz. jar whole stuffed olives, drained
1 8 oz. can tiny whole carrots, drained
1 8 oz. can tiny whole onions, drained
1 4 oz. can whole mushrooms, drained
1 16 oz. can whole white potatoes, drained

Mix wine and soups together. Add meat and stir. Bake in a covered pot at 250° for 3½ hours. Add remaining ingredients and cook for 1½ hours more. Works beautifully in crock pot cooking all day on low.

BURGUNDY BEEF STEW

Average

3 Tbsp. oil
1 clove garlic, crushed
2½ lbs. lean beef, cubed
  (top round steak
  preferred)
¼ cup flour
4 medium onions,
  quartered
4 cups beef bouillon
1 cup Burgundy wine
10 small carrots
4-5 stalks celery, sliced
6-8 small potatoes, (if
  medium, cut in half)
4 whole tomatoes, peeled
  and seeded
1½ tsp. salt
1 bay leaf
1 tsp. paprika
½ tsp. oregano
4-5 whole cloves, crushed
½ tsp. basil
1 tsp. Worcestershire
  sauce
¼ tsp. freshly ground
  pepper
5-6 peppercorns

Heat oil with garlic until it is smokey hot. Roll meat in flour and brown in hot oil. Add onions and saute for 2 minutes. Add bouillon. Cover and simmer for 45 minutes. Add remaining ingredients and simmer for 2 hours, or until meat is tender and liquid is well blended. Best if served in bowls.

BEEF BRISKET

Easy

Beef brisket (4 lb.)
Lawry's salt
Paprika
½ cup onion, chopped

Sprinkle beef brisket with salt and paprika; top with onions. Bake at 350° for 15 minutes. Add 1 cup boiling water; reduce oven to 325° and bake 3 more hours, basting occasionally. Thinly slice on diagonal. Great on Kimmelwick rolls.

BEEF GOULASH

A real Hungarian rhapsody!

Average

6 Servings
Make Ahead

6 Tbsp. oil or drippings
3-4 lbs. chuck steak, cut
  into large cubes
4 large onions, sliced
4 Tbsp. paprika
4 Tbsp. flour
2 Tbsp. tomato paste
1 clove garlic, crushed
4 cups beef stock
Bouquet garni
Salt and pepper to taste
2 red peppers or 1 4 oz.
  jar pimiento, chopped
4 large tomatoes, peeled
  and chopped
8 oz. sour cream or plain
  yogurt

Heat oil or drippings and brown meat. Remove meat, lower heat, and saute onions for a few minutes. Add paprika and cook 1 minute. Add flour, tomato paste, garlic and stock. Stir until boiling; add meat, bouquet garni, salt and pepper. Cover and simmer gently on stove or in oven for 2 hours. Blanch red peppers. When meat is tender, add peppers and tomatoes. Simmer for 2-3 minutes. Place into casserole for serving and spoon sour cream or yogurt on top. Serve with noodles.

BEEF ROLL-UP

Average

6 Servings
Make Ahead

6 beef cube steaks
1 tsp. salt
¼ tsp. pepper
¾ cup bottled low-cal
  French dressing
1½ cups carrot, shredded
¾ cup onion, finely
  chopped
¾ cup green pepper, finely
  chopped
¾ cup celery, finely
  chopped
¼ cup water
6 slices bacon

Sprinkle meat with salt and pepper. Marinate in French dressing 30-60 minutes, at room temperature. In saucepan, simmer vegetables, covered, in water until tender-crisp, about 7-8 minutes; drain. Drain steaks; place about ⅓ cup vegetable mixture on each steak. Roll up jelly roll fashion. Cut bacon slices in half, crosswise. Wrap two half pieces bacon around each roll-up; secure with wooden toothpicks. Grill steaks over hot coals, or broil 3-4 inches from heat, 20-25 minutes, turning steaks occasionally. Best when done over charcoal.

STEAK AND KIDNEY PIE

God will save The Queen and you will save this recipe!

Average   4-6 Servings

½ lb. kidney
1½ lbs. stewing beef
Seasoned flour
2 Tbsp. vegetable oil
1 onion, sliced
½ lb. mushrooms, finely
  chopped
Pinch of mixed herbs
2¼ cups stock
Salt and freshly ground
  pepper
1 lb. flaky pastry
  (Pepperidge Farm
  preferred)
1 egg
2 Tbsp. milk

Remove core from kidney and cut into small pieces. Roll meats in seasoned flour and brown quickly in oil. Lift meat into saucepan. Add onion and mushrooms to pan with mixed herbs. Add stock, salt and pepper. Cover and simmer for 1½ hours. Strain off ¾ of gravy and reserve. Prepare pastry. Roll out and line bottom of 10 inch pie plate. Spoon meat and remaining gravy into pie. Cover with pastry top and seal edges. Make a hole in center of pie; decorate with pastry leaves cut from any remaining pastry. Mix egg and milk together and brush pie. Bake at 425° for 30 minutes; reduce oven to 350° and bake 40-60 minutes longer. It may be necessary to cover pie during baking to prevent over-browning. Serve hot with reserved gravy.

BEEF KROMESKIES

Average   2-4 Servings

4 Tbsp. butter
½ cup flour
1 beef bouillon cube
1¼ cups milk
½-¾ lb. cooked, cold beef,
  minced or finely
  chopped (may substitute
  lamb with chopped mint)
1 egg, beaten
1½ Tbsp. parsley,
  chopped
Salt and pepper to taste

Melt butter in pan; blend in flour and cook for 1 minute. Crumble bouillon cube in milk, then blend into flour paste. Bring to boiling point and simmer for 2 minutes, stirring well. Remove from heat and add beef. Stir in egg, parsley and seasoning. Set aside until cold. Divide mixture into 8 portions and shape into cylinders.

COATING:
¼ cup flour
1 egg, beaten
Bread crumbs, toasted
Oil or fat for deep frying

Coat each with flour, then egg and bread crumbs. Heat oil or fat; add kromeskies and fry for about 4 minutes or until golden brown. Drain on paper towels. Serve at once.

BEEF FILLET WITH HORSERADISH SAUCE

Easy

**8 Servings
Make Ahead**

1 3-4 lb. beef tenderloin
½ cup butter

MARINADE:

1 cup red wine (Burgundy
    or Madeira preferred)
1 Tbsp. Worcestershire
    sauce
Juice of 1 lemon
Dash of freshly ground
    pepper

Combine all marinade ingredients. Marinate beef at room temperature for several hours. Heat butter in skillet and brown beef on all sides. Remove to shallow roasting pan. Insert meat thermometer into thickest part of meat. Bake, uncovered, at 375° until desired degree of doneness. This beef is served to best advantage at room temperature.

HORSERADISH SAUCE:

¼ cup prepared
    horseradish, drained
¼ tsp. salt
1 cup sour cream

Combine all ingredients. Cover and chill until ready to serve with meat.

ZESTY POT ROAST

**6 Servings
Make Ahead**

Easy

1 3-4 lb. pot roast
2 Tbsp. shortening
Salt and pepper to taste
½ cup tomato or V-8 juice
¼ cup prepared
    horseradish
½ cup onion, chopped
1 Tbsp. cornstarch or flour

Brown pot roast in shortening and pour off drippings. Add salt, pepper, juice, horseradish and onion. Cover tightly and cook slowly for 3 hours or until meat is tender. Remove pot roast to heated platter. Add water to cooking liquid to make 2 cups and then thicken with cornstarch to make gravy. After roast has cooked for 2 hours, vegetables such as potatoes, carrots and onions may be added for the third hour of cooking.

BAR-B-CUE BRISKET

A real Texas taste!

6-8 Servings
Make Ahead

Average

½ of a 3 oz. bottle liquid
  smoke
Beef brisket (3-5 lbs.)
Garlic powder
Onion powder
Celery salt
Meat tenderizer
Salt and pepper
2 Tbsp. Worcestershire
  sauce
1 16 oz. bottle barbecue
  sauce

Pour liquid smoke on meat and rub on all sides. Sprinkle garlic powder, onion powder, celery salt, meat tenderizer, salt and pepper on both sides of meat. Cover with foil and place in refrigerator overnight. When ready to bake, sprinkle with Worcestershire sauce. Bake, covered with foil, at 275° for 5 hours. Uncover and add ½ bottle barbecue sauce. Bake another hour, uncovered. Let cool. Remove any hardened fat. Slice thin and place on platter. Make sauce using ½ drippings and remaining barbecue sauce. Pour sauce over sliced brisket. Reheat before serving. Also good cold for sandwiches on hard rolls.

MARVELOUS MEAT MARINADE

2½ Cups
Make Ahead

Easy

½ cup brown sugar
½ cup wine vinegar
½ cup pineapple juice
2 tsp. salt
½ tsp. garlic powder
1 cup soy sauce

Mix all ingredients and bring to a boil. Marinate meat (use beef or pork tenderloin cubes) for a minimum of 4 hours.

SWEET'N EASY MARINADE

The name says it all!

Easy

⅓ Cup

2 Tbsp. soy sauce
2 Tbsp. sherry
2 Tbsp. honey
1 clove garlic, sliced

Combine all ingredients. Use to marinate sirloin or flank steak. Marinate meat in refrigerator for at least 2 hours or overnight.

FRENCH VEAL

Average   **6 Servings**

2 Tbsp. flour
6 veal steaks
6 Tbsp. butter
3 Tbsp. oil
1 large onion, finely
  chopped
3 carrots, peeled and
  sliced
2-4 cloves garlic, finely
  chopped
2-3 ripe tomatoes, peeled,
  seeded and chopped
½ cup white wine
1 tsp. rosemary, crushed
¼ cup parsley, chopped
Salt and pepper
12 mushroom caps
Butter

Flour steaks; heat butter and oil until bubbly, then quickly brown steaks on both sides. Place on heated plate. Add onion, carrots and garlic to pan and saute until browned. Add tomatoes and cook down 5 minutes; add steaks, wine, rosemary and parsley. Cover and simmer 25-30 minutes. Do not over cook. Season with salt and pepper, if needed. Saute mushroom caps in butter and add to veal when ready to serve.

TANGY VEAL

Average   **2-4 Servings**

1½ lbs. veal steak, ½-¾
  inch thick
2 Tbsp. olive oil
½ tsp. salt
⅛ tsp. pepper
½ fresh lemon, thinly
  sliced
1 cup Burgundy wine
1 chicken bouillon cube
1 Tbsp. cornstarch

Cut meat into serving pieces. In pressure cooker, heat oil and brown veal on all sides. Season. Lay lemon slices on veal; pour on wine combined with bouillon cube. Close pressure cooker, place regulator on vent pipe set at number 10; bring cooker to pressure. With regulator rocking, gently cook for 15 minutes. Remove from heat; let pressure drop of its own accord. Remove veal to warm dish. Heat liquid in cooker; add cornstarch mixed with a little cold water to thicken the wine sauce. Pour over veal and serve. Recipe may be done in covered casserole by increasing cooking time to 45 minutes.

VEAL PICCATA

Average   **6-8 Servings**

8 boneless veal cutlets
All-purpose flour
2 eggs, well beaten
1½ tsp. salt
½ cup milk
½ cup dry white wine
1 tsp. parsley, minced
½ tsp. ground black
   pepper
¾ cup unsalted butter
¼ cup fresh lemon juice
Parsley, minced
8 lemon wedges

Pound veal cutlets with a wooden mallet until very thin. Sprinkle lightly with flour and pound flour into cutlets. Combine eggs, salt, milk, wine, parsley and pepper. Dip cutlets into egg mixture, coating well. Heat ½ cup butter in large skillet and saute cutlets until golden brown. Remove to a heated serving platter. Melt remaining 4 Tbsp. butter in pan. Stir in lemon juice until just blended. Pour over cutlets and garnish with parsley and lemon wedges.

VEAL STEW

Average

6 Servings
Make Ahead
Freeze

4 large onions, chopped
1 lb. fresh mushrooms,
   sliced
3 Tbsp. butter
2 lbs. stewing veal
½ cup flour
1 tsp. salt
¾ tsp. pepper
¼ tsp. garlic powder
½ cup butter
1 clove garlic
Pinch of rosemary or
   marjoram
½ cup sherry
1 10 oz. can beef
   consomme
Noodles, cooked

Saute onions and mushrooms in 3 Tbsp. butter. Place in 1½ quart oven-proof casserole. Dust veal with flour, salt, pepper and garlic powder. Brown in skillet using ½ cup butter. When browned, place veal in casserole; add clove garlic, rosemary or marjoram, sherry and consomme. Cover and bake at 350° for 2 hours or until tender. Add more sherry if it becomes dry. Spoon over cooked noodles, if desired.

VEAL FRANCAIS

COMPLIMENTS OF MORETTI'S RESTAURANT, ELMIRA, N.Y.

Average   **4 Servings**

4 Tbsp. butter
1 clove garlic, chopped
1/3 tsp. dried thyme,
  crumbled
2 lbs. veal medallions (4
  oz. pieces)
All-purpose flour for
  dredging
3 eggs, whisked
3 oz. white table wine
2 lemons
Parsley

In large non-stick skillet, melt butter and add chopped garlic and thyme. Dredge veal medallions in flour; then dip in eggs. Fry on both sides until golden brown. When finished, place on a pre-heated platter. Using the same hot skillet, heat wine with juice of 1 fresh lemon. Be sure this is very hot. Pour over veal medallions and garnish with lemon slices and sprigs of parsley.

THREE LAYER CASSEROLE

Average

4 Servings
Make Ahead
Freeze

1 lb. ground veal or beef
1/3 cup onion, minced
1 8 oz. can tomato sauce
1 tsp. basil
3/4 tsp. parsley
1/4 tsp. oregano
1/8 tsp. garlic salt
Dash of pepper
1 4 oz. can mushrooms,
  drained or equivalent
  fresh
1 10 oz. pkg. frozen
  chopped spinach,
  thawed
6 oz. cottage cheese
4 oz. Mozzarella cheese

Saute meat and onion until onion is transparent. Add tomato sauce, spices and mushrooms. Squeeze liquid from thawed spinach and combine with cottage cheese. In 7x11 inch baking dish, arrange in layers spinach mixture, meat mixture and then Mozzarella cheese. Repeat, ending with cheese. Bake at 375° until bubbly, about 30-40 minutes.

BARBECUED LEG OF LAMB

COMPLIMENTS OF GLENORA WINE CELLARS, DUNDEE, N.Y.

Average   **6-8 Servings**

1 medium-size leg of lamb,
  boned and butterflied
2 cups sherry
½-1 cup fresh mint
Dry mustard
Pepper
Garlic
Onion juice

Before cooking, marinate lamb for 2 hours with sherry and mint. Rub lamb with dry mustard, pepper, garlic and onion juice.

SAUCE:
4 Tbsp. butter
1 clove garlic
1 Tbsp. onion, grated
½ cup fresh mint, chopped

Combine sauce ingredients and cook gently for 5 minutes. Barbecue lamb slowly until medium to well done (slightly pink in middle). While barbecuing, brush with sauce. Serve with Glenora Wine Cellars' Baco Noir Rose or other dry rose or light red wine.

 # GRILLED LEG OF LAMB

A real snap for a summer meal!

Easy

**6-8 Servings
Make Ahead**

1 leg of lamb, butterflied
  (your butcher can do
  this)
2 8 oz. bottles spicy
  French dressing
  (Catalina preferred)

Marinate lamb overnight, turning periodically, in dressing. Grill as you would a steak, and cut on the bias.

HELPFUL HINT

Use waxless dental floss for tying roasts.

188

CHUTNEY GRILLED LAMB CHOPS

Easy

4 Servings
Make Ahead

½ cup chutney, chopped
2 Tbsp. butter, melted
1 Tbsp. lemon juice
1 tsp. curry powder
4 loin lamb chops, cut ¾
 inch thick

Combine all ingredients except chops. Place chops on rack and brush with half the mixture. Broil until half done and turn chops. Brush with remaining mixture and complete broiling.

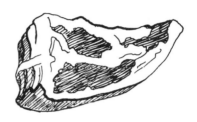

SHISH KEBOBS

Average

4-6 Servings
Make Ahead

MARINADE:
¼ cup vinegar
¼ cup salad oil
2 tsp. salt
½ cup onion, thinly sliced
¼ cup A-1 sauce
½ tsp. pepper
1½ to 2 inch thick lean
 cubes of lamb or beef,
 ½ lb. per person

Combine all ingredients, except meat, and mix thoroughly. Add meat and marinate several hours, preferably overnight.

VEGETABLES:
Whole mushrooms, canned
 or fresh
Cherry tomatoes
Green peppers, parboiled
Onions, parboiled
1 16 oz. can potatoes or
 fresh potatoes, parboiled

Make shish kebobs using meat and vegetables. Cook 5-6 inches from heat source, 10-12 minutes per side. Baste with sauce while broiling. Sauce can be made ahead of time and refrigerated.

SPIEDIES

Average

1½ onions, sliced and
    separated
1 lemon, sliced and
    squeezed on meat
2 cloves garlic, crushed
½ tsp. fennel seed
2 tsp. salt
1 tsp. pepper
⅓ cup oregano
2 cups oil
5 lbs. lamb, venison or
    beef, cubed

Combine first 8 ingredients in large bowl. Add meat, and marinate overnight. Grill over a charcoal fire on skewers. Serve as sandwich on Italian bread or on a bed of rice.

SAUCE:
½ cup vinegar
¼ cup oil
3 garlic cloves, crushed
2 tsp. mint leaves, crushed

Mix and serve cold or warm over cooked meat.

HELPFUL HINT

Meat may be tenderized with a few drops of vinegar or wine.

EASY HAM DIVAN

Easy

1 10 oz. pkg. frozen
  broccoli spears
4 slices white or French
  bread, toasted and
  buttered
4 large thin slices baked
  ham
1 cup sour cream
1 tsp. prepared mustard
½ cup Cheddar cheese,
  grated

Cook broccoli; drain well. Place toast slices in single layer in a large shallow baking dish or in individual baking dishes. Cover each with a slice of ham, folding ham to fit toast, if needed. Top with hot broccoli. Blend sour cream with mustard. Spoon in ribbons over broccoli; sprinkle with cheese. Bake at 400° for 15 minutes or until heated through and cheese is melted.

HAM POLYNESIAN

4 Servings
Make Ahead

Easy

3 cups cooked ham, diced
2 Tbsp. butter
1 13 oz. can pineapple
  chunks
2 medium green peppers,
  cut into strips
½ cup brown sugar
2 Tbsp. cornstarch
½ cup vinegar
½ cup chicken bouillon
2 tsp. soy sauce
3 cups rice, cooked

Brown ham pieces lightly in butter. Add pineapple chunks with syrup and green pepper strips. Cover and simmer for 15 minutes. Mix brown sugar and cornstarch; add vinegar, bouillon and soy sauce. Add to ham mixture and stir until thickened. Serve over hot rice.

HAM LOAF

Easy

2 lbs. ground ham
1½ lbs. ground fresh pork
1 cup milk
2 eggs
1 cup bread crumbs
1½ cups brown sugar
½ cup water
½ cup vinegar
1 tsp. dry mustard

If possible have butcher grind ham and fresh pork together. Mix all ingredients. Bake at 325° for 1 hour. Reduce oven to 300° and bake 1 hour longer. May be served hot or cold.

HAM STUFFED ACORN SQUASH

Average

4 Servings
Make Ahead

2 medium acorn squash,
 cut into halves
1 lb. cooked ground ham
1 egg
½ cup soft bread crumbs
½ cup celery, chopped
¼ cup green peppers,
 chopped
2 Tbsp. prepared mustard
½ cup brown sugar
2 Tbsp. butter, softened

Scoop out seeds from acorn squash. Cut off bottoms to enable squash to evenly sit in bottom of pan. Mix ham, egg, bread crumbs, celery, peppers and mustard together. Mash together brown sugar and butter and place in center of each squash half. Fill squash with ham mixture and place in a shallow baking dish filled with 1 inch of water. Bake at 350° for 1 to 1½ hours. May also individually wrap the squash in aluminum foil and bake the same as above.

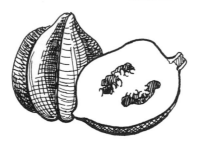

HAM AND SPINACH ROLLS

Average

4-6 Servings
Make Ahead

1 10 oz. pkg frozen
  chopped spinach,
  cooked and drained
1 cup of pkg. cornbread
  stuffing mix
1 cup sour cream
12 thin slices cooked ham
3 Tbsp. butter
3 Tbsp. flour
1½ cups milk
¼ cup Cheddar cheese,
  shredded
2 Tbsp. Parmesan cheese,
  grated

Combine spinach, stuffing mix and sour cream in medium bowl. Spread on ham slices, dividing evenly. Roll up slices and arrange seam-side down, in one layer, in shallow baking dish. Melt butter in small saucepan. Stir in milk slowly and continue to cook, stirring until sauce thickens and bubbles. Add Cheddar cheese, remove from heat and stir until cheese melts. Pour over ham; sprinkle on Parmesan cheese. Cover dish and bake at 350° for 15 minutes. Uncover, and bake 15 minutes longer.

STUFFED HAM ROLLS

Average

1 Dozen
Make Ahead

½ cup rice
½ cup onion, finely
  chopped
½ cup celery, finely
  chopped
1½ tsp. salt
1½ tsp. mustard (Dijon
  preferred)
1 egg
12-14 thin slices boiled or
  baked ham

Cook rice according to package directions. Combine rice with onion, celery, salt, mustard and egg. Place mixture on ham slice and roll up. Place seam-side down in greased 7x12 inch baking dish.

SAUCE:
½ cup orange or peach
  marmalade
½ cup brown sugar
2 Tbsp. vinegar
1 tsp. dry mustard
¼ tsp. cinnamon
¼ tsp. ground cloves

Combine all ingredients and spread on top of rolls. Bake at 350° for 25 minutes.

SPECIAL PORK CHOPS

Easy   **4 Servings**

4 thick pork chops
1½ Tbsp. olive oil
1½ Tbsp. butter
Salt and freshly ground
   pepper
¼ lb. Gruyere or Swiss
   cheese, finely grated
1-2 tsp. dry mustard
Light cream

In heavy frying pan, brown chops in oil and butter; season to taste with salt and pepper. Cook slowly for 30 minutes or until done. Remove from pan and spread with a thick paste made from Gruyere cheese, mustard and enough cream to form a spreading consistency. Place chops under broiler until sauce is golden.

MARINATED PORK ROAST

Easy

8-10 Servings
Make Ahead

½ cup soy sauce
½ cup dry sherry
2 cloves garlic, minced
1 Tbsp. dry mustard
1 tsp. ginger
1 tsp. crushed thyme
1 4-5 lb. pork roast, boned,
   rolled and tied

Combine all ingredients, except pork roast. Place roast in large clear plastic bag. Pour in marinade and close bag. Let stand 2-3 hours or refrigerate overnight. Shake occasionally to coat all sides of pork. Remove from bag. Place roast on rack in shallow pan and bake at 325° for 3 hours. Baste with marinade during last hour of cooking.

ROAST PORK WITH OLIVES

A colorful company dish!

Easy   **8 Servings**

1 4 lb. pork loin
3 cloves garlic, slivered
1½ cups chicken broth or
   bouillon
¾ cup dry Vermouth
½ tsp. ground sage
¼ tsp. pepper
¾ cup pimiento stuffed
   olives, sliced
2 Tbsp. cornstarch
Rice, cooked

Score fat side of pork; insert garlic in slits. Place in shallow roasting pan and cover with mixture of broth, Vermouth, sage and pepper. Bake at 325° for 35 minutes per pound. Baste occasionally. Add ½ cup olives to pan liquid for last hour of baking. Skim off fat and add enough water to make 1¾ cups liquid. Thicken with cornstarch and ¼ cup water. If desired, add the remaining olives to rice and use the thickened liquid as gravy.

SAUSAGE STUFFED PEPPERS

Average

2 Servings
Make Ahead
Freeze

2 large green peppers
Salt
½ lb. mild bulk sausage
1 small onion, chopped
1 10 oz. can tomato soup
1½ cups rice, cooked
½ cup sharp Cheddar
  cheese, shredded
2 tsp. Worcestershire
  sauce
Salt and pepper
Parsley

Slice tops off green peppers and remove seeds. Parboil peppers in boiling, salted water for 5 minutes and drain. Season cavity of each pepper with salt; set aside. In skillet, brown sausage, then add onion and cook until tender. Pour off drippings. Add tomato soup, rice, cheese and Worcestershire sauce. Season to taste with salt and pepper. Simmer 5 minutes. Stuff peppers with sausage mixture and place in a 1 quart casserole, packing any extra stuffing around peppers. Bake at 350° for 30 minutes. Garnish with parsley.

SAUSAGE CASSEROLE

Average

6 Servings
Make Ahead
Freeze

1 lb. bulk Italian sausage
1 cup celery, chopped
1 cup onion, chopped
½ cup green pepper,
  chopped
¼ cup pimiento, chopped
1 10 oz. can cream of
  mushroom soup
1¼ cups rice, uncooked
¼ tsp. salt
1 cup soft bread crumbs
3 Tbsp. butter, melted

Cook sausage until done but not brown. Pour off fat and add celery, onion and pepper. Cook until tender. Stir in pimiento, soup, rice and salt. Pour into a 1½ quart ungreased casserole and bake at 350° for 50 minutes. Top with crumbs tossed with melted butter and return to oven for 20 minutes.

SKILLET SAUSAGE ITALIANO

Perfect for Dad's night in the kitchen!

Average   **4 Servings**

1½ lbs. link Italian
   sausage, cut into pieces
2 medium onions, sliced
1 green pepper, sliced
¼ tsp. oregano
¼ tsp. garlic powder
5-6 slices bread
Butter
2 cups Mozzarella cheese,
   grated
1 to 1½ cups spaghetti
   sauce

Lightly brown sausage in skillet. Lay onion and green pepper slices on top; cover and simmer 15-20 minutes. While sausage is simmering, sprinkle oregano and garlic on bottom of an iron skillet (oven-proof). Butter one side of bread and cut into quarters. Place buttered side down in bottom of pan and arrange to cover the pan. Sprinkle Mozzarella cheese over bread, being sure to cover. Top with sausage. Spread onions and peppers over sausage. Cover all with spaghetti sauce. Sprinkle more Mozzarella cheese over top and bake at 350° for 20 minutes or until bubbly.

SWEET AND SOUR SAUSAGE

4 Main Dish Servings
16 Hors d'oeuvres Servings
Easy   **Make Ahead**

2 lbs. sweet Italian
   sausage
1 13½ oz. can pineapple
   chunks
4 tsp. cornstarch
½ tsp. salt
½ cup maple flavored
   syrup
⅓ cup water
⅓ cup vinegar
1 large green pepper, cut
   into ¾ inch squares
½ cup Maraschino
   cherries, drained

Saute sausage; cut into bite-size pieces. Drain pineapple, reserving syrup for sauce. Blend cornstarch, salt, pineapple syrup, maple syrup, water and vinegar. Heat to boiling, stirring constantly. Add all other ingredients. Cook for 5 minutes. More sausage may be added using same amount of sauce. For main dish, serve with rice; as hors d'oeuvres serve using toothpicks. This may be made ahead, refrigerated and reheated to serve.

BAKED SPARERIBS AND ONIONS

Average

4-6 Servings
Make Ahead

3 lbs. country-style
  spareribs
2 Tbsp. shortening
2 cups onion, sliced
2 cloves garlic, minced
⅓ cup vinegar
⅔ cup water
¼ cup chili sauce
2 Tbsp. lemon juice
2 Tbsp. Worcestershire
  sauce
3-4 Tbsp. brown sugar
1 tsp. salt
1 tsp. dry mustard

Bake ribs in 9x13 inch pan at 450° for 30 minutes. Drain fat. Meanwhile, cook onion and garlic in shortening until tender. Add remaining ingredients and simmer for 10 minutes. Pour sauce over browned ribs. Cover pan tightly with foil. Reduce oven to 350° and bake for another 1 to 1½ hours. Check after 1 hour. If well-done, reduce heat to 250° and hold until ready to serve.

BARBECUED SPARERIBS

Average

4-6 Servings
Make Ahead
Freeze

3-4 lbs. spareribs, cut into
  pieces (ribs)
  (country-style preferred)
1 lemon, sliced
1 large onion
3 cups catsup
2 cups water
½ cup Worcestershire
  sauce
1 tsp. chili powder
1 tsp. salt
2 dashes of tabasco sauce

Place ribs in shallow roasting pan, meaty-side up. Place slices of lemon on top of meat. Slice onion and separate into rings; place on top of meat. Roast at 450° for 30-45 minutes. Drain off fat. Combine catsup, water, Worcestershire sauce, chili powder, salt and tabasco sauce in saucepan. Bring to a boil and pour over ribs. Continue baking at 350°, basting ribs every 15 minutes with sauce, for 45-60 minutes or until tender. May be pre-cooked in oven and then barbecued on outdoor grill.

SWEET PINEAPPLE SPARERIBS

Easy   **4-6 Servings**

2-3 lbs. spareribs
¾ cup brown sugar
½ cup pineapple juice
½ cup crushed pineapple
¼ cup prepared mustard
   (French's preferred)

Place ribs in baking dish. Combine all remaining ingredients and pour over ribs. Bake, covered, basting occasionally, at 350° for 45 minutes. Uncover and bake for additional 35 minutes. Serve with sauce.

LUAU PORK SAUCE

A spicy taste men love!

Easy   **2 Cups**
Make Ahead

1 7½ oz. jar baby food
   peaches
⅓ cup catsup
⅓ cup vinegar
2 Tbsp. soy sauce
½ cup brown sugar
2 tsp. ground ginger
1 tsp. salt
Dash of pepper
2 cloves garlic, minced

Combine all ingredients. This is delicious when added to a pork roast during the last 30 minutes of baking. May also be used as a basting sauce when cooking pork on the rotisserie. Heat any extra sauce and serve with fried rice.

RAISIN SAUCE

Easy   **2 Cups**
Make Ahead

½ cup brown sugar
1 tsp. dry mustard
2 Tbsp. cornstarch
2 Tbsp. vinegar
2 Tbsp. lemon juice
¼ tsp. lemon peel
1½ cups water
½ cup raisins

Mix brown sugar, dry mustard and cornstarch. Slowly add vinegar. Add lemon juice, lemon peel, water and raisins. Stir over low heat until thickened. Serve over baked ham.

JOHNSON MUSEUM — CORNELL UNIVERSITY

The Herbert F. Johnson Museum of Art on the Cornell University campus in Ithaca was designed by the acclaimed architect I.M. Pei. From the top of the museum, the visitor is treated to a view of the Cornell University campus and the hills surrounding Cayuga Lake.

POULTRY AND SAUCES

CHICKEN

GAME HENS

DUCK

SAUCES

CHICKEN TARRAGON

Easy

6 Servings
Make Ahead

2 frying chickens, cut into pieces
½ cup margarine
4 cloves garlic, minced
2 tsp. fresh tarragon leaves, snipped
1 tsp. salt
½ tsp. ground black pepper
½ cup dry Vermouth

Place chicken in a large foil-lined pan (broiler pan). In a small saucepan, melt margarine. Stir in remaining ingredients. Brush basting sauce over chicken. May refrigerate until ready to bake. Bake in preheated 350° oven, basting every 15 minutes, for 1¼ hours or until chicken is tender and light golden brown.

GOLDEN CHICKEN TARRAGON

Easy

6 Servings

6 Tbsp. butter
2 onions, chopped
2 small frying chickens, quartered
Salt and pepper to taste
1 tsp. tarragon
2 cups heavy cream
5 egg yolks
2 Tbsp. lemon juice
Parsley

In large heavy skillet, melt butter. Add onions and chicken pieces. Lightly brown chicken on both sides. Season with salt, pepper and tarragon; cover and cook slowly about 40-60 minutes or until done. Pour cream over chicken and let simmer about 10 minutes. Remove from heat. Remove chicken to heated platter. Beat egg yolks and add to pan together with lemon juice. Stir until blended; pour sauce over chicken. Garnish with parsley and serve immediately.

CORNELL BARBECUED CHICKEN

Add some class to your cook-out!

Easy

1¾ Cups
Make Ahead

½ cup oil
1 cup vinegar
2 Tbsp. salt
1½ tsp. poultry seasoning
¼ tsp. pepper
1 egg
1 frying chicken or up to 5 halves

Mix all ingredients together, except chicken. Pour over chicken and marinate at least 4 hours. Barbecue chicken.

199

CHICKEN MARENGO

Easy

1 medium onion, chopped
2 Tbsp. butter
1 10 oz. can tomato soup
1 10 oz. can cream of
    mushroom soup
½ cup sauterne
1 clove garlic, crushed
¼ tsp. oregano
Salt and pepper to taste
5-7 chicken pieces
Rice, cooked

In large saucepan, saute onion in butter. Mix in soups, sauterne, garlic, oregano, salt and pepper. Add chicken and cook, covered, on stove top for 30 minutes over medium-low heat, stirring frequently. Uncover, and cook 20 minutes longer, stirring frequently. Serve over rice.

MONDAY NIGHT CHICKEN

Easy

6-8 chicken pieces
2 Tbsp. margarine
1 10 oz. can cream of
    mushroom or chicken or
    celery soup
¼ cup white wine or
    sherry
1 3 oz. can sliced
    mushrooms, drained
¼ tsp. thyme
¼ tsp. parsley

Remove skin and brown chicken in margarine. Remove from pan and heat soup, wine, mushrooms and seasonings. Arrange chicken in baking dish; pour soup mixture over it. Cover and bake at 325° for 1¼ hours. Uncover for last 15 minutes.

HELPFUL HINT

For crispier skin on roasting poultry or potatoes, substitute mayonnaise for butter or margarine.

OVEN BAR-B-CUED CHICKEN

Easy

4 Servings
Make Ahead
Freeze

1 chicken, cut into pieces,
   salt and peppered
1 cup celery, chopped
1 cup onion, chopped
1 green pepper, chopped
1 4 oz. can mushrooms,
   drained or equivalent
   fresh
½ cup catsup
½ tsp. Worcestershire
   sauce
2 Tbsp. butter
3 cups water
½ cup sherry

Place chicken in baking dish. Bring all other ingredients, except sherry, to a boil and pour over chicken. Bake, covered, at 350° for 30 minutes. Remove cover and bake 30-60 minutes longer, or until chicken is tender. Add sherry during the last ½ hour.

SPRING CHICKEN

One bite and you feel years younger!

Easy

6 Servings
Make Ahead

4 whole chicken breasts,
   split, skinned and boned,
   if desired
2 Tbsp. butter or
   margarine
1 cup water
½ cup sauterne
1 pkg. sour cream sauce
   mix
1 pkg. chicken gravy mix
Parsley flakes

Brown breasts in butter. Combine water, wine, sour cream mix and gravy mix in a saucepan. Bring to a boil and beat if lumpy. Place browned chicken breasts in an ovenware dish. Pour sauce over all. Cover with foil or lid. Bake at 325-350° for 1½ hours. Sprinkle with parsley flakes and serve.

201

ELEGANT CHICKEN PATTIES

Complicated

10 Servings
Make Ahead
Freeze

6 chicken breasts,
  skinned, boned and cut
  into small pieces
1¾ cups cream
1 small onion
2 slices white bread, no
  crusts, cut into cubes
½ lb. ground round steak
1 egg
2½ tsp. salt
⅛ tsp. pepper
4 Tbsp. butter
Lemon-parsley butter

Using a blender or food processor, blend chicken, 1 cup cream and add onion. Add bread to ¾ cup cream. Add to round steak and combine with chicken mixture. Stir in egg, salt and pepper and beat until light and fluffy. Chill 2 hours. Beat again. Melt butter in skillet. With wet hands, mold chicken mixture into patties and drop into hot butter. Sear quickly on both sides. Reduce heat and cook for 20 minutes, turning twice. Serve with lemon-parsley butter ball.

CHICKEN DIVAN

Keep in freezer for unexpected guests!

Easy

8 Servings
Make Ahead
Freeze

2 10 oz. pkgs. frozen
  broccoli spears *or* 1
  small bunch fresh
  broccoli
8 split chicken breasts,
  boned, skinned and
  cooked
2 10 oz. cans cream of
  chicken soup
1 cup mayonnaise
1 tsp. lemon juice
¼ tsp. curry powder
½ cup yellow sharp
  cheese, grated
½ cup seasoned bread
  crumbs, buttered
Slivered almonds

Cook broccoli until tender-crisp. Slice into 1 inch chunks and place in bottom of 9x13x2 inch casserole. Top with chicken breasts. Heat soup, mayonnaise, lemon juice, curry powder and cheese until cheese is melted. Pour over chicken and broccoli. Top with bread crumbs and almonds. Bake, covered, at 350° for 20 minutes. Uncover and continue baking 25 minutes, or until browned and bubbly. This dish can be prepared the day before. Add bread crumbs and almonds just prior to baking.

CHICKEN MOZZARELLA

Average

**16 Servings
Make Ahead
Freeze**

8 whole chicken breasts,
  boned, skinned and cut
  into strips
4-6 eggs, beaten
Salt and pepper to taste
2 cups bread crumbs
½-1 cup butter and/or
  vegetable oil
1 lb. fresh mushrooms,
  sliced
1 8 oz. pkg. Mozzarella
  cheese, sliced
1 13 oz. can chicken broth

Let chicken stand in beaten eggs, salt and pepper for 5 hours or overnight. Roll in bread crumbs and fry in butter and/or oil about 3-4 minutes, or until golden brown. Place chicken in casserole; top with mushrooms and cheese. Pour broth over all and bake at 350° for ½ hour, covered, and ½ hour, uncovered.

HERB CHICKEN ROLLS

Average

**2-3 Servings
Make Ahead
Freeze**

4 split chicken breasts,
  skinned and boned
½ cup butter
Salt and pepper
4 slices Mozzarella cheese
Flour
1 egg, beaten
Bread crumbs
1 Tbsp. parsley
¼ tsp. sage
¼ tsp. rosemary
¼ tsp. thyme
½ cup white wine

Flatten breasts between wax paper; spread ¼ cup butter on chicken. Season to taste with salt and pepper. Place a piece of Mozzarella cheese in the center; wrap chicken up and secure with toothpicks. Dredge in flour; dip in beaten egg and roll in bread crumbs. Melt ¼ cup butter and add parsley, sage, rosemary and thyme. Pour over each rolled breast. Bake at 350° for ½ hour, basting occasionally. Then add wine and cook another ½ hour, basting often.

IMPERIAL CHICKEN

Average

4-6 Servings
Make Ahead

¾ cup margarine, melted
2 cloves garlic, minced
1 cup fine dry bread
   crumbs
⅔ cup Parmesan cheese,
   grated
¼ cup fresh parsley,
   minced
½ tsp. salt
¼ tsp. pepper
4 whole chicken breasts,
   split, boned and skinned
2 Tbsp. lemon juice

Combine margarine and garlic; set aside. Combine bread crumbs, cheese, parsley, salt and pepper. Dip chicken in margarine and coat with crumb mixture. Tuck ends under and place seam side down in large greased baking dish. Sprinkle leftover crumbs on top. Sprinkle with lemon juice. Bake at 350° for 1 hour.

SPICY ORANGE CHICKEN

Average

4 Servings

2 whole chicken breasts,
   boned and cut into strips
1 Tbsp. cornstarch
2 tsp. ginger
Red pepper flakes to taste
Peanut oil
1 onion, cut into 1 inch
   pieces
¼ cup orange zest (rind,
   cut into thin strips)
2 Tbsp. soy sauce
3 Tbsp. orange juice
1 tsp. sugar
1 tsp. vinegar
½ cup slivered almonds,
   cashews or peanuts

Combine chicken, cornstarch, ginger and red pepper. In wok, stir-fry chicken mixture in peanut oil for approximately 3 minutes. Add onion and orange zest. Combine soy sauce, orange juice, sugar and vinegar. Add to wok. Cook for 2 minutes. Add nutmeats. Serve hot with rice.

CHICKEN WITH ORANGE AND HONEY

Average

6 Servings
Make Ahead

¾ cup fine dry bread
crumbs
1 Tbsp. orange rind,
grated
½ tsp. salt
¼ tsp. pepper
1 3 lb. frying chicken, cut
into pieces
½ cup orange juice
1 chicken bouillon cube
½ cup boiling water
4 Tbsp. butter
½ cup honey

Mix together bread crumbs, orange rind, salt and pepper. Dip each piece of chicken in orange juice, then coat with crumb mixture. Place coated chicken on a lightly greased, foil-lined, 9x14 inch pan. Bake at 350° for 30 minutes. Dissolve bouillon cube in boiling water, add butter and honey. Stir until butter melts. After chicken has baked for 30 minutes, baste with honey glaze. Bake chicken 35-40 minutes longer, or until chicken is browned and tender, basting several times with glaze.

APRICOT CHICKEN AU VIN

Average

4 Servings
Make Ahead

1 frying chicken, cut into
pieces
3 Tbsp. butter or
margarine
Salt and pepper
1 cup celery, chopped
1 6 oz. can water
chestnuts, drained and
sliced
½ tsp. dried rosemary
¼ tsp. salt
2 cups long-grain rice,
cooked
½ cup dry white wine

Brown chicken in butter. Season with salt and pepper; remove and set aside. In same skillet, add celery, water chestnuts, rosemary and salt. Cook until celery is tender. Remove from heat and add rice and wine. Turn into 11x7x2 inch baking dish; top with chicken. Cover and bake at 375° for 1 hour.

TOPPING:
1 16 oz. can apricot halves
4 tsp. cornstarch
¼ tsp. salt
¼ cup dry white wine

Drain apricots, reserving syrup. Combine syrup, cornstarch, and salt; cook until thickened. Add remaining wine. Arrange apricots around chicken. Pour glaze over all. Bake, uncovered, 10 minutes longer.

COQ AU VIN

A welcome dish from a European friend!

Average

½ lb. bacon
½ lb. small white onions
  (or medium onions,
    sliced)
8 pieces chicken
½ cup butter
½ bottle Burgundy wine
2 cloves garlic, crushed
  with salt
Bouquet garni (bay leaf,
  sprig of thyme and 3-4
  stalks of parsley, tied
  together)
1¼ cups chicken stock *or*
  remaining ½ bottle wine
Kneaded butter (2 Tbsp.
  butter and 1 Tbsp. flour
  mixed to form paste)
French bread for croutons,
  sliced (optional)
Butter or oil (optional)
Parsley, chopped

Cut bacon into strips and blanch in cold water with onions; drain well. Brown chicken slowly in butter; remove and keep warm. In same pan, brown onions and bacon. Return chicken pieces to pan. Flame chicken with wine; add garlic, bouquet garni and chicken stock (or balance of wine). Cover pan and cook very slowly for 1 hour, either in medium oven or on top of stove. When chicken is tender, remove bouquet. Thicken slightly with kneaded butter and adjust seasoning. Brown bread croutons in butter or oil. Place chicken in serving dish, surround with croutons and sprinkle with parsley.

GINGER BAKED CHICKEN

Easy

**3-6 Servings
Make Ahead**

½ cup honey
½ cup catsup
1 Tbsp. margarine
1 tsp. lemon juice
3 Tbsp. soy sauce
1 tsp. ground ginger
3 whole chicken breasts,
  split

Combine all ingredients, except chicken, in saucepan and bring to a boil. Place chicken in oven-proof casserole. Pour sauce over chicken. Bake, uncovered, at 375° for 50 minutes.

CHICKEN AND SAUSAGE CASSEROLE

Average

6-8 Servings
Make Ahead
Freeze

1½ cups long-grain and
  wild rice
4 cups water
1 tsp. salt
1 lb. bulk sausage (Jones
  Farm preferred)
1 4 oz. can whole
  mushrooms, drained or
  equivalent fresh
3 10 oz. cans cream of
  mushroom soup
1 tsp. Worcestershire
  sauce
Chicken stock or milk, if
  necessary
12 chicken pieces, partially
  cooked
1½ cups bread crumbs
4 Tbsp. butter, melted

Cook rice in salted water according to directions on box. Brown sausage, breaking into small bits. Drain fat. Stir in mushrooms, soup, cooked rice and Worcestershire sauce. Add chicken stock or milk to reach sauce consistency, if necessary. In greased casserole, layer chicken and sausage mixture. Top with crumbs that have been tossed in melted butter. Bake at 350° for 45 minutes.

CHICKEN CORDON BLEU

Don't be afraid to try this one — it's outstanding!

Average

4 Servings

4 split chicken breasts,
  boned
2 slices Swiss cheese
2 thin slices ham
Salt and pepper
Flour
4 Tbsp. butter
½ cup dry white wine
Pinch of sage
Pinch of basil
¼ cup heavy cream

Put chicken between wax paper and pound until meat is double in size. Cut cheese and ham in half. Lay cheese and ham on chicken and roll up, tucking in ends. Secure with toothpicks. Sprinkle with salt and pepper and roll in flour. Heat butter in pan and brown chicken on both sides. Cook 5-6 minutes on each side. Remove to serving dish. Add wine to pan and boil down. Add sage, basil and cream. Pour over meat.

CHICKEN MARSALA

Average

3 whole chicken breasts, split, skinned and boned
1 egg, beaten
¼ cup milk
½ cup flour
3 Tbsp. olive or vegetable oil
3 Tbsp. butter
¼ green pepper, chopped
1 small onion, chopped
½ lb. mushrooms, sliced
1 small garlic clove, mashed (optional)
1 chicken bouillon cube dissolved in ¾ cup water
1 cup Marsala wine or dry sherry
Salt and pepper to taste

Place chicken breasts between 2 sheets of wax paper and pound with wooden or metal mallet. Make as thin as possible. Combine egg and milk. Dip chicken pieces into egg mixture, then dredge with flour. Combine oil and butter in an iron skillet and brown chicken over medium-high heat. Add more butter and oil, if necessary. Remove chicken, drain on paper towels and place in oven-proof casserole. Remove excess fat from skillet and add peppers, onion, mushrooms, garlic, bouillon with water, wine and salt and pepper to taste. Bring to boil and simmer for 10 minutes. Pour mixture over chicken. This dish may be made ahead up to this point. Bake at 350° for 1 hour or until gravy is thickened.

CHICKEN CARUSO

Easy

2 whole chicken breasts, skinned, boned and cut into small pieces
Garlic salt
Pepper
3 Tbsp. margarine
1 15½ oz. jar spaghetti sauce or 2 cups homemade
1 8 oz. can tomato sauce
1 tsp. oregano
1 tsp. Italian seasoning
2 cups celery, sliced
Parmesan cheese, grated

Season chicken with garlic salt and pepper. Saute in margarine 2 minutes. Add spaghetti sauce, tomato sauce and seasonings. Cover and simmer 10 minutes. Add celery and continue cooking until celery is tender crisp. Sprinkle with Parmesan cheese. Good served over beds of hot fluffy rice.

CHICKEN TETRAZZINI

Complicated

CHICKEN AND BROTH:
1 3 lb. frying chicken, cut
   into pieces
1 small onion, coarsely
   chopped
1 sprig parsley
1½ tsp. salt
⅛ tsp. thyme, crushed
2 cups water

In a large frying pan or Dutch oven, combine all ingredients. Bring to a boil. Reduce heat, cover, and simmer for about 1½ hours or until chicken is very tender. Strain and reserve broth. Remove chicken from bones in large pieces, discarding bones and skin.

SAUCE AND SPAGHETTI:
⅓ cup butter or margarine
1 cup mushrooms, sliced
   or 1 4 oz. can, drained
⅓ cup flour
¾ tsp. salt
⅛ tsp. nutmeg
⅛ tsp. white pepper
⅛ tsp. paprika
1 cup milk
1 cup half and half
½ cup cooked smoked
   pork, shoulder picnic or
   leftover ham, cut into
   julienne strips
¼ cup dry sherry
½ lb. spaghetti
Boiling water, salted
1 cup Parmesan cheese,
   grated

In 3 quart saucepan, heat butter and cook mushrooms until lightly browned. Remove mushrooms with slotted spoon and reserve. To butter in pan, add flour, salt, nutmeg, pepper and paprika and cook until bubbly. Remove from heat and gradually stir in 1½ cups of reserved, strained chicken broth. Mix in milk and half and half. Return to heat and cook, stirring constantly, until thickened and bubbly. Mix in chicken, ham, sherry and reserved mushrooms. Cook spaghetti in boiling water according to package directions until al dente. Drain, rinse and drain again. Mix spaghetti with chicken sauce mixture. Place in buttered 3 quart casserole and sprinkle with cheese. Bake, uncovered, at 375° for ½-1 hour or until heated through.

KEUKA LAKE CHICKEN

A summer favorite for years!

Average

8 Servings
Make Ahead

1 4-5 lb. roasting chicken,
  cut into pieces
Olive oil
1 onion, sliced
½ cup white wine
1 cup chicken stock
2 cloves garlic, crushed
1 16 oz. can Italian-style
  tomatoes
½ tsp. thyme
1 bay leaf
2 tsp. parsley, minced
1 lb. mushrooms, sliced
1 16 oz. jar small white
  onions, drained
½ cup butter
¼ cup lemon juice
1 cup black olives

Brown chicken in olive oil with onion. Drain the excess oil. Add wine, chicken stock, garlic, tomatoes, thyme, bay leaf and parsley. Cover and simmer for 1 hour. Reduce sauce a bit by uncovering and simmering. In frying pan, saute mushrooms and small white onions in butter and lemon juice. Mix chicken mixture with mushroom mixture in large casserole. Add black olives. Reheat in 350° oven. Serve over wild rice. This can be made ahead and reheated.

CHICKEN ZUCCHINI BAKE

Average

4 Servings
Make Ahead

4 split chicken breasts,
  skinned
2-4 Tbsp. Italian salad
  dressing
3 cups zucchini, sliced and
  diced
¼ cup fresh onion, minced
½ cup fresh green pepper,
  diced (optional)
1 16 oz. can whole
  tomatoes
1 15 oz. can tomato sauce
Parmesan cheese, grated

In baking dish, place chicken breasts; sprinkle with salad dressing. Bake, uncovered, at 350° for 30 minutes. Add all vegetables and tomato sauce and continue baking for 1½ hours. During the last 5-10 minutes, sprinkle with Parmesan cheese. This is a low calorie recipe if low-cal dressing is used, or if regular dressing is used sparingly.

CHICKEN CURRY

Great fun for a large crowd!

Average

6 chicken pieces, skinned and boned, if desired
1½ Tbsp. oil
4 Tbsp. butter or margarine
1 medium onion, chopped
3 Tbsp. curry powder (more if hot curry is desired)
2 Tbsp. flour
2 cups chicken stock
1 clove garlic, crushed
½ cup coconut milk (made from 2 Tbsp. shredded coconut steeped with ½ cup water for 1 hour and strained well before using)
1 Tbsp. red currant jelly *or* juice of ½ lemon and 1 Tbsp. sugar
¼ cup cream

Fry chicken to golden brown in oil and 1 Tbsp. butter; remove and keep warm. Melt remaining butter; add onion and cook gently until color begins to change. Add curry powder and continue cooking for 3-4 minutes. Stir in flour and cook for 1 minute. Pour in stock gradually; add garlic and simmer for 20 minutes. Adjust seasonings. Replace chicken in pan, cover tightly and continue to cook in pan or oven for 45 minutes or until chicken is tender. Cut into bite-size pieces, if desired. Arrange chicken in serving dish. Add coconut milk and jelly to sauce and simmer another 2 minutes. Add cream and spoon over chicken. Serve with rice, fresh chutney, cucumber Raiti and several coolers (recipes follow). Serve coolers in small containers on table, 1 Tbsp. per serving.

FRESH CHUTNEY:

1 apple
1 onion
3 tomatoes
1 clove garlic
3 stalks celery
1 pimiento
2 Tbsp. mint, chopped
2 Tbsp. horseradish, grated
2 Tbsp. sugar
3 Tbsp. vinegar

Peel and grate apple and onion; skin tomatoes, squeeze out seeds. Crush garlic and chop celery and pimiento. Place all ingredients in saucepan. Bring to boil; adjust seasonings and serve hot or cold.

CUCUMBER RAITA:

2 cucumbers
Salt
1 cup sour cream or yogurt
Dash of pepper

Peel and grate cucumber; salt lightly. Leave 15 minutes. Strain off liquid and mix with sour cream and pepper.

(Continued)

COOLERS:

Bananas, sliced	Green grapes
Tomatoes, sliced	Olives
Raisins	Apples, sliced
Peanuts	Pickles
Coconut, shredded	Green peppers, sliced

SPICY CHICKEN WINGS

Easy

**2 Dozen
Make Ahead**

½ cup cooking oil
¾ cup cider or wine
  vinegar
2 tsp. salt
Dash of tabasco sauce
¼ tsp. black pepper
1 clove garlic, minced
⅛ tsp. onion powder
⅛ tsp. nutmeg
⅛ tsp. celery salt
Dash of ground cloves
1 egg
2 Tbsp. cayenne pepper
2 dozen chicken wings,
  cut up

Place all ingredients, except wings, in a glass jar. Shake well. Place wings in a glass bowl and cover with marinade. Marinate for 8-10 hours. Remove wings to a non-stick or foil-lined cookie sheet and bake at 375° for 25 minutes. To crisp wings, place under broiler for a few minutes, turning once or twice. May also be served as an hors d'oeuvre.

CHICKEN LIVERS AND MUSHROOMS MARSALA

Average

2 Servings

¾ lb. chicken livers
Flour
Butter
¼ lb. mushrooms, sliced
¼ cup Marsala
1 chicken bouillon cube
  with ¼ cup water
Salt and pepper
Rice, cooked

Dredge chicken livers in flour, shaking off excess. Brown in butter over high heat. Add mushrooms and saute for 1 minute. Add wine, chicken bouillon cube with water and salt and pepper to taste. Cook, stirring, for 1-2 minutes. Serve over rice.

CHICKEN LIVERS PAPRIKASH

A liver lover's dream!

Easy

3-4 Servings

1 lb. chicken livers
1 medium onion, diced
3 Tbsp. butter
½ tsp. salt
½ tsp. pepper
1 Tbsp. Hungarian paprika
1 clove garlic, minced or
   pressed
½ tsp. thyme
1 Tbsp. flour
¼ cup sour cream

Clean livers. Saute onion in butter until soft. Add livers and brown. Add salt, pepper and paprika. Stir until paprika loses raw smell. Add ½ cup water or enough to half cover livers. Add garlic and thyme. Cover and simmer for 10-15 minutes or until livers are cooked. Blend flour into sour cream. Stir into livers and warm. Serve on bed of hot rice. May also serve with toothpicks as an appetizer.

 # CANARD AU NICAISE

An unbeatable duck recipe, moist yet not greasy!

Average

4-6 Servings

2 small ducks
6 tomatoes, peeled,
   seeded and quartered or
   equivalent canned
½ cup pitted green olives,
   coarsely chopped
2 Tbsp. parsley, chopped
1 small clove garlic,
   crushed
½ cup dry white wine
¼ cup brandy
¼ cup beef stock
½ tsp. sugar
Salt and pepper

Preheat oven to 450°. Dry ducks thoroughly and season with pepper. Truss ducks and pierce skin several times. Place on rack and roast for 20 minutes. Lower heat to 350° and cook 1 to 1½ hours. Remove ducks from rack, season with salt and return to oven to keep warm. Pour off fat from pan and add remaining ingredients. Stir and cook until most of the moisture has evaporated. Cut ducks into serving pieces; pour juices into sauce. Season to taste. Place duck on serving platter and serve with sauce.

CORNISH GAME HENS WITH CUMBERLAND SAUCE

Average

2-3 Servings

CORNISH GAME HENS:
Salt and pepper
2-3 medium game hens
4 Tbsp. butter, melted

Preheat oven to 500°. Salt and pepper cavities of hens and tie legs together. Brush hens with butter and bake for 15 minutes. Reduce heat to 350°; turn hens breast side down; pour ¼ cup water over all. Cover pan with foil and bake for 30 minutes. Remove foil, turn hens breast side up and bake, uncovered, for 30 minutes. Split hens in half on heated platter. Pour sauce into cavities and let soak in for several minutes. Turn hens and baste quickly with sauce from platter. Serve with extra sauce in gravy boat.

CUMBERLAND SAUCE:
1 lemon
1 orange
Frozen orange juice
1 10 oz. jar currant jelly
¾ cup sherry
1½ tsp. dry mustard
¾ tsp. ginger
½ tsp. salt
Dash of tabasco sauce

Coarsely grate peel of lemon and orange. Squeeze juice from each, adding enough frozen orange juice to fresh to yield 1 cup. Simmer rind in juices until tender, about 10 minutes. Add jelly, sherry, dry mustard, ginger, salt and tabasco sauce. Simmer 15 minutes. Serve with game hens.

SHERRIED GAME HEN

Easy

1 Serving

1 Rock Cornish game hen
1 Tbsp. golden raisins
1 Tbsp. sweet onion, coarsely chopped
Pinch of tarragon
Cream sherry

Place raisins, onion and a pinch of tarragon in stomach cavity of hen. Place in roasting pan. Pour enough sherry over hen to baste and cover bottom of pan. Roast at 400° for 45-60 minutes or until done, basting frequently with sherry, pouring some into cavity. This will steam onion and raisins. When legs move freely, the hen is done. Baste frequently during last 5 minutes. Serve with rice.

BREAD SAUCE

A pleasant change from traditional gravy!

Average   **6-8 Servings**

1¼ cups milk
2 onions, peeled
2 small bay leaves
4 oz. fresh white bread
　crumbs (4 slices)
2 Tbsp. butter
Salt and freshly ground
　pepper
¼ cup cream

Place milk in pan. Add onions and bay leaves to milk. Bring almost to a boil, then remove pan from heat, cover and allow to steep for about 30 minutes. Remove onions and bay leaves and add bread crumbs. Place bread sauce over heat, add butter, and cook gently, stirring frequently, until mixture is fairly thick. Add salt and pepper to taste (quite a bit is needed). Stir in cream. Serve with roast chicken or turkey.

TARRAGON WINE SAUCE

2½ Cups
Make Ahead

Easy

2 Tbsp. butter
2 Tbsp. flour
1 cup chicken broth
½ cup dry white wine
½ tsp. tarragon
Salt and pepper to taste
1 4 oz. can mushrooms,
　drained
1 egg yolk
½ cup half and half

Melt butter; add flour to butter, but do not brown. Slowly add chicken broth, wine, tarragon, salt and pepper and simmer for 2-3 minutes. Add mushrooms and simmer 5 minutes longer. Mix egg yolk and half and half. Remove sauce from heat and stir in half and half and egg yolk mixture. Reheat, but do not boil.

NOTES

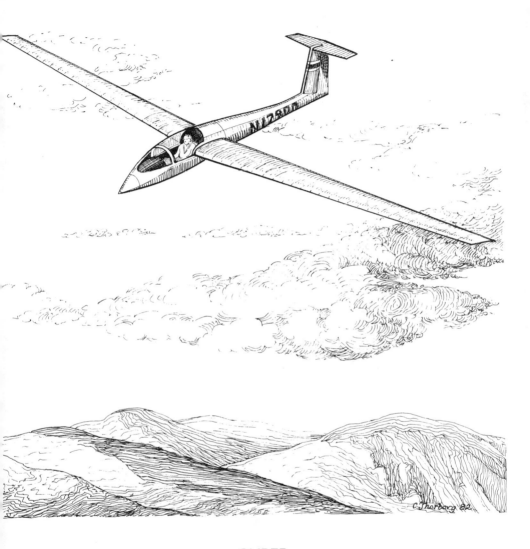

GLIDER
Graceful sailplanes soar high above Elmira, "The Soaring Capital of America."

FISH, SEAFOOD AND SAUCES

SOLE A LA BONNE FEMME

Complicated

4-6 Servings

2 lbs. fillet of sole
Butter
1 shallot or 1 scallion,
  finely chopped
Salt and pepper
¼ lb. mushrooms
Juice of ½ lemon
½-⅔ cup dry white wine
Parsley, chopped

Bone and skin fish, reserving bones and skin for sauce. Butter large saucepan or skillet. Add shallot and then add fillets with both ends folded under to make a neat shape. Season with salt and pepper. Remove stems from mushrooms. Reserve stems for sauce; slice caps. Add sliced mushrooms, lemon juice, wine and parsley to fish. Cover with a buttered piece of wax paper and lid and poach gently for about 10 minutes, or until fish is tender.

SAUCE:
1¼ cups fish stock (see
  directions)
2 Tbsp. butter
¼ cup flour
6¼ Tbsp. half and half
Swiss cheese, shredded
  (optional)

Place fish bones, skin and mushroom stems in saucepan. Cover with cold water and bring to a boil. Simmer for 20 minutes, then strain and reserve 1¼ cups fish stock. When cooked, lift fish and mushrooms from pan and place on a hot serving platter and keep warm. Reduce liquid in pan by boiling rapidly to about 2 Tbsp. Add reserved 1¼ cups fish stock. Cream butter and flour together to make a smooth paste. Add by pieces to fish stock, stir until boiling, then remove pan from heat. Stir in half and half; check seasoning and strain over fillets of sole. Top with cheese, if desired. Place under preheated grill and brown before serving, if desired.

SOLE ALMONDINE

Average

6 Servings

6 pieces of sole
¼-½ cup flour
3 Tbsp. and 1 tsp.
  margarine
Juice of 1 lemon
1 clove garlic, minced
¼ cup slivered almonds
¼ cup dry white wine
1 Tbsp. parsley, chopped
White pepper to taste

Dust fish lightly with flour. Heat 3 Tbsp. margarine in skillet. Add fillets and saute 2-3 minutes on each side. Remove fish to heated serving platter and sprinkle with lemon juice. Melt 1 tsp. margarine in skillet placed over medium heat. Add garlic, almonds and wine. Cook, stirring briskly, for 30 seconds or until light brown color. Spoon sauce over fish and sprinkle with parsley and pepper.

EASY SOLE FLORENTINE
Easy   **4 Servings**

2 pkgs. Stouffer's Spinach
   Souffle
Onion flakes
1 lb. sole or flounder or
   scallops
½ cup dry Vermouth
½ cup sour cream
Sharp Cheddar cheese,
   grated
Paprika

Partially thaw spinach. Press into a greased 8 inch square baking dish. Sprinkle with onion flakes; cover with sole. Mix wine and sour cream and spread over sole. Sprinkle liberally with cheese. Bake at 350° for 30 minutes. Sprinkle with paprika before serving.

STUFFED SOLE MORNAY
Average   **6 Servings**

STUFFING MIXTURE:
1 small onion, chopped
½ cup celery, chopped
2 Tbsp. butter or
   margarine
1 4½ oz. can tiny shrimp,
   chopped
1 cup bread crumbs

Saute onion and celery in butter. Add shrimp and bread crumbs; set aside.

MORNAY SAUCE:
4 Tbsp. butter or
   margarine
2 Tbsp. flour
1 cup milk
¼ tsp. salt
⅛ tsp. pepper
½ cup white wine
2 Tbsp. Parmesan cheese,
   grated
2 Tbsp. Swiss cheese,
   grated

Melt 2 Tbsp. butter; add flour and blend over low heat for approximately 5 minutes. Add milk and stir constantly until thickened. Season with salt and pepper. Add wine, remaining 2 Tbsp. butter, Parmesan and Swiss cheeses.

6 fillets of sole

Stuff fillets with stuffing mixture; secure with toothpick. Place in shallow ovenproof dish. Pour Mornay sauce over fish. Bake at 350°, uncovered, for ½ hour.

218

STUFFED SOLE

A light and delicious dish!

Easy   **4 Servings**

Onion
Celery
Green pepper
4 Tbsp. butter, melted
¼ cup bread crumbs
1 7 oz. can crab meat
Fillet of sole for four
Parsley
Lemon slices

Dice onion, celery and green pepper. (The amount depends on your taste.) Mix butter and bread crumbs. Break up crab meat and add it along with onion, celery and peppers to bread crumb mixture. Place mixture on sole and roll up. Bake at 350° for 20 minutes. Serve with parsley and lemon slices.

SALMON LOAF WITH CUCUMBER SAUCE

6 Servings
Easy   **Make Ahead**

LOAF:
1 1 lb. can salmon
½ cup mayonnaise
1 10 oz. can cream of
   celery soup
1 egg, beaten
½ cup bread crumbs
½ cup onion, chopped
¼ cup green pepper,
   chopped
1 Tbsp. fresh lemon juice
Salt to taste

Combine all ingredients and put into greased loaf pan. Bake at 350° for 1 hour. Serve with sauce.

SAUCE:
¼ cup mayonnaise
½ cup sour cream
½ cup cucumber, chopped
Dill weed

Combine all ingredients and serve with loaf.

SALMON POTATO BAKE

Average   **4 Servings**

3 Tbsp. butter
3 Tbsp. flour
1 tsp. salt
Dash of pepper
2 cups milk
1 15 oz. can salmon,
   drained, boned and
   skinned
4 cups potatoes, cooked
   and sliced
½ cup mayonnaise
½ cup sharp cheese,
   shredded
2 tsp. Worcestershire
   sauce
1 tsp. prepared mustard
Paprika

Make cream sauce; melt butter and stir in flour, salt and pepper. Add milk, cook, stirring until thickened. Add salmon; stir until blended. Arrange in 9 inch square pan in alternate layers with potatoes. Mix mayonnaise, cheese, Worcestershire sauce and mustard. Spread over top. Sprinkle with paprika and bake at 350° for 30 minutes.

TROUT PECAN

COMPLIMENTS OF OLDPORT HARBOUR, ITHACA, N.Y.

Average   **4 Servings**

4 trout (each 8 oz.) fresh
   or frozen
½ lb. pecans
½ cup plus 2 Tbsp. butter
1 Tbsp. Lea & Perrins
   Worcestershire sauce
Dash of tabasco sauce
Juice of 1 lemon
3 eggs
1 cup milk
2 cups flour
2 Tbsp. oil

Fillet trout, removing backbone and rib cage; leave skin on. In food processor, place pecans, ½ cup butter, Worcestershire sauce, tabasco sauce and lemon juice. Puree; set aside. Beat eggs and milk together for an egg wash. Divide flour evenly into 2 pie plates. Set egg wash between the pie plates. Pass trout fillets through flour, then egg wash, then the second plate of flour, one at a time. Heat 2 Tbsp. each butter and oil in a frying or saute pan. Let it get hot. Lay fillets in pan (it should sizzle) and cook to a golden brown, turning them carefully. Place fillets on a cookie sheet and top with equal portions of pecan butter. Place under a hot broiler to melt butter.

FLOUNDER WITH ALMOND SAUCE

Easy   **4-6 Servings**

2 lbs. flounder fillets
¼ cup butter
¼ cup lemon juice
2 tsp. paprika
Salt and pepper
½ cup slivered almonds

Place fillets in well greased baking dish. Combine butter, lemon juice, paprika, salt and pepper to taste, and pour over fillets. Sprinkle with almonds and bake at 350° for 20-25 minutes. Put under broiler for 2-3 minutes.

MICROWAVED ROQUEFORT FLOUNDER

Easy   **4-6 Servings**

TOPPING:
3 Tbsp. butter
4 oz. Roquefort cheese,
   crumbled
½ cup Parmesan cheese,
   grated
½ cup seasoned bread
   crumbs
4 Tbsp. milk
1 Tbsp. lemon juice
1 Tbsp. fresh parsley,
   chopped
1½ tsp. Worcestershire
   sauce
⅛ tsp. pepper
Dash of cayenne pepper

In a 1 quart glass bowl, melt butter in microwave 30-45 seconds. Add remaining topping ingredients and mix thoroughly. Topping may be prepared up to 24 hours ahead. Before using, heat for 30 seconds to soften.

FISH:
2 lbs. flounder fillets (if
   frozen, thawed)
¼ cup fresh lemon juice

Pat fish dry with paper towels and arrange in one layer in an 11x7x1 inch glass baking dish. Sprinkle with lemon juice. Cover with clear plastic wrap, leaving one corner folded back. Put in microwave and cook a total of 5-7 minutes, turning a quarter turn halfway through. Drain off any liquid. Add topping; then either broil 4-5 minutes, until browned, or continue to microwave 5 minutes longer.

ARTICHOKE CRAB AMBROSIA

Makes a divine first course as well!

Average

4 Servings
Make Ahead

2 cups lump crab meat
  (backfin)
1 cup fine bread crumbs
1 cup light cream
1½ cups mayonnaise
1 Tbsp. parsley, chopped
1 Tbsp. onion, chopped
Pepper to taste
1 8½ oz. can artichokes,
  drained and cut into
  halves
Thin slices of lemon for
  garnish

Gently mix all ingredients, except artichokes and lemon, in large bowl. Lightly butter a 2 quart casserole or baking dish. Distribute artichokes on bottom. Place crab mixture in casserole and bake at 350° for 20 minutes. Thinly slice lemons; make cut from center to edge, twist and place on top of each serving. This recipe may be assembled the day before and refrigerated. Remove from refrigerator several hours before baking.

CRAB MEAT MORNAY

COMPLIMENTS OF HILLTOP INN, ELMIRA, N.Y.

Average

4 Servings

1 cup white sauce
1 lb. Alaskan King crab
  meat, well drained
½ cup mushrooms, sliced
½ cup Great Western
  cooking sherry
Two year old sharp red
  New York Cheddar
  cheese, grated
Toast tips

Make a white sauce of butter, flour and milk. To the warm sauce, add crab meat, mushrooms and sherry. (If not using Great Western cooking sherry, make sure the cooking sherry has no salt added; many do.) Fold this mixture gently, so as not to break the meat. Heat until bubbly, taking care not to burn the cream sauce. Place heated crab meat mixture into an oven-proof dish and top with cheese. Place under the broiler until browned. Remove and serve with toast tips.

CRAB AND AVOCADO ELEGANT

Add a spinach salad for a spring luncheon!

Average   **4-6 Servings**

4 Tbsp. butter
¼ cup flour
½ tsp. salt
½ tsp. prepared mustard
2 cups milk
2 6 oz. pkgs. frozen crab
  meat, drained (do not
  use canned)
1 3 oz. can mushrooms,
  drained (whole or sliced)
3 Tbsp. white wine
Dash of tabasco sauce
1 avocado, sliced into
  wedges
1 Tbsp. lemon juice
Garlic salt
½ cup Swiss cheese,
  shredded
Patty shells (Pepperidge
  Farm preferred)

Melt butter, add flour and salt, making a paste-like mixture. Add remaining ingredients in the order listed. When all are combined, heat through completely. Do not cook too long or boil, or the mixture may become too thin. Serve over patty shells.

CLASSY CRAB MEAT

Equally good as an appetizer!

Average   **4-6 Servings**

4 Tbsp. butter
4 Tbsp. flour
1 cup cream
Salt and pepper to taste
Dash of cayenne
Dash of dry mustard
4 Tbsp. sherry
1 lb. white crab meat
  (backfin preferred)
Parmesan cheese, grated

Melt butter in a saucepan over medium heat. Stir in flour until mixture is bubbly. Add cream and continue stirring until mixture begins to thicken. Add salt, pepper, cayenne, mustard and sherry. Remove from heat and add crab meat. Pour mixture into a buttered casserole or individual baking dishes. Sprinkle with grated cheese and bake at 375° until cheese melts. Do not overcook. (May substitute 1½ lbs. shrimp.)

223

OYSTER-CELERY BROIL

COMPLIMENTS OF ONTARIO HISTORICAL SOCIETY, CANANDAIGUA, N.Y.

Average   **4 Servings**

1 quart good rich milk
2 thin slices onion
1 blade mace
   (approximately ⅛ tsp.
   ground)
3 Tbsp. flour
Red pepper to taste
1 tsp. salt
1 good stalk celery
1 quart oysters, large or
   medium
1 generous Tbsp. butter

Place milk to come to a boil, with onion and mace; mix flour with a little milk and put in pepper. Put salt in last thing before adding celery. While waiting for milk to come to a boil, after thickening is in, put oysters in their own liquor to heat until edges curl. Celery should be very crisp and cut with silver knife in quarter (¼) inch pieces and added after oysters are added to thickened milk, and allow all to just come to a bubble. If mixture is too thick for taste, add a little oyster liquor, and serve on toast. Remove mace before adding oysters. From the *Kanandarque Kook Book* published in 1903 by the First Presbyterian Church in Canandaigua.

SCALLOPED OYSTERS

4 Servings
Make Ahead

Easy

1 pint oysters
2 cups medium-coarse
   oyster cracker crumbs
½ cup butter, melted
Dash of pepper
¾ cup light cream
¼ tsp. Worcestershire
   sauce
½ tsp. salt

Drain oysters, reserving ½ cup liquid. Combine cracker crumbs and melted butter. Spread ⅓ crumbs in greased 8 inch round or square pan. Cover with ½ of the oysters. Sprinkle with pepper. Using another ⅓ crumbs, spread a second layer; cover with remaining oysters. Sprinkle with pepper. Combine cream, reserved oyster liquid, Worcestershire sauce and salt. Pour over oysters. Top with remaining crumbs. Bake, uncovered, at 350° for about 40 minutes. Recipe may be doubled and the more oysters the better the dish.

TERRINE DE JACQUES AU COULIS DE TOMATES —SCALLOP MOUSSE TERRINE WITH SALMON— CHILLED TOMATO SAUCE

COMPLIMENTS OF CHEF GREG BROMAN,
STRATHALLON HOTEL, ROCHESTER, N.Y.

Complicated   **6-8 Servings**

SCALLOP MOUSSE
  TERRINE:
1 4 lb. salmon
2 Tbsp. vinegar
1 Tbsp. plus 2 tsp. salt
Bouquet garni
  (cheesecloth bag
  containing 6 parsley
  sprigs, 6 peppercorns, 1
  tsp. thyme, 1 bay leaf)
1 lb. sea scallops, rinsed
½ tsp. white pepper
3 egg whites
1⅓ cups heavy cream

In a large baking dish, combine salmon with water to cover, vinegar, 1 Tbsp. salt and bouquet garni. Bring liquid to a boil and poach salmon over low heat for 5 minutes. Let salmon cool in the liquid; transfer it with a slotted spatula to a cutting board, and skin and bone it. Reserve 1 cup liquid from salmon for fish stock. In a small heavy saucepan, reduce 1 cup white fish stock over high heat to 2 Tbsp. In food processor fitted with the steel blade, puree sea scallops with 2 tsp. salt and white pepper. Transfer puree to a metal bowl; set bowl in a larger bowl filled with cracked ice, and beat puree until it is cold and thick. Beat in egg whites, one at a time, and reduce fish stock. Beat in heavy cream about ⅓ cup at a time, until it is incorporated and mousse is fluffy. Chill mousse, covered, for 25 minutes. Spoon ⅓ of the mousse into a buttered 1½ quart rectangular ceramic or glass terrine, cover it with half of the salmon, and continue to layer mousse and salmon, ending with a layer of mousse. Rap pan sharply to expel any bubbles and smooth top with a spatula. Put terrine in a baking pan, add enough water to pan to reach halfway up sides of the terrine, and bake terrine, covered with a buttered sheet of wax paper and a layer of foil, in pre-heated 325° oven for 2 hours. Remove terrine from baking pan, let cool and chill for at least 12 hours. Remove foil and wax paper and run a thin knife around the inside of terrine. Dip pan in hot water for 2 seconds and invert a platter over it. Invert the terrine with a sharp rap onto the platter. Slice the terrine with a serrated knife and serve it surrounded with chilled tomato sauce.

(Continued)

225

TOMATO SAUCE:

¾ lb. tomatoes, peeled,
   seeded and chopped
3 Tbsp. white wine vinegar
2 Tbsp. olive oil
1 Tbsp. tarragon, minced
2 mint leaves, snipped

In a food processor fitted with steel blade, puree tomatoes and force puree through a fine sieve into a bowl. Stir in vinegar and add olive oil in a stream, beating the sauce until it is well combined. Add tarragon and mint leaves.

MICROWAVED COQUILLES ST. JACQUES
Average
4 Servings

4 Tbsp. butter
¼ cup celery, chopped
1 4 oz. can sliced
   mushrooms, drained
2 medium green onions,
   sliced
2 Tbsp. green pepper,
   chopped (optional)
2 Tbsp. flour
½ tsp. salt
⅛ tsp. pepper
1 bay leaf
½ cup dry white wine
1 lb. scallops
1 Tbsp. pimiento
¼ cup light cream
1 egg yolk
2 Tbsp. butter, melted
2 Tbsp. bread crumbs
2 Tbsp. Parmesan cheese,
   grated

Combine 4 Tbsp. butter, celery, mushrooms, onions and green pepper in 2 quart glass casserole. Microwave on 75% power for 3-4 minutes or until tender. Stir in flour, salt, pepper, bay leaf and wine. Mix well. Add scallops and pimiento. Microwave on 75% power for 6 minutes. Stir and continue cooking for 2-3 minutes or until thickened. Combine cream and egg yolk in custard cup and stir into scallop mixture. Microwave on roast level for 2 minutes until hot. Remove bay leaf and spoon into 4 shells. Mix 2 Tbsp. melted butter, bread crumbs and Parmesan cheese together. Sprinkle 1 Tbsp. crumbs on each serving. Microwave on 85% power until hot. Cover and let stand for 5 minutes.

SCALLOPS IN WINE SAUCE
Easy
2-4 Servings

½ cup butter or margarine
1 lb. scallops
2 Tbsp. flour
½ tsp. salt
⅛ tsp. pepper
½ cup dry white wine
Parsley or paprika

Melt butter in skillet. Add scallops and saute until barely cooked. Sprinkle flour, salt and pepper over scallops. Stir until flour is moistened; add wine. Stir and simmer until a creamy sauce appears. Be careful not to overcook. Garnish with parsley or paprika.

226

SHRIMP AND SCALLOP NEWBURG

Average

6 Servings
Make Ahead

1 lb. Bay scallops
½-¾ cup New York State white wine
1 Tbsp. butter
1 bay leaf
A few black peppercorns
1 lb. fresh or frozen shrimp
2 cups heavy cream
4 egg yolks, well beaten
Salt and pepper to taste
Dash of cayenne pepper
¼ cup cream sherry

Saute scallops in wine, butter, bay leaf and peppercorns until done. Remove from pan and reserve. Saute shrimp in the same way after checking to make sure all veins and shells are removed. When shrimp are done, reserve with scallops. Reduce wine, butter and fish juices to about 2 Tbsp. Heat cream and whisk into egg yolks. Cook in double boiler over hot water until thickened and mixture coats a spoon. Add fish, salt, pepper, cayenne and strained fish reduction. Add sherry. Serve over puff pastry shells or rice. This may be chilled and reheated in the microwave at 6 or 7 level. This multiplies beautifully for parties.

LOUISIANA BOILED SHRIMP

The subtle seasoning is shrimp at its best!

Easy

4 Servings
Make Ahead

2 quarts water
3 cups celery, diced (may substitute instant celery flakes)
1 cup onion, chopped (may substitute instant minced onion)
2 lemons, quartered
2 cloves garlic, minced (may substitute garlic powder)
6 bay leaves
3 Tbsp. salt
2 tsp. cayenne pepper
2 Tbsp. vinegar
2-3 lbs. headless frozen or fresh shrimp with shells

In large kettle bring water to a boil. Add all ingredients, except shrimp. Simmer 15-20 minutes. Add shrimp; bring back to boil; simmer 5-10 minutes or until shells turn pink and shrimp is tender. Remove kettle from heat. Let shrimp stand 20 minutes in shrimp broth. To serve hot: drain and place shrimp in "community" bowl. Guests shell their own (messy, but fun). Good served with tossed salad, garlic bread or wild rice. To serve cold: drain; peel off shells and remove black vein. Serve on platter/-bowl of cracked ice with favorite cocktail or horseradish sauce.

MICROWAVED SCAMPI
Easy   **2-4 Servings**

1 lb. jumbo shrimp
½ cup butter
2 Tbsp. lemon juice
½ tsp. garlic powder or 1
   clove garlic, minced
2 Tbsp. parsley
3-4 Tbsp. dry white wine

Shell and devein shrimp. If desired, butterfly shrimp. Combine remaining ingredients in measuring cup and heat for 1-2 minutes to melt butter. Pour over shrimp evenly. Cook on high for 3-6 minutes until shrimp are pink and opaque, stirring once. Let stand for 5 minutes before serving.

SHRIMP CREOLE
Average   **4 Servings**

⅓ cup shortening
¼ cup flour
1 lb. shrimp, peeled and
   deveined
1 garlic bud, minced
½ cup onion, minced
2 Tbsp. parsley, minced
½ cup bell peppers,
   chopped
1 cup water
2 tsp. salt
2 bay leaves
1 8 oz. can tomato sauce

Melt shortening in heavy skillet over high heat. Add flour and stir until light brown. Lower heat, add shrimp and cook for 3 minutes or until shrimp are pink. Add garlic, onion, parsley and peppers and cook 2 more minutes. Raise heat and gradually add water, then remaining ingredients. Bring to a boil, then simmer, covered, 20-30 minutes. Serve very hot over fluffy rice.

SHRIMP DEJONGHE
Easy   **4-6 Servings**

½ cup butter, softened
1 tsp. salt
1 clove garlic, minced
⅔ cup fine bread crumbs
2 Tbsp. parsley, chopped
⅓ cup dry sherry
⅛ tsp. cayenne pepper
2 lbs. shrimp, cooked
Lemon slices for garnish

Combine all ingredients, except shrimp and lemon slices. Arrange shrimp in shallow casserole and top with crumb mixture. Bake at 375° for 20-25 minutes. Don't overcook. Garnish with lemon slices, if desired.

SHRIMPS FOURNIER

COMPLIMENTS OF GOLD SEAL VINEYARDS,
HAMMONDSPORT, N.Y.

Average   **4 Servings**

1 medium onion, chopped
1 clove garlic, chopped
Butter
1 lb. frozen shrimp,
  defrosted
2 oz. Gold Seal sherry
2 oz. Charles Fournier
  Chablis Superieur
1 tsp. oregano
1 tsp. parsley
Pinch salt
Pinch pepper
2 oz. LeRoux Cognac

Brown onion and garlic in butter until slightly done. Add shrimp, Gold Seal Sherry, Charles Fournier Chablis Superieur, oregano and parsley. Salt and pepper to taste. Simmer until juices are reduced. Warm cognac and flambee over shrimp. Serve on bed of rice with a salad.

SHRIMP MORNAY

6 Servings
Make Ahead

Average

¼ cup onion, finely
  chopped
4 Tbsp. butter or
  margarine
¼ cup flour
½-1 tsp. salt
½ tsp. dry mustard
2 cups milk
½ cup Swiss cheese,
  shredded
¼ cup Parmesan cheese,
  grated
2 10 oz. pkgs. spinach,
  cooked and drained
1 8 oz. can water
  chestnuts, drained and
  sliced
1½ tsp. lemon juice
1½ lbs. shrimp, cooked

Cook onion in butter until tender, not brown. Stir in flour, salt and mustard. Add milk, cook stirring constantly, until thickened. Remove sauce from heat and add Swiss and Parmesan cheeses. Fold in until melted. In shallow greased baking dish, mix cooked spinach and water chestnuts. Drizzle lemon juice over vegetables. Arrange shrimp over top and pour cheese sauce over all. Sprinkle more Parmesan cheese on top and bake at 400° for 15-20 minutes.

SHRIMP THERMIDOR

The taste of shrimp stands out in this one!

Average

8 Servings
Make Ahead

2 lbs. fresh or frozen
   shrimp or 2 7½ oz. cans
   white tuna and 1 lb.
   shrimp
1 lb. mushrooms
½ cup butter
½ onion, chopped
1 cup celery, chopped
2-3 Tbsp. flour
Salt to taste
½ tsp. Accent
Pinch of saffron (optional)
1½ cups half and half or
   milk
¼ cup sherry
½ cup sharp cheese,
   grated
Dash of paprika

Cook shrimp. Saute mushrooms in butter, then add onion and celery. Blend in flour, salt, Accent and saffron. Gradually add half and half or milk to smooth sauce. Stir in shrimp and sherry. Turn into greased casserole; cover with cheese and paprika. Bake at 350° for about 10-15 minutes or until cheese is golden brown and bubbly. If made a day ahead, allow approximately 40 minutes to heat thoroughly.

SOPHISTICATED SHRIMP

Average

4 Servings

4 Tbsp. butter
2 garlic cloves, minced
16 medium-size shrimp,
   shelled and deveined
1 Tbsp. parsley, chopped
4 oz. dry white wine
3 Tbsp. fresh tomatoes,
   peeled and sliced
Salt and pepper

Melt butter in a saute pan. When foam subsides, add minced garlic. Cook gently for a minute, then add shrimp. Saute until shrimp are partially cooked (about 3 minutes). Add parsley and wine. Let simmer 3-4 minutes. Add tomatoes. Season with salt and pepper. Pour into a casserole and bake at 375° for 5 minutes.

HELPFUL HINT

To eliminate odors, add celery leaves to water when boiling shrimp.

SHRIMP AND CHEESE CASSEROLE

Average

4 Servings
Freeze

¼ lb. fresh mushrooms,
  sliced
2 Tbsp. butter
½ cup milk
3 Tbsp. catsup
½ tsp. Worcestershire
  sauce
12 oz. shrimp, cooked
1½ cups rice, cooked
1½ cups American
  cheese, crumbled
Salt and pepper to taste

Saute mushrooms in butter until tender. In small bowl, mix milk, catsup and Worcestershire sauce. In 2½ quart casserole, mix shrimp, rice, cheese, mushrooms, salt and pepper. Add catsup mixture and lightly stir with wooden spoon to mix. Bake at 325° for 25 minutes. May be frozen before baking.

WILD RICE AND SHRIMP CASSEROLE

Average

4 Servings
Make Ahead

½ cup onion, thinly sliced
¼ cup green pepper, thinly
  sliced
½ cup fresh mushrooms,
  thinly sliced
4 Tbsp. butter
1 Tbsp. Worcestershire
  sauce
A few drops of tabasco
  sauce
2 cups wild rice, cooked
1 lb. shrimp, cooked
2 cups thin cream sauce
  (use chicken broth in
  place of milk)

Saute onion, green pepper and mushrooms in butter until soft. Add seasonings, rice, shrimp, and cream sauce. Place in buttered casserole and bake at 350° until thoroughly heated. Serve piping hot.

LOBSTER CREOLE

Average

1 large or 2 small (1 lb.)
  lobsters

In large pot, bring salted water to a rolling boil. Plunge lobster into water upside-down and head first. Cover pot, simmer for 5 minutes for first pound and 3 minutes for each additional pound. Drain and reserve liquid. Cool lobster. Pull apart and cut tail into 3 or 4 sections. Leave shell on. Cut off very end and discard. Crack claws leaving meat in shell.

SAUCE:
¼ cup olive oil
1 clove garlic, minced
1 large onion, chopped
1 large green bell pepper,
  chopped
½ cup tomato sauce
¼ tsp. pepper
1 tsp. salt
6 Tbsp. pale dry white
  wine
1 bay leaf
¼ tsp. paprika

Heat oil in skillet. Saute garlic, onion and green pepper until soft. Add tomato sauce, ground pepper, salt, wine, bay leaf and paprika. Simmer 10 minutes. Add lobster and ½ cup reserved liquid to sauce. Simmer until sauce thickens. Serve over steamed white rice or less formally with French bread for dipping. Shrimp may be substituted for lobster, using 1½ lbs. fresh shrimp, peeled and ½ cup cooking liquid. May be made a day ahead.

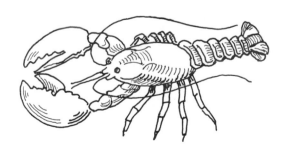

SEAFOOD CASSEROLE

Average

1 lb. Velveeta cheese, cut into cubes
1 cup margarine
1½ to 2 cups evaporated milk
½ lb. fresh mushrooms
1 medium onion, chopped
4 Tbsp. pale dry sherry
4 6½ oz. cans seafood (either lobster, shrimp or crab meat) *OR*
2 lbs. fresh seafood (lobster, shrimp, crab meat)
4 cups noodles, cooked and drained
Bread crumbs
Butter

Melt cheese, ¾ cup margarine and milk in top of double boiler. Saute mushrooms and onion in ¼ cup margarine. Add to first mixture. Remove from stove and add sherry. Add seafood and noodles to cheese-vegetable mixture. Put into a buttered casserole, top with bread crumbs and dot with butter. Bake, uncovered, at 350° for 60-90 minutes.

BAKED SEAFOOD DELUXE

Average

4 cups crab meat, lobster or shrimp
2 cups celery, thinly sliced
2 Tbsp. lemon juice
1 to 1½ cups mayonnaise
¼ cup onion, minced
¼ cup green pepper, chopped
¼ cup pimiento, chopped
½ tsp. salt
1 Tbsp. Worcestershire sauce
2-4 drops tabasco sauce
1 cup bread crumbs
2 Tbsp. butter, melted
½ cup cheese, grated (optional)
Parsley
Lemon wedges

Combine all ingredients except crumbs, butter and cheese and place in casserole. Toss bread crumbs with melted butter and sprinkle over seafood mixture. Top with grated cheese, if desired. Bake at 350° for 30 minutes or until hot. Serve with parsley and lemon wedges.

TUNA DIVAN

Easy

4-6 Servings
Make Ahead
Freeze

2 10 oz. pkgs. frozen
   broccoli
2 6½ oz. cans tuna
1 10 oz. can cream of
   chicken soup
⅓ cup milk
⅓ cup Parmesan cheese,
   grated
1 Tbsp. lemon juice

Cook broccoli according to directions on package. Place broccoli in shallow baking dish. Arrange tuna over broccoli. Combine soup, milk, cheese, and lemon juice. Pour over tuna. Bake at 375° for 20 minutes, or until heated through.

LEMONY BUTTER AND WINE BASTING SAUCE FOR GRILLED LAKE TROUT

COMPLIMENTS OF WAGNER VINEYARDS, LODI, N.Y.

Easy

1⅛ Cups

¾ cup butter, melted
¼ cup lemon juice
⅛ cup Wagner's Aurora
   wine
Fresh parsley, chopped

Melt butter over low heat; add lemon juice, wine and parsley. Baste fish frequently with this mixture during grilling. Serve with potatoes baked in the coals and Bill Wagner's Favorite Salad (see salad section), accompanied with a chilled bottle of Wagner's Aurora for a meal you're sure to enjoy!

TARTAR SAUCE

Great with deep-fried batter-dipped vegetables!

3 Cups
Make Ahead

Easy

2 cups mayonnaise
¼ cup fresh or frozen
   lemon juice
¼ cup sweet pickle relish
1 Tbsp. Dijon mustard
¼ cup fresh parsley,
   minced
2 Tbsp. capers

Put all ingredients in food processor and mix thoroughly. Refrigerate. It will keep a long time in refrigerator.

TAUGHANNOCK FALLS

Taughannock Falls, just north of Ithaca, is the highest waterfall in the eastern United States. Water plunges 215 feet between rocky walls that ascend 400 feet into the air.

234a

VEGETABLES AND SIDE DISHES

234b

BRAISED GREEN BEANS
Average   8-10 Servings

2 small bunches green
  onions, chopped
3 Tbsp. olive or salad oil
4 tomatoes, chopped
4 cloves garlic, minced (or
  less, if preferred)
½ cup parsley, chopped
2 16 oz. cans French-style
  green beans, drained or
  2 lbs. fresh beans
Salt and pepper to taste

Saute onions in oil until glazed. Add
other ingredients, cover and simmer for
10 minutes. A small amount of water
may be added to prevent burning.
Simmer for 20-30 minutes, if fresh
beans are used.

GREEN BEAN AND MUSHROOM CASSEROLE

10-12 Servings
Make Ahead

Average

1 lb. fresh mushrooms or 2
  4 oz. cans mushrooms,
  drained
1 medium onion, minced
½ cup butter
¼ cup warm milk
1 cup light cream
¾ lb. sharp Cheddar
  cheese, grated
½ tsp. tabasco sauce
2 tsp. soy sauce
Salt and pepper to taste
3 10 oz. pkgs. frozen
  green beans
1 5 oz. can sliced water
  chestnuts, drained
¾ cup slivered almonds

Saute mushrooms and onion in butter;
add milk and cream. Stirring constantly,
add cheese, tabasco sauce, soy sauce
and salt and pepper to taste. Simmer
gently until cheese melts. Cook green
beans until just tender; drain and mix
with sauce. Add water chestnuts. Pour
into casserole and sprinkle almonds on
top. Bake at 350° for 30 minutes.

GREEN BEANS PARISIENNE

Even stick-in-the-mud bean haters like this one!

Average   **4 Servings**

1 lb. fresh green beans
⅓ cup butter
4 Tbsp. water
1 tsp. lemon juice
1 tsp. salt
¼ tsp. cayenne pepper
1 cup blanched, slivered
    almonds
1 tsp. fresh garlic, minced

Top and tail beans. Cut into 2 inch slices diagonally. Put in cold water and slowly bring to a boil. Drain. Melt half the butter in a very heavy pan. Add water, lemon juice, salt and pepper. Add beans, cover and cook gently, stirring occasionally, until just soft, about 20 minutes. In another pan, melt remaining butter; add almonds and brown slowly. Add garlic. Put beans in a serving dish and pour almonds, garlic and butter mixture over beans.

THREE BEAN CASSEROLE

Perfect picnic fare!

8-10 Servings
Make Ahead

Average

1 lb. ground beef
½ lb. bacon, cut into
    chunks; reserve 2 slices
½ onion, diced
1 16 oz. can kidney beans
1 16 oz. can pork-n-beans
    (Campbells preferred)
1 8 oz. can lima beans
¼ tsp. salt
Dash of pepper
½ cup catsup
2 Tbsp. vinegar
¾ tsp. dry mustard
½ cup brown sugar

Brown beef, bacon chunks and onion. Drain off fat. Combine remaining ingredients, including all can liquids, into large casserole. Place bacon strips on top and bake at 350° for 1 hour.

LIMA BEAN CASSEROLE

Who said lima beans have to be dull?

Easy

12 Servings
Make Ahead

3 10 oz. pkgs. frozen large
   lima beans
1 10 oz. can clear onion
   soup
1 10 oz. can cream of
   celery soup
2 cups Cheddar cheese,
   shredded
Bread crumbs, buttered

Partially cook lima beans; drain. Add soups. Put into 9x12 inch pan and top with cheese and bread crumbs. Bake at 350° for 30 minutes.

SWEET CABBAGE

Easy

6 Servings
Make Ahead

1 medium head cabbage
3 tsp. sugar
3 tsp. salt
Butter or margarine

Break cabbage into small pieces. Soak in large pan of water with 2 tsp. sugar and 2 tsp. salt for at least 3-4 hours. Drain. Cover with water. Add 1 tsp. sugar and 1 tsp. salt to water. Boil 5 minutes. Drain and serve with butter or margarine.

HARVARD BEETS

Easy

6 Servings
Make Ahead

½ cup sugar
1 heaping Tbsp.
   cornstarch
¼ cup vinegar
¼ cup water
1 16 oz. can diced beets,
   drained
1-2 Tbsp. butter

Bring sugar, cornstarch, vinegar and water slowly to boil, stirring frequently. Add beets and butter; simmer 20 minutes. Serve hot or cold.

BROCCOLI CASSEROLE

Easy

6-8 Servings
Make Ahead

2 10 oz. pkgs. frozen
   chopped broccoli,
   cooked and drained
1 8 oz. jar Cheese Whiz
1 cup rice, cooked
1 10 oz. can cream of
   chicken soup
Cheddar cheese, grated
Flavored croutons
   (optional)

Combine cooked broccoli, Cheese Whiz, rice and soup. Spoon into 1½ to 2 quart casserole. Top with cheese or croutons. Bake at 350°, uncovered, for 30-45 minutes.

STIR-FRIED BROCCOLI

Average

6-8 Servings

2 bunches broccoli
¼ cup oil
1 large onion, sliced and
   separated into rings
½ lb. small mushrooms,
   halved
1 cup chicken broth
¼ cup sherry
¼ cup soy sauce
4 tsp. cornstarch
2 Tbsp. water

Trim and discard bottom inch or two of broccoli stems. Cut off flowers and break into bite-size pieces. Cut wide stems in half lengthwise, then into 1 inch pieces. Add broccoli to pot of boiling water and parboil 3-4 minutes. Quickly drain and rinse in ice cold water. Prepare onion and mushrooms, as directed. Mix broth, sherry and soy sauce together. Combine cornstarch and water. Do all this ahead. At serving time, heat oil in wok or 1 quart fry pan. Stir fry onions 2 minutes; add mushrooms and stir fry 2-3 more minutes. Stir in broccoli; add broth mixture and bring to a boil and simmer, covered, 2 minutes. Stir in cornstarch mixture and cook until mixture thickens.

CARROTS AND WATER CHESTNUTS
Average

8 Servings

1 lb. carrots, peeled, cut ½ inch thick diagonally
2 Tbsp. butter
¼ tsp. ground ginger
¾ tsp. crushed thyme
1 6 oz. can sliced water chestnuts, drained
3 Tbsp. white wine
1 Tbsp. parsley, snipped

In covered pan, cook carrots in small amount of boiling water, 15 minutes or until crisp tender. Drain and set aside. In pan melt butter, add ginger, thyme and water chestnuts; cook and stir for 2 minutes. Add wine, parsley and carrots. Cook and stir until heated through.

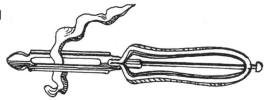

CAULIFLOWER CASSEROLE

6-8 Servings
Make Ahead

Average

2 10 oz. pkgs. frozen cauliflower or equivalent fresh
3 Tbsp. butter
¼ cup flour
2 cups milk
¾ tsp. salt
⅛ tsp. pepper

Cook and drain cauliflower. Place in a 2 quart casserole. Melt butter, stir in flour and cook a few minutes, stirring constantly. Remove from heat and blend in milk. Return to stove and bring to a boil, stirring constantly. Simmer until thickened. Add salt and pepper. Pour over cauliflower in casserole.

TOPPING:
½-1 8 oz. pkg. herb stuffing mix (crumbs, not cubes)
½-1 cup water
¼-½ cup butter, melted

Combine stuffing mix, water and butter. Spoon on top of casserole, pressing down. Bake at 350° for 30 minutes. If a thick layer of topping is desired, use full amounts of ingredients. If a thinner layer is desired, use the smaller amounts.

CORN-ZUCCHINI BAKE

Average

8 Servings
Make Ahead

2 medium zucchini (1 lb.),
  sliced
¼ cup onion, sliced
1 16 oz. can corn, drained
1 egg, beaten
1 cup Swiss or Cheddar
  cheese, grated
¼ tsp. salt
¼ cup bread crumbs
2 Tbsp. Parmesan cheese,
  grated
1 Tbsp. butter, melted

Cook zucchini and onion in small amount of water until tender, about 5 minutes. Drain. Combine zucchini, onion, corn, egg, cheese and salt; mix well. Pour mixture into 2 quart greased casserole. Combine bread crumbs, Parmesan cheese and butter; sprinkle over zucchini mixture. Bake at 350° for 30-40 minutes.

SCALLOPED CORN

Easy

6-8 Servings
Make Ahead

4 eggs
½ cup milk
2 16 oz. cans creamed
  corn
20 round crackers,
  crushed (Ritz preferred)
2 Tbsp. butter or
  margarine, melted
Salt and pepper to taste

Beat eggs until foamy. Add remaining ingredients and blend thoroughly. Place in greased 8 or 9 inch deep-dish pie pan or other comparable round baking pan. Bake at 350° for 1 hour.

HELPFUL HINTS

Fresh corn on the cob is best when steamed for 8 minutes, not boiled.

240

CORN PUDDING

The taste of fresh corn without the mess!

Easy

6 Servings
Make Ahead

12 ears fresh corn,
   scraped
Pinch of salt
Pinch of pepper
2 eggs
1-2 Tbsp. sugar (for fully
   ripe corn)
1 cup cream

Mix scraped corn with other ingredients in buttered casserole. Dot with butter. Bake at 350° for 1 hour.

GOURMET MUSHROOMS

Easy

4 Servings
Make Ahead

1 lb. mushrooms, sliced
2 tsp. onion, grated
4 Tbsp. butter
2 cups sour cream
4 tsp. flour
1 tsp. salt
¼ tsp. pepper

Saute mushrooms and onion in butter. Mix together sour cream, flour, salt and pepper. Add to mushrooms. Refrigerate. When ready to serve, cook over very low heat until thickened. Stir.

BAKED ONIONS

Easy

6-8 Servings

2 16 oz. jars whole small
   onions
2 Tbsp. brown sugar
Paprika
2 Tbsp. butter

Put onions and juice into casserole. Sprinkle with brown sugar and paprika, and dot with butter. Bake at 350° for at least 1 hour. Drain before serving.

FRENCH-FRIED ONION RINGS

You'll never eat frozen onion rings again!

Easy

Spanish onions
Milk or sour cream
Flour
Fat or oil
Salt

Peel onions and slice into ¼ inch slices. Separate into rings. Soak in whole milk or sour cream for 1 hour or more. Drain and dip in flour. Fry in deep fat at 370°. (The old-fashioned way is to fry them in oil that is hot enough to light a kitchen match when it is dropped in.) Drain on a brown paper bag. Sprinkle with salt.

DUCHESSE POTATOES

Average

**4 Servings
Make Ahead**

1½ lbs. potatoes
Salt
Freshly ground pepper
2 Tbsp. butter
2 eggs
1 Tbsp. butter, melted

Peel potatoes. Cut large potatoes in half. Place potatoes in cold, salted water. Bring to a boil and cook 15-20 minutes or until tender. Drain at once and put back on heat for a minute to dry off excess water. Mash potatoes. Beat in salt, pepper, butter and enough beaten egg to give a smooth piping consistency. Spoon mixture into piping bag with rosette piping tube or into cookie press. Pipe out whirls of potatoes onto buttered baking tray. Brush each one with melted butter. Bake at 400° for about 10 minutes or until heated through and golden brown. May be made ahead and refrigerated until ready to bake and serve.

AU GRATIN POTATOES

Easy

6 Servings

1 2 lb. pkg. frozen hash
   brown potatoes
10 oz. mild yellow Cheddar
   cheese, grated
3 cups heavy cream
Salt and pepper

Place ½ potatoes in 8x12 inch (2 quart) shallow baking dish. Put ½ cheese over potatoes; put remaining ½ potatoes on top; then remaining ½ cheese. Add salt and pepper to taste. Pour heavy cream over all. Bake at 350°, covered, for 45 minutes. Uncover, and bake for another 45 minutes.

BACON-TOPPED BLEU CHEESE POTATOES
Average   **4 Servings**

4 medium baking potatoes
Shortening
½ cup sour cream
¼ cup milk
4 Tbsp. butter
¼ cup Bleu cheese,
  crumbled
¾ tsp. salt
Dash pepper
4 slices bacon, cooked
  and crumbled

Wash potatoes and rub skins with shortening. Bake at 400° for 1 hour or until done. Allow potatoes to cool to touch; slice skin away from top of each potato. Carefully scoop out pulp, leaving shells intact. Combine warm potato pulp and remaining ingredients, except bacon, in a medium mixing bowl. Beat until fluffy. Stuff shells. Bake at 400° for 15 minutes. Top with bacon.

 # TWICE-BAKED POTATOES

The perfect potato for entertaining!

Easy

6 Servings
Make Ahead
Freeze

3 baking potatoes, baked
½ cup sour cream
¼-⅓ cup milk
1 Tbsp. onion, grated
1 tsp. salt
½ cup Cheddar cheese,
  grated

Cut potatoes in half lengthwise and scoop out pulp (it's easier when hot). Add all ingredients, except cheese, and whip until fluffy. Fold in cheese and mix well. Stuff mixture back into potato shells and bake at 350° for 30 minutes, or until tops are browned and bubbly.

HELPFUL HINT

It's easier to remove baked potato from skins while they're still hot.

CREAMY GARLIC POTATOES

These are not for the faint of heart or stout of hip!

8 Servings
Make Ahead

Easy

6-8 large potatoes, peeled
and diced
Celery salt
Seasoning salt
2-3 fresh cloves garlic,
pressed
1 5½ oz. can evaporated
milk
2 cups sour cream
½ cup butter, melted

Place potatoes in large buttered casserole layering with generous shakings of both salts. Stir until salts are well distributed. Mix garlic, milk, sour cream and butter. Pour over potatoes. If necessary, cover with more evaporated milk. Bake at 275° for 2½-3 hours or at 325° for 3 hours with a roast.

EASY SCALLOPED POTATOES

6-8 Servings
Make Ahead

Easy

8-10 medium Idaho or
baking potatoes, thinly
sliced
Salt and pepper
Garlic powder
3 cups heavy cream

Arrange potatoes and seasonings in layers in a 2½ to 3 quart casserole. Pour heavy cream over all to cover potatoes. Bake at 350°, uncovered, for 1 to 1½ hours.

MASHED POTATOES

10-12 Servings
Make Ahead

Easy

8-10 potatoes
4 Tbsp. butter
4 oz. cream cheese
½ cup sour cream
1 tsp. onion salt (optional)
Butter

Boil potatoes. Peel and mash potatoes. Add remaining ingredients, adding butter and cream cheese by chunks. Place potatoes into casserole. Dot with extra butter. Refrigerate until ready to use — up to 2 weeks. Bring to room temperature. Bake at 350° for 30 minutes.

GOLDEN CHEESE POTATOES

Easy

8-10 Servings
Make Ahead

1 medium onion, chopped
4 Tbsp. butter, melted
4 Tbsp. flour
2 tsp. salt
½ tsp. dry mustard
½ tsp. paprika
¼ tsp. pepper
2 cups milk
8 medium potatoes,
    cooked and diced
2 pimientos, diced
2 8 oz. pkgs. Velveeta
    cheese, cut in cubes

Saute onion in butter until tender; blend in flour and seasonings. Slowly add milk; stir until sauce thickens. Add potatoes, pimientos and cheese. Spoon into buttered shallow 2 quart baking dish. Bake at 350° for 40 minutes.

SWEET POTATO AND APPLE CASSEROLE

Average

6-8 Servings
Make Ahead
Freeze

5 medium sweet potatoes
4 cooking apples, peeled
    and sliced ½ inch thick
Dash of salt
½-1 cup maple syrup
½ cup butter or margarine
¾ cup soft bread crumbs

Cook sweet potatoes in boiling, salted water for 30-35 minutes or until fork tender. Remove from heat, cool, peel and slice 1 inch thick. Place sliced apples, salt, maple syrup and butter in saucepan. Simmer 10 minutes or until almost tender. Place half the potato slices in a layer in buttered 1½ quart casserole. Spoon half the apple mixture over potatoes. Repeat, layering potatoes and apple mixture. Put crumbs on top and bake at 400° for about 20 minutes.

CREAMED SPINACH

6 Servings
Make Ahead

2 10 oz. pkgs. frozen
   spinach or 2 lbs. fresh
   spinach
1 Tbsp. instant minced
   onion
1 tsp. salt
6 oz. cream cheese, cut
   into pieces
1 Tbsp. milk
Pepper
Parsley

Place spinach, onion and salt in boiling water and cook, covered, 10-12 minutes. Drain, pressing out excess liquid. Return spinach to saucepan and add cheese, milk and pepper. Cook over low heat until cheese melts and mixture is well blended, stirring constantly. Garnish with parsley.

SPINACH SAVOY

Easy

4-6 Servings
Make Ahead

2 10 oz. pkgs. frozen,
   chopped spinach,
   thawed and drained
½ envelope dried onion
   soup mix (Lipton's
   preferred)
8 oz. sour cream
4 Tbsp. margarine, melted
½ cup bread crumbs
¼ cup Cheddar, Swiss or
   Mozzarella cheese,
   grated

Combine spinach, soup mix and sour cream; put into greased casserole. Mix margarine, bread crumbs and cheese; sprinkle on top of spinach mixture. Bake at 350° for 20 minutes.

CREAMY BAKED SQUASH

Easy

6 Servings

1 quart Hubbard or other
   winter squash, peeled
   and thinly sliced
2 tsp. salt
¼ cup sugar
½ cup heavy cream
1 tsp. cinnamon

Place squash in a 2 quart buttered casserole. Sprinkle with salt and sugar. Pour cream over squash. Sprinkle with cinnamon. Bake, uncovered, at 250-300° for 50 minutes or until tender.

246

SUMMER SQUASH AND CARROT CASSEROLE

A delightful blend of fresh vegetables!

Average

10 Servings
Make Ahead

2 lbs. (6 cups) yellow
  summer squash or
  zucchini, sliced
¼ cup onion, chopped
1 10 oz. can cream of
  chicken soup
1 cup sour cream
1 cup carrot, shredded
1 8 oz. pkg. herb
  seasoned stuffing
½ cup butter, melted

Cook squash and onion in boiling, salted water for 5 minutes; drain. Combine soup and sour cream; stir in carrots. Fold in squash and onion. Combine stuffing and butter. Spread half of stuffing in bottom of 9x13 inch pan. Spoon squash mixture on top of stuffing. Sprinkle remaining stuffing over top. Bake at 350°, uncovered, for 25-30 minutes.

WINTER SQUASH CASSEROLE

Easy

4-6 Servings

2 12 oz. pkgs. frozen
  squash or equivalent
  fresh
⅓ cup butter or margarine
¼ cup light cream or half
  and half
2 Tbsp. dark brown sugar
½ tsp. salt
½ tsp. pepper
⅛ tsp. ground nutmeg

Cook and mash squash. Add butter, cream, brown sugar, salt, pepper and nutmeg. Mix well. Place in a buttered 1½ quart casserole.

TOPPING:
¼ cup dark brown sugar
2 Tbsp. light corn syrup
2 Tbsp. butter, melted
1 cup walnuts, coarsely
  chopped

Combine all ingredients and spread over squash. Bake at 350° for 30 minutes.

247

GLAZED PEANUT SQUASH

Easy   **4 Servings**

2 medium acorn squash
¼ tsp. salt
3 Tbsp. margarine
3 Tbsp. light brown sugar
2 Tbsp. peanuts, finely
   chopped
½ tsp. cinnamon

Wash squash and cut in half lengthwise. Remove seeds and pulp. Place cut side down in baking dish and bake at 400° for 30 minutes. Place cut side up and dot with margarine. Combine brown sugar, peanuts and cinnamon. Sprinkle in cavities and bake 15 minutes longer, or until tender.

RATATOUILLE

                                              4 Servings
Average   **Make Ahead**

4 Tbsp. oil
1 onion, sliced
2 cloves garlic, minced
2 eggplant, seeded and
   sliced
2 small zucchini, seeded
   and sliced
Salt and pepper
2-3 medium tomatoes,
   skinned, seeded and
   sliced
1-2 green peppers, cored,
   seeded and finely
   shredded

Heat oil in large frying pan; add onion and garlic and cook for 2-3 minutes. In same pan, fry eggplant and zucchini for 2-3 minutes on each side, adding extra oil, if necessary. Season. Add tomatoes and peppers. Cover pan and cook very gently for at least 1 hour. Serve hot or cold.

STACKED TOMATOES

Can even make winter hot-house tomatoes taste good!

Easy   **4 Servings**

4 ripe tomatoes, peeled
Salt and pepper to taste
½ cup mayonnaise
½ cup green onion,
   minced
1 cup Cheddar cheese,
   grated

Thickly slice tomatoes and arrange in a buttered casserole. Layer remaining ingredients in order. Bake at 325° for 20 minutes or until cheese is bubbly.

248

VERACRUZ TOMATOES

Average

4 Servings
Make Ahead

3 slices bacon
¼ cup onion, chopped
8 oz. fresh spinach,
  snipped
½ cup sour cream
Dash tabasco sauce
4 medium tomatoes
Salt
½ cup Mozzarella cheese,
  shredded

Cook bacon until crisp; drain, reserving 1 Tbsp. drippings. Crumble bacon and set aside. Cook onion in reserved drippings until tender; stir in spinach. Cook, covered, until tender, 3-5 minutes. Remove from heat; stir in sour cream, bacon and tabasco sauce. Cut tops from tomatoes; remove centers, leaving shells. Reserve tomato centers for another use. Drain shells. Salt shells and fill with spinach mixture. Place in 8 inch square pan. Bake at 375° for 20-25 minutes. Top with cheese and bake 2-3 minutes more or until cheese is melted.

ZUCCHINI WITH CHERRY TOMATOES

Easy

4 Servings

1½ lbs. small zucchini
3 Tbsp. butter
1 tsp. salt
⅛ tsp. freshly ground
  black pepper
1 pint cherry tomatoes,
  halved
2 tsp. lemon juice
¼ tsp. sugar

Wash, but don't peel zucchini. Slice ½ inch thick. Place in large skillet and add boiling water to cover. Cook, covered, until barely tender. Drain well. Return to skillet and add remaining ingredients. Toss gently; cover and simmer until tomatoes are heated through. Do not overcook.

OVEN BAKED ZUCCHINI SLICES

Easy

4 Servings

¼ cup plain or Italian
  bread crumbs
¼ cup Parmesan cheese,
  grated
3 Tbsp. mayonnaise
1 medium zucchini, sliced
  ½ inch thick

Mix bread crumbs and cheese in one bowl. In another bowl, put mayonnaise. With fingers, dip each piece of zucchini first into mayonnaise and then into cheese mixture. Put zucchini on ungreased cookie sheet and bake at 350° for 20 minutes. If crispier zucchini is desired, bake in hotter oven.

249

ZUCCHINI PANCAKES

Easy   **4 Servings**

2 cups zucchini, shredded
2 eggs
3 Tbsp. flour (more, if
  needed)
2 Tbsp. Parmesan cheese
1 Tbsp. sherry
1 tsp. chives
¼ tsp. parsley
Garlic salt
Salt and pepper

Drain zucchini; put in bowl and mix in rest of ingredients. If mixture is too thin, add more flour. Fry like pancakes, over medium heat until brown.

ZUCCHINI-TOMATO CASSEROLE

8 Servings
Easy   **Make Ahead**

1-2 medium zucchini,
  sliced
1 onion, sliced
2 fresh tomatoes, sliced or
  1 16 oz. can tomatoes
1 cup Swiss cheese,
  grated
Salt and pepper
Butter
Parmesan cheese, grated

Parboil zucchini and onion. In 1½ to 2 quart casserole, layer zucchini, onion and tomato slices. On **each** layer sprinkle some Swiss cheese, salt and pepper and dot with butter. Sprinkle top layer with a mixture of Swiss and Parmesan cheese. Bake at 350° for 20-30 minutes, or until golden brown.

ZUCCHINI MORNAY

Average   **8 Servings**

3 8 inch zucchini
½ tsp. salt
1 cup onion, sliced
1 clove garlic, minced
4 Tbsp. butter
3 Tbsp. flour
⅓-½ cup light cream
Salt and pepper
⅔ cup Swiss cheese,
  grated
3 Tbsp. bread crumbs,
  buttered

Grate zucchini. Add salt and let stand for 20 minutes. Wring out zucchini and save juice. Saute onion and garlic in butter until tender. Add flour; blend and cook 2 minutes. Add reserved juice and thicken; add zucchini. Thin with light cream. Season to taste. Add ⅓ cup Swiss cheese. Turn into buttered shallow baking dish. Sprinkle ⅓ cup Swiss cheese over zucchini; top with bread crumbs. Bake at 425° for 15-20 minutes.

ZUCCHINI STUFFED TOMATOES

A delicious way to serve home grown goodies!

Average   **4 Servings**

4 tomatoes (nicely shaped
   and uniform in size)
4 Tbsp. butter or
   margarine
3 medium zucchini, diced
½ lb. mushrooms, sliced
1 medium onion, chopped
½ tsp. salt
½ tsp. sugar
¼ tsp. basil
Pepper
1 cup croutons

Cut a thin slice from each tomato top; scoop out pulp and chop, leaving a ¼ inch shell. In skillet, melt butter, then add tomato pulp and all remaining ingredients, except croutons. Cook about 10 minutes, until most of the liquid evaporates. Stir in croutons. Fill tomato shells with mixture and bake at 350° for 20 minutes.

COUNTRY STIR-FRY VEGETABLES

8 Servings
Make Ahead

Average

9 Tbsp. oil
1¼ tsp. salt
4 large carrots, thinly
   sliced diagonally
½ lb. Chinese pea pods or
   1 6 oz. pkg. frozen
   Chinese pea pods,
   thawed
1 lb. mushrooms, cut into
   halves
1 pint cherry tomatoes
1 small bunch broccoli, cut
   into 2x1 inch pieces
1 small head cauliflower,
   separated into florets
1 medium onion, quartered
½ cup water
2 Tbsp. soy sauce

In 8 quart Dutch oven over medium-high heat, in 2 Tbsp. hot oil, cook carrots with ¼ tsp. salt, stirring often, until carrots are tender-crisp, about 3-5 minutes. With slotted spoon, remove carrots to a large bowl. In 1 more Tbsp. oil, cook pea pods with ¼ tsp. salt, stirring, 1-2 minutes. Remove to bowl. In 3 more Tbsp. oil, stir mushrooms with ¼ tsp. salt until mushrooms are coated. Cover and cook, stirring, 3-5 minutes. Remove to bowl. In 1 more Tbsp. oil, cook tomatoes, stirring until heated through, about 1 minute. Remove to bowl. In 2 more Tbsp. oil stir broccoli, cauliflower and onion until well coated; add water and ½ tsp. salt; cover and cook, stirring, 5-10 minutes. Remove pan from heat. Return all vegetables to pan; add soy sauce and mix well. Spoon vegetables onto large platter. Serve hot or refrigerate to serve cold.

MARINATED TOMATOES AND CUCUMBERS

Easy

8 Servings
Make Ahead

1 cup olive or salad oil
¼ cup red wine or cider
  vinegar
1½ tsp. salt
1 tsp. pepper
1 tsp. garlic powder
2 tsp. parsley, chopped
⅛ tsp. thyme
5 medium cucumbers,
  peeled and sliced
5 medium tomatoes,
  peeled and sliced

Combine all ingredients except cucumbers and tomatoes; mix well. Add vegetables. Marinate at least 8 hours, stirring occasionally.

 # MARINATED BROCCOLI AND MUSHROOMS

Easy

6 Servings
Make Ahead

1 lb. fresh broccoli or 2 10
  oz. pkgs. frozen broccoli
1½ cups fresh mushrooms,
  sliced
1 cup Italian dressing
¾ cup mayonnaise
⅓ cup sour cream
¼ cup pimiento, chopped
1 hard-boiled egg, finely
  chopped

Cook broccoli according to package directions or until crisp-tender, if fresh. (May also be made with raw broccoli, broken into pieces.) Marinate mushrooms and broccoli overnight in Italian dressing. When ready to serve, drain marinade and arrange vegetables on platter. Mix mayonnaise, sour cream and pimiento together. Spoon dressing over vegetables and garnish with egg. May also be used as an hors d'oeuvre.

WINTER FRUIT COMPOTE

Average

4-6 Servings
Make Ahead
Freeze

1 30 oz. can apricot
  halves, drained,
  reserving syrup
½ cup dry white wine
¾ Tbsp. cornstarch
1½ Tbsp. cold water
½ Tbsp. curry powder
¼ cup brown sugar, firmly
  packed
½ cup dried prunes, pitted
  and cut in half
1 16 oz. can pear halves,
  drained

Pour 1 cup apricot syrup into a non-stick skillet. Add wine to syrup and boil until volume is reduced by a quarter. Blend cornstarch and water in saucepan; stir in curry powder and sugar. Heat mixture and stir until blended. Add syrup mixture and simmer 1 minute. Add apricot halves, prunes and pear halves; simmer 5 minutes, or until heated through. Serve warm.

HOT FRUIT COMPOTE

Easy

12 Servings
Make Ahead

1 16 oz. can *each* of:
  pineapple slices
  peach halves or slices
  pear slices
  apricot halves
  spiced apple rings
2 Tbsp. flour
½ cup butter or margarine
¼-½ cup brown sugar
1 cup sherry

Drain fruit. Cut into desired sizes. Arrange in casserole. In double boiler, combine flour, butter, sugar and sherry; cook, stirring, until smooth and thickened. Pour over fruit. Refrigerate overnight. Heat at 350° for 20-25 minutes or until hot and bubbly.

PINEAPPLE CASSEROLE

Average

8 Servings
Make Ahead

½ cup sugar
3 Tbsp. flour
3 eggs
1 20 oz. can crushed
  pineapple in
  unsweetened juice
4 slices white bread,
  cubed
⅓ cup butter or margarine

Mix together sugar, flour and eggs. Add pineapple with juice and mix. Saute bread cubes in butter until butter is absorbed. Put pineapple mixture into a 1½ quart casserole. Place bread cubes on top. Bake at 350° for 75 minutes. Good with ham or pork.

NOTES

WATKINS GLEN GORGE

Watkins Glen Gorge, at the southern end of Seneca Lake, provides the hiker with 1½ miles of spectacular waterfalls, cascades and grottos.

CAKES, PIES AND DESSERTS

Other

Sauces and Frostings

SCANDINAVIAN ALMOND RING

COMPLIMENTS OF
PIERCE'S 1894 RESTAURANT, ELMIRA HEIGHTS, N.Y.

Average   **1 10 Inch Ring**

½ lb. granulated sugar
½ lb. almond flour or finely ground almonds
15 egg whites (divided into 5 and 10)

Blend sugar, almond flour and 5 of the egg whites over a bain marie until thoroughly blended and warm. Meanwhile, whip remaining 10 egg whites until stiff peaks form; fold gently into almond mixture. Pour into a prebuttered 10 inch ring mold and bake in a water bath at 400° for about 40 minutes. When done, turn out cake and let cool. Glaze with chocolate coating and place on a serving dish. Serve with fresh fruit in the center and ice cream.

APPLESAUCE SPICE CAKE

Average   **9-12 Servings**
Make Ahead
Freeze

CAKE:
⅓ cup margarine, softened
¾ cup brown sugar
1 egg
1 cup applesauce
1¾ cups flour
1 tsp. baking soda
1 tsp. salt
¼ tsp. mace
¼ tsp. ground cloves
½ tsp. cinnamon
½ cup raisins

Beat together margarine and sugar; beat in egg and applesauce. Beat in dry ingredients gradually, a third at a time. Fold in raisins. Pour into a greased and floured 9x9 inch pan. Bake at 350° for 30-35 minutes, or until toothpick inserted in center comes out clean.

FROSTING:
3 Tbsp. margarine, softened
½ lb. confectioners' sugar
⅛ tsp. salt
½ tsp. vanilla
2 Tbsp. milk

Blend margarine and sugar. Beat in remaining ingredients until smooth.

APPLE COCONUT POUND CAKE

Average

12 Servings
Make Ahead
Freeze

CAKE:
1½ cups oil
2 cups sugar
3 eggs
3 cups flour
1 tsp. salt
1 tsp. baking soda
1 4 oz. can coconut
1 cup nuts, chopped
3 cups apples, chopped
1½ tsp. vanilla

Mix oil and sugar and add eggs one at a time. Add dry ingredients. Add coconut, nuts, apples and vanilla. Mix well; pour into greased and floured tube pan. Bake at 325° for 80 minutes. Do not open door while baking.

ICING:
½ cup nuts, chopped
4 oz. cream cheese, softened
2 cups confectioners' sugar
4 Tbsp. butter, melted
1 tsp. vanilla

Mix all ingredients together. Spread on cooled cake.

APPLE NUT CAKE

Average

8 Servings
Make Ahead
Freeze

2 cups apples, finely diced
1 cup granulated sugar
¼ cup vegetable oil
1 egg
1 cup flour
1 tsp. cinnamon
1 tsp. baking soda
¼ tsp. salt
1 tsp. vanilla
½ cup walnuts, chopped

Toss apples and sugar together and let stand 15 minutes. Mix in oil, egg, flour, cinnamon, baking soda, salt, vanilla and walnuts. Pour into greased and floured 8 inch pan. Bake at 350° for 45-50 minutes and turn onto rack. Dust with confectioners' sugar, or serve with ice cream or whipped cream.

APPLE CHIP CAKE

Simply delicious!

Average

12 Servings
Make Ahead
Freeze

1½ cups salad oil
2 cups sugar
2 eggs
3-4 cups apples, diced
1 cup nuts, chopped
1 tsp. baking soda
1 tsp. cinnamon
1 tsp. vanilla
3 cups flour
½ cup chocolate chips
    and/or ½ cup raisins
½ tsp. salt

Blend oil, sugar and eggs with mixer. Blend in remaining ingredients with spoon in order given. Batter will be stiff. Bake at 350° in ungreased 9x13 inch pan for 1 hour. No frosting is necessary.

FESTIVE CAKE

So simple, the only danger is eating it before the guests arrive!

Easy

12 Servings
Make Ahead
Freeze

2 cups flour
1½ tsp. salt
1 tsp. nutmeg
1 tsp. cinnamon
1 tsp. baking soda
1 tsp. vanilla
1¼ cups oil
2 eggs
2 cups sugar
2 fresh apples, thinly
    sliced
1 cup nuts, chopped
⅓ cup brandy

Sift together flour, salt, nutmeg, cinnamon and baking soda. In another bowl, combine vanilla, oil, eggs, sugar, apples, nuts and brandy. Combine the two mixtures. Batter will be stiff. Place in **well** greased tube or bundt pan. Bake at 350° for 40-45 minutes. Great for the Fall and holidays.

YE OLDE CARROT CAKE

Average

2 cups sugar
1½ cups vegetable oil
4 eggs
2 cups flour
2 tsp. baking soda
2 tsp. baking powder
1 tsp. salt
2 tsp. cinnamon
3½ cups carrots, grated
1 cup walnuts, chopped
Dash of nutmeg

Beat sugar and oil until fluffy. Add eggs and blend well. Sift together all dry ingredients and add to sugar mixture. Mix thoroughly. Fold in carrots and nuts. Pour into greased 9x13 inch pan and bake at 350° for 1 hour. May also be made in two 9 inch round pans and baked at 350° for 45 minutes. Cool.

ICING:
½ cup butter or margarine, softened
8 oz. cream cheese, softened
1 lb. confectioners' sugar
1 tsp. vanilla
½ tsp. lemon extract (optional)
1 cup nuts, chopped (optional)

Cream together butter and cheese. Gradually add sugar, vanilla and lemon extract; blend until smooth. Fold in nuts. Spread on cooled cake.

VARIATION:
1 8 oz. can crushed pineapple, drained

Substitute 2 cups grated carrots and pineapple for 3 cups grated carrots. Prepare the same as above.

HELPFUL HINT

A pinch of salt added to sugar in icing will prevent graining.

APRICOT BRANDY POUND CAKE

Average

16 Servings
Make Ahead
Freeze

1 cup butter (no substitute)
3 cups sugar
6 eggs
3 cups flour, sifted
¼ tsp. baking soda
½ tsp. salt
1 cup sour cream
½ tsp. rum flavoring
1 tsp. orange extract
¼ tsp. almond extract
½ tsp. lemon extract
1 tsp. vanilla extract
½ cup apricot brandy

Grease and flour a large tube or bundt pan. In a large bowl, cream butter and sugar thoroughly with electric mixer. Add eggs, one at a time, beating well after each addition. Sift together flour, baking soda and salt three times. Combine sour cream, flavorings and brandy. Add dry ingredients alternately with cream mixture, beginning and ending with dry ingredients. Pour into prepared pan and bake at 325° for 60-70 minutes, or until cake tests done. Cool in pan for 15 minutes before removing from pan.

CHEESECAKE

Average

12 Servings
Make Ahead

CRUST:
1⅓ cups graham cracker crumbs
1½ tsp. sugar
½ cup butter, melted

In medium bowl, combine graham cracker crumbs, sugar and butter. Press onto bottom and sides of 9 inch spring-form pan. Bake at 200° for 10 minutes. Set aside to cool.

CAKE:
1½ lbs. cream cheese, softened
2 cups sugar
3 eggs
1 Tbsp. vanilla
Pinch of salt
3 cups sour cream

In large bowl, beat cream cheese for 4 minutes. Add sugar and beat 3 minutes longer. Add eggs, vanilla and salt. Gently fold in sour cream. Pour into prepared crust and bake at 375° for 30-40 minutes or until done. This amount of baking time produces a soft creamy cake. For a firmer texture, bake 15 minutes longer. Allow cake to cool, then refrigerate for 24 hours before serving.

EASY CHEESECAKE

Easy

2 lbs. cream cheese,
  softened
4 eggs
1¾ cups sugar
1 tsp. vanilla
Butter or margarine,
  softened
5 graham crackers,
  crushed into crumbs
1 21 oz. can cherry pie
  filling (optional)

Place first four ingredients in large mixing bowl. Beat until creamy and only a few small lumps remain. Grease an 8 or 9 inch spring-form pan with butter and dust with graham cracker crumbs to coat. Pour cheese mixture over crumbs. Place spring-form pan in a larger, shallow pan containing ½ inch of water. Bake at 325° for 1½ hours. Gently remove pan of water, turn off oven and leave cheesecake in closed oven for ½ hour longer. Remove cheesecake from oven and cool on rack. When completely cooled, remove spring-form. Cooled cake may be topped with cherry pie filling.

MOCK CHEESECAKE

Top with fresh berries for summer parties!

Average

1½ cups graham cracker
  crumbs
¼ cup sugar
4 Tbsp. butter, melted
1 3 oz. pkg. lemon gelatin
1 cup hot water
1 cup evaporated milk
8 oz. cream cheese,
  softened
½ cup sugar
2 Tbsp. vanilla

Mix crumbs, sugar and butter. Put crumbs in pie plate or 9 inch square pan, reserving small amount to sprinkle on top. Refrigerate. Mix gelatin and water, and cool. Whip evaporated milk until foamy; add cream cheese, sugar and vanilla. Mix well. Add gelatin mixture and mix until blended. Pour on top of crust and sprinkle with remaining crumbs. Refrigerate until firm.

CHOCOLATE CHEESECAKE

So rich it's like a mousse!

Average

10-12 Servings
Make Ahead
Freeze

CRUST:
1/3 cup butter
2 Tbsp. sugar
1½ cups Zwieback crumbs
 (12-16 Zwieback pieces)

Melt butter in small saucepan. Stir in sugar and Zwieback crumbs. Press mixture on bottom and partially up sides of 8 inch spring-form pan. Refrigerate until cool and firm.

FILLING:
16 oz. cream cheese,
 softened
1¼ cups sugar
1/3 cup unsweetened cocoa
 powder
1 tsp. vanilla
2 eggs

Beat cream cheese in medium-size bowl with electric mixer until smooth. Add sugar, cocoa, vanilla and eggs, beating until smooth. Pour into prepared crust. Bake at 375° for 25 minutes. Remove, but do not turn off oven.

TOPPING:
1 cup sour cream
2 Tbsp. sugar
½ tsp. vanilla
½ cup heavy cream,
 whipped
1 Tbsp. semi-sweet
 chocolate, shaved

Combine sour cream, sugar and vanilla. Spread on top of baked filling. Return to oven and bake 10 minutes. Cool and chill thoroughly. Garnish with whipped cream and shaved chocolate.

BUNDT FUDGE CAKE

Average

12-15 Servings
Make Ahead
Freeze

1½ cups butter, softened
6 eggs
1½ cups sugar
2 cups flour
1 box fudge frosting mix
2 cups walnuts, chopped

Beat butter at high speed until fluffy. Beat in eggs, one at a time. Gradually add sugar and beat until fluffy. Mix in flour, dry frosting mix and walnuts until well blended. Bake in **well** greased bundt pan at 350° for 60 minutes or until top is dry and shiny. Cool at least 2 hours.

CHOCOLATE CAKE ROLL

A chocolate lover's dream!

Average

6 Servings
Make Ahead
Freeze

5 eggs, separated
1 cup confectioners' sugar
3 Tbsp. cocoa
1 Tbsp. flour
¼ tsp. salt
1-2 cups heavy cream,
   whipped and sweetened
Fudge sauce

Beat egg whites until stiff. Beat egg yolks and add dry ingredients; beat until smooth. Fold in egg whites. Pour mixture into jelly roll pan greased and floured with cocoa or lined with wax paper, and bake at 375° for 20 minutes. Turn cake onto sugared towel. Roll. When cool, unroll and fill with sweetened whipped cream. Reroll cake and refrigerate. Slice and serve with fudge sauce.

HERSHEY CHOCOLATE CAKE

Average

16-24 Servings
Make Ahead

1 cup sugar
½ cup margarine
4 eggs
1 tsp. vanilla
1 cup flour
1 tsp. baking powder
¼ tsp. salt
1 16 oz. can Hershey
   syrup

Cream sugar and margarine. Add eggs, one at a time, and beat well. Add vanilla. Sift together flour, baking powder and salt. Add flour mixture to sugar alternately with Hershey syrup. Pour into 13x9 inch greased pan and bake at 350° for 30 minutes.

ICING:
1 cup confectioners' sugar
4 Tbsp. margarine
½ cup evaporated milk
½ cup semi-sweet
   chocolate pieces
1 cup pecans, chopped

Combine sugar, margarine, milk and chocolate pieces in saucepan. Heat until melted. Ice cake while hot. Sprinkle with nuts. Cool before serving.

261

CHOCOLATE WHIPPED CREAM CAKE

Complicated

3 1 oz. squares
   semi-sweet chocolate
4 oz. (½ cup) almond
   paste, crumbled
¼ cup milk
2 eggs
2 egg yolks
½ cup all-purpose flour,
   sifted
¼ cup almonds, toasted
   and ground
¼ cup semi-sweet
   chocolate pieces
2 egg whites
¼ cup sugar

Combine chocolate squares, almond paste and milk. Cook and stir until melted; cool. Beat eggs and egg yolks until foamy; gradually blend in chocolate mixture. Stir in flour, almonds and ¼ cup chocolate pieces. Beat egg whites until frothy; gradually add sugar, beating until stiff peaks form. Gently fold egg whites into chocolate mixture until well blended. Turn into greased and floured 10¼ x 3⅝ x 2⅝ inch loaf pan. Bake at 350° for 40 minutes. Cool. Split into 2 layers.

GLAZED LAYER:
¾ cup semi-sweet
   chocolate pieces
½ cup evaporated milk

Combine chocolate pieces and evaporated milk. Cook and stir over low heat 3-5 minutes or until smooth and thickened. Cool and spread on tops and sides of both layers of cake. This dessert can be made ahead up to this point.

WHIPPED CREAM LAYER:
1 cup whipping cream
1 Tbsp. sugar
Whole almonds, toasted
Confectioners' sugar

Beat whipping cream and sugar until stiff. Spread on 1 glazed layer, top with the 2nd layer. If desired, trim with whole toasted almonds and dust lightly with confectioners' sugar.

HELPFUL HINT

A pinch of salt makes heavy cream whip faster.

CHOCOLATE POUND CAKE

This will keep beautifully, if there is any left!

Easy

10-12 Servings
Make Ahead
Freeze

1½ cups margarine
3 cups sugar
2 tsp. vanilla
5 eggs
3 cups flour
½ tsp. salt
½ tsp. baking powder
½ cup cocoa
1 cup milk

Cream together margarine, sugar, vanilla and eggs, adding eggs one at a time. Sift together flour, salt, baking powder and cocoa and add to creamed mixture alternately with milk. Use electric mixer. Bake in greased and floured tube pan at 325° for 1½ hours.

FRENCH CHOCOLATE TORTE

Average

12 Servings
Make Ahead

1 angel food cake

Cut cake into 2 or 3 layers.

FILLING:
½ cup butter, softened
1⅓ cups confectioners' sugar
1 tsp. vanilla
3 tsp. hot water
2 oz. unsweetened chocolate, melted

Combine and beat to spreading consistency. Spread filling between layers of cake.

FROSTING:
6 Tbsp. confectioners' sugar
4 Tbsp. cocoa
½ tsp. vanilla
1⅓ cups heavy cream, whipped
¼ cup nuts, chopped

Add sugar, cocoa and vanilla to whipped cream. Frost cake and sprinkle with nuts.

DOUBLE CHOCOLATE CAKE

No icing, no mess, but so moist!

Easy

1 box chocolate cake mix
  (Duncan Hines preferred)
1 3 oz. pkg. chocolate
  instant pudding mix
4 eggs
½ cup salad oil
¾ cup water
1 cup sour cream
1 6 oz. pkg. semi-sweet
  chocolate chips
Confectioners' sugar

Mix all ingredients, except chocolate chips and sugar, and beat 3 minutes with electric mixer. Add chips. Pour into greased bundt pan and bake at 350° for 40-50 minutes or until toothpick inserted in center comes out clean. Cool in pan 20 minutes. Remove from pan. When cooled, sprinkle cake with confectioners' sugar, if desired.

MISSISSIPPI MUD CAKE

Average

CAKE:
2 cups sugar
⅓ cup cocoa
1½ cups margarine,
  softened
4 eggs
1 tsp. vanilla
1½ cups flour
1⅓ cups coconut
1½ cups pecans, chopped
1 7 oz. jar marshmallow
  creme

Cream sugar, cocoa and margarine. Add eggs and vanilla; mix well. Add flour, coconut and pecans and mix well. Bake in greased 9x13 inch pan at 350° for 35-40 minutes. When done, spread marshmallow creme on hot cake. Cool.

FROSTING:
1 lb. confectioners' sugar
1 tsp. vanilla
⅓ cup cocoa
½ cup margarine, softened
½ cup evaporated milk

Mix all ingredients together and spread on cooled cake.

NEW ENGLAND BUTTER CRUNCH LOAF

Bliss with every crunchy bite!

Average

12 Servings
Make Ahead

½ cup butter, melted
½ cup brown sugar
⅔ cup walnuts, chopped
1½ cups graham crackers, crushed
1 box chocolate cake mix
Vanilla cream frosting

Cover jelly roll pan (approximately 15x10 inch) with foil. Combine butter, sugar, walnuts and graham crackers; spread evenly on jelly roll pan. Prepare chocolate cake mix according to directions on box. Spread evenly over crumb mixture. Bake at 350° for 22-28 minutes. Cool in pan for 5 minutes; then remove cake from pan by inverting pan. Cut cake into 3 equal parts. Using your favorite vanilla cream frosting, ice the 3 layers, placing one on top of the other. Finally, frost the ends.

TEXAS SHEET CAKE

Easy

32 Servings
Make Ahead
Freeze

CAKE:
2 cups sugar
2 cups flour
1 cup butter or margarine
1 cup water
4 Tbsp. cocoa
2 eggs
1 tsp. baking soda
½ cup buttermilk
1 Tbsp. vinegar
1 tsp. vanilla
1 tsp. cinnamon (optional)

Sift together sugar and flour in large bowl. In pan, bring butter, water and cocoa to a boil. In a small bowl, beat eggs, baking soda, buttermilk, vinegar, and vanilla together. Add mixture in pan and egg mixture to dry ingredients. Pour into a greased 11x17 inch jelly roll pan. Bake at 375° for 20 minutes. The cinnamon adds a slight hint of spice and makes this cake delicious.

FROSTING:
½ cup butter or margarine
4 Tbsp. cocoa
⅓ cup milk
1 Tbsp. vanilla
1 lb. confectioners' sugar
½-1 cup nuts, chopped

Bring to boil, butter, cocoa and milk; cook 2-3 minutes. Add vanilla, sugar and nuts. Mix until smooth. Spread on hot cake.

FANCY CUPCAKES

Loved by all ages!

Easy

**2 Dozen
Make Ahead
Freeze**

CUPCAKES:
1 box double fudge
  chocolate cake mix
  (Duncan Hines preferred)
2 Tbsp. oil

Prepare cake mix according to directions, adding oil to cake mix.

FILLING:
8 oz. cream cheese,
  softened
2 Tbsp. milk
1 egg
6 oz. chocolate chips
Frosting of choice

Combine all filling ingredients. Grease cupcake tins and fill ½ full with batter. Place 1 tsp. of filling mixture on top of cupcake batter. Bake as directed on package. Frost when cupcakes are cool.

HEATH BAR CAKE

Average

**24 Servings
Make Ahead
Freeze**

1 cup brown sugar
1 cup granulated sugar
2 cups flour
½ cup butter or margarine
½ cup pecans, chopped
6 Heath Bars, crushed
1 cup buttermilk
1 tsp. baking soda
1 egg
1 tsp. vanilla

Mix brown sugar, white sugar, flour and butter as for pie crust. Remove ½ cup of crumbs and mix with pecans and Heath Bars; reserve for topping. To remaining mixture, add buttermilk in which baking soda has been dissolved. Add egg and vanilla; mix well. Pour into buttered and floured 9x13 inch pan and sprinkle with topping. Bake at 350° for 35 minutes.

FILLED DATE-NUT CAKE

Average

12 Servings
Make Ahead

CAKE:
½ cup butter, softened
1 cup sugar
1 egg
1½ cups flour
1 tsp. baking soda
1 tsp. cinnamon
¾ cup sour milk
½ cup dates, chopped
½ cup nuts, chopped

Cream butter and sugar. Add egg and mix. Add dry ingredients alternately with sour milk, and beat until mixed. Stir in dates and nuts. Pour into 2 greased 8 inch pans and bake at 350° for 25 minutes. Let cake cool.

FILLING:
1 heaping Tbsp.
  cornstarch
½ cup sugar
1 cup milk, scalded
2 egg yolks, slightly
  beaten
½ tsp. vanilla

Mix cornstarch and sugar; add milk and blend. Add egg yolks and cook until thickened. Cool; add vanilla. Spread filling between layers of cooled cake. Frost with favorite vanilla icing.

Vanilla icing

COCONUT CAKE

Easy

14 Servings
Make Ahead

1 box yellow cake mix
2 cups sugar
1 cup sour cream
10-14 oz. flaked coconut
8 oz. Cool Whip

Bake a 2 layer cake according to directions on box. Split cake into 4 layers. Mix sugar, sour cream and coconut. Reserve 1 cup mixture for icing. Put sugar-coconut mixture between layers. Mix 1 cup reserved mixture with Cool Whip and spread on top and sides of cake. Refrigerate for 3 days in an air-tight container. Keep cake in refrigerator until finished — which won't be long.

GINGERBREAD

COMPLIMENTS OF CORNING-PAINTED POST
HISTORICAL SOCIETY

½ cup sugar
½ cup butter
1 large egg
1 tsp. cinnamon
1 tsp. ginger
½ tsp. salt
1 cup dark molasses
1 cup sour milk
2 cups flour
1 tsp. baking soda

Cream together sugar and butter. Add egg and beat until fluffy. Add cinnamon, ginger and salt. Stir in dark molasses and add alternately the sour milk and flour with soda. Pour into two greased pans and bake until it springs back when touched with the finger. Glaze with lemon, when cooled. Bake at 350° for 50 minutes.

LEMON GLAZE:
Juice of 1 lemon
Sugar to taste

Mix lemon juice with "enough" sugar. Spread on cooled gingerbread and glaze with hot shovel. An adapted recipe from the Lippitt Farmhouse.

MICROWAVED GINGERBREAD

Easy

6-8 Servings
Make Ahead
Freeze

1½ cups all-purpose flour
½ cup sugar
1 tsp. baking soda
½ tsp. ginger
½ tsp. cinnamon
½ tsp. salt
½ cup shortening
1 egg
½ cup light molasses
½ cup very hot water

In mixing bowl, stir together flour, sugar, baking soda, ginger, cinnamon and salt. Add shortening, egg, molasses and water. Beat 2 minutes on medium speed of mixer until well blended. Pour batter into greased 8 inch round dish. Microwave on high 8-10 minutes, rotating dish ½ turn after 4 minutes. When cake is done let stand directly on heat-proof counter or wooden board.

KENTUCKY JAM CAKE

Average

16-20 Servings
Make Ahead
Freeze

CAKE:
2/3 cup butter, softened
1½ cups sugar
4 eggs, separated
2/3 cup buttermilk
1 tsp. baking soda
2 cups flour, sifted
1 cup jam (any flavor)
½ cup nuts, chopped
1 tsp. ground cinnamon
1 tsp. ground cloves
1 tsp. ground allspice

Cream butter and sugar. Beat in egg yolks. Mix buttermilk with baking soda and add to egg yolks. Mix in flour. Add jam, nuts, cinnamon, cloves, and all-spice. Fold in stiffly beaten egg whites. Bake in 13x9x2 inch greased pan at 325° for 45-60 minutes. Cake is done when it begins to pull from sides of pan. When cool, frost.

CARAMEL FROSTING:
½ cup butter or margarine
1 lb. brown sugar
1 cup cream
Pinch of salt

In heavy pan, melt butter and stir in sugar. Add cream. Cook until it forms soft ball stage (235° on a candy thermometer). Add pinch of salt. Cool, beat and spread on cake. Cake should be refrigerated during warm weather.

LEMON ANGEL CAKE

Average

10 Servings
Make Ahead
Freeze

2/3 cup margarine, softened
1½ cups sugar
1 tsp. vanilla
1½ tsp. lemon rind, grated
¼ cup lemon juice
5 eggs, separated
2/3 cup heavy cream,
    whipped
1 large angel food cake
Maraschino cherries
Whipped cream

Cream margarine and sugar; add vanilla, lemon rind, lemon juice and mix well. Add egg yolks, one at a time, beating well after each addition. Fold in stiffly beaten egg whites and whipped cream. Line a 13x9x2 inch pan with wax paper. Cut cake into 16 slices; arrange 8 slices on bottom of pan, spread ½ of filling, place remaining slices on top and cover with remaining filling. **Freeze** at least 1 hour before serving. Garnish with whipped cream and Maraschino cherries, if desired.

PEPPERMINT ANGEL FOOD CAKE

Average

1 box angel food cake mix
   (Duncan Hines preferred)
2 pints heavy cream
1 cup granulated sugar
Dash of salt
1 tsp. peppermint flavoring
6 heapng Tbsp. cocoa
Almonds
Chocolate, grated

Prepare cake according to directions on box. When cake has cooled, slice into 4 layers. Mix cream, sugar, salt, flavoring and cocoa together and put in refrigerator for 1 hour. Don't whip. Remove from refrigerator and whip to proper consistency. Ice each layer and sides. Almonds and chocolate may be added on top. Refrigerate overnight.

OATMEAL CAKE

Average

1¼ cups boiling water
1 cup quick oats
½ cup oil
1 cup brown sugar
1 cup white sugar
2 eggs
1½ cups flour
1 tsp. baking soda
1 tsp. salt
¾ cup nuts, chopped

Pour water over quick oats. Stir and let cool. Cream oil, sugars and eggs; add oatmeal mixture. Add flour, baking soda, salt and nuts. Place mixture into greased and floured 13x9 inch pan and bake at 350° for 30-40 minutes.

ICING:
1 egg
1 cup evaporated milk
1 cup sugar
½ cup margarine
1 cup coconut
1 cup nuts, chopped
1 tsp. vanilla
¼ tsp. salt

Slightly beat egg in heavy saucepan. Add milk, sugar and margarine. Cook over medium heat, stirring constantly, until mixture boils and thickens slightly. Remove from heat. Add coconut, nuts, vanilla and salt. Stir occasionally while cooling. When cake has cooled, frost.

ORANGE-PINEAPPLE PRALINE CAKE

12 Servings
Make Ahead

Complicated

CAKE:
1 box yellow cake mix
2 eggs
Orange juice
2 Tbsp. orange peel,
   grated
1½ cups crushed
   pineapple, well drained
   (measure after it is
   drained)

Preheat over to 350°. Line two 9 inch cake pans with wax paper. Grease and flour bottoms and sides. Prepare cake mix according to box directions, with 2 eggs and substituting orange juice for water. Add orange peel. Turn ¼ cake batter into each pan; spread each with half of the pineapple. Cover each with remaining cake batter. Bake for 25-30 minutes. While cake is baking, make praline.

PRALINE:
3½ oz. coconut, flaked
½ cup light brown sugar,
   packed
½ cup pecans, coarsely
   chopped
4 Tbsp. butter, melted

In a small bowl, combine coconut, brown sugar, pecans and butter. Mix well. At the end of the baking time, spread surface of 1 layer of cake with praline mixture; bake this layer 10 minutes longer. Let cake cool slightly in pans; remove to cake rack to cool completely.

2 cups heavy cream,
   whipped
5-6 cherries with stems

Spread half of the whipped cream between layers, then frost sides. Make 5-6 rosettes on top. Refrigerate several hours or overnight before serving. Decorate with cherries. A beautiful cake!

HELPFUL HINT

For whipped cream with better texture, refrigerate beaters and bowl before whipping heavy cream.

ORANGE PINEAPPLE DREAM CAKE

Average

CAKE:
1 box yellow or white cake
   mix (Duncan Hines
   preferred)
1 3 oz. pkg. vanilla instant
   pudding mix
1 cup oil
3 eggs
1 11 oz. can Mandarin
   oranges and juice

Combine all ingredients and beat for 2 minutes. Pour into two 9 inch or one 13x9 inch greased pan and bake according to directions on box. It may also be baked in 3 layers at 325° for 25 minutes.

FROSTING:
1 3 oz. pkg. vanilla instant
   pudding mix
1 20 oz. can crushed
   pineapple and juice
9 oz. Cool Whip
Coconut or pecans for
   garnish

Combine pudding mix and pineapple with juice and beat for 2 minutes. Fold in Cool Whip. Frost cake. Garnish with coconut or pecans, if desired. This cake must be refrigerated.

SOCK-IT-TO-ME-CAKE

Also packs a punch as a coffee cake!

Easy

½ cup sugar
½ cup oil
4 eggs
1 tsp. vanilla
1 cup sour cream
1 box pound cake mix
1 cup pecans *or* walnuts,
   chopped
1 Tbsp. cinnamon
1½ Tbsp. brown sugar

Mix together sugar, oil, eggs, (adding one at a time), vanilla and sour cream. Add cake mix and nuts. In a separate bowl, mix cinnamon and brown sugar. Grease and flour tube pan. Alternate layers of batter and sugar mixture. Bake at 325° for 60-75 minutes.

7-UP CAKE

Easy

1 box yellow cake mix
4 eggs
¾ cup oil
1 3¾ oz. pkg. instant vanilla pudding mix
1 cup 7-Up

Mix together dry cake mix, eggs, oil and dry pudding mix; add 7-Up and beat 4 minutes with electric mixer. Pour into greased 13x9x2 inch pan and bake at 350° for 35-40 minutes.

BUTTER RUM CAKE

Average

12 Servings
Make Ahead
Freeze

1 cup butter, softened
½ cup shortening, softened
2½ cups sugar
5 eggs
3½ cups flour
½ tsp. baking powder
½ tsp. salt
1 cup milk
1 Tbsp. rum extract
1 cup pecans, chopped

Cream butter, shortening and sugar well. Add eggs, one at a time, beating well after each egg. Sift together flour, baking powder and salt. Add alternately with milk and extract. Grease sides and bottom of tube pan with butter. Line pan with wax paper and grease. Sprinkle pecans in bottom, then sprinkle with flour before pouring in cake batter. Bake at 225° for 1 hour, then increase oven to 300° and bake 1 hour longer or until done when tested with toothpick. Turn cake immediately out of pan.

GLAZE:
⅓ cup water
1 cup brown sugar
½ cup butter
1-2 Tbsp. rum extract

Boil water, sugar and butter for 2-3 minutes. Remove from heat and add rum extract. Cool until almost cold. Prick cake with toothpick and spread glaze on cake.

273

WHISKEY CAKE

Easy

CAKE:
1 box yellow cake mix
1 3 oz. pkg. instant vanilla
  pudding mix
4 eggs
1 cup milk
1½ oz. whiskey
1 cup nuts, chopped

Combine all ingredients and beat on medium speed for 3 minutes. Grease tube or bundt pan. Pour batter into pan and bake at 350° for 50-60 minutes.

TOPPING:
½ cup butter, melted
½ cup sugar
½ cup whiskey

Mix topping ingredients together. Pour ½ over hot cake while still in pan. Let stand for 15-20 minutes. Remove cake from pan and pour remaining mixture over it. This should be made ahead to let whiskey penetrate.

SHERRY-POPPY SEED CAKE

Easy

12-16 Servings
Make Ahead
Freeze

CAKE:
1 box yellow cake mix
  (Duncan Hines preferred)
1 3¾ oz. pkg. instant
  vanilla pudding mix
4 eggs
1 cup sherry
½ cup oil
¼ cup poppy seeds

Mix all ingredients with electric mixer for 3 minutes. Bake in greased 10 inch tube pan at 350° for 40-45 minutes. Cool and frost.

FROSTING:
1 cup confectioners' sugar
2 Tbsp. sherry

Combine frosting ingredients and drizzle over cooled cake.

KEUKA LAKE WINE CAKE

Be prepared to share this recipe!

Easy

10-12 Servings
Make Ahead
Freeze

CAKE:
1 box yellow cake mix
  (Duncan Hines preferred)
1 3¾ oz. pkg. instant
  vanilla pudding mix
4 eggs
½ cup vegetable oil
½ cup cold water
½ cup white, fruity wine
1 to 1¼ cups walnuts or
  pecans, chopped

Mix all ingredients, except nuts, with electric mixer for 3 minutes. Fold in ¾ cup nuts. Grease and flour 10 inch tube pan. Sprinkle remaining ¼-½ cup nut-meats on bottom of pan. Pour batter into pan. Bake at 325° for 50-60 minutes. (If using a cake mix with pudding already in the mix omit instant pudding, use 3 eggs instead of 4 and ⅓ cup of oil instead of ½ cup.)

GLAZE:
½ cup margarine, softened
1 cup sugar
¼ cup water
¼ cup same wine as used
  in cake recipe

Combine all ingredients and boil for about 1 minute. Drizzle over cake which has been pricked with toothpicks. Leave in pan overnight or at least 3 hours. Better if made 2-3 days ahead.

HELPFUL HINT

A recipe for a 9 inch tube pan will also make two 9 inch layers or 2½ dozen cupcakes.

APPLE WALNUT PIE

Average

6-8 Servings

**PASTRY FOR TOP AND
    BOTTOM CRUST:**
**Foolproof Pie Crust (see
    recipe in book)**
2 Tbsp. sugar
1 egg yolk
Water

Combine crust ingredients with sugar. Combine egg yolk with water (small amount to thin.) Toss into crust 1 tsp. at a time. Roll ½ dough and place in pie plate. Reserve remaining ½ for top crust.

FILLING:
**2 lbs. tart cooking apples,
    peeled, cored and sliced
    (about 5 apples)**
**1 cup walnuts, coarsely
    broken**
1 cup sugar
3 Tbsp. flour
½ tsp. salt
½ tsp. cinnamon
¼ tsp. nutmeg
1 Tbsp. lemon juice

Combine all ingredients and fill pastry shell. Seal with top crust. Make slits in crust. Bake at 400° for 45-55 minutes.

NORWEGIAN APPLE PIE

**6-8 Servings
Make Ahead**

Average

1 cup flour, sifted
2 tsp. baking powder
½ tsp. salt
1½ cups sugar
½ tsp. cinnamon
2 eggs
½ tsp. lemon juice
1 tsp. vanilla
2 cups apples, diced
1 cup nuts, chopped

Mix flour, baking powder, salt, sugar and cinnamon together. Set aside. Beat eggs. Add lemon juice and vanilla to eggs. Add dry ingredients to egg mixture. Stir until moist. Add apples and nuts. Mix thoroughly. Pour into a greased 10 inch pie plate. Bake at 375° for 30-35 minutes.

SOUR CREAM APPLE PIE

Average

8 Servings
Make Ahead

4 cups apples, peeled,
   cored, and sliced (early
   tart, preferred)
¾ cup sugar
Pinch salt
1 egg, beaten
2 Tbsp. flour
1 cup sour cream
1 9 inch pie shell, unbaked

Mix first six ingredients and pour into pie crust. Bake at 375° for 30 minutes or until custard sets. Remove, but don't turn off oven.

TOPPING:
⅓ cup sugar
⅓ cup butter, softened
1 tsp. cinnamon

Mix all ingredients until creamy. Spread on top of pie, mixing some of it into pie with fork. Return to 350° oven for 30-40 minutes. Best eaten the day it's baked.

ORANGE GALLIANO PIE

Complicated

8 Servings
Make Ahead

¾ cup fresh orange juice
1 envelope gelatin
⅓ cup sugar
¼ tsp. salt
3 eggs, separated
½ cup Galliano
1 Tbsp. orange peel,
   grated
¼ tsp. cream of tartar
¼ cup sugar
1 cup heavy cream,
   whipped
½ cup coconut, toasted
   (optional)
1 9 inch pie shell, baked

Combine juice and gelatin in saucepan. Add sugar, salt and egg yolks and stir to blend. Cook over low heat, stirring constantly, until gelatin is dissolved and mixture is hot but **not** boiling. Remove from heat; add Galliano and peel; stir well. Chill until mixture starts to thicken. Add cream of tartar to egg whites; beat to soft peak stage. Gradually beat in sugar until well mixed. Fold in gelatin mixture; fold in half of whipped cream. Pour into pie crust and chill several hours. Spread with remaining cream and sprinkle with toasted coconut. (Toast by spreading in pan and baking at 375° until golden brown.) Chill several more hours.

GRAPE STREUSEL PIE

A seasonal favorite!

Complicated

8 Servings
Make Ahead
Freeze

4½ cups Concord grapes
1 cup sugar
¼ cup flour
1 Tbsp. lemon juice
Dash of salt
1 9 inch pie shell, unbaked

Wash grapes and remove skins. Reserve skins. Place pulp in saucepan and bring to a boil; cook until seeds separate out. Put through a food mill or sieve to remove seeds. Mix strained pulp with reserved skins. Stir in sugar, flour, lemon juice and salt. Put mixture into pastry lined pie plate.

STREUSEL TOPPING:
½ cup quick-cooking oats
½ cup brown sugar
¼ cup flour
4 Tbsp. butter

Mix oats, sugar and flour; cut in butter. Place on top of pie. Bake at 450° for 35-40 minutes.

GRAPE PIE

Complicated

8 Servings
Make Ahead
Freeze

5 cups purple Concord
  grapes
1 cup sugar
3½ Tbsp. flour *or*
  cornstarch
1 tsp. cinnamon
1 top and bottom 9 inch
  pie crust, unbaked

Remove pits from grapes by slitting in half with knife **or** pop grape pulp into bowl, reserving skins. Cook pulp until seeds separate and go to bottom of pan, about 10 minutes. Press through strainer to remove pits. Put grape pulp and skins in bowl; add sugar, flour and cinnamon; mix well. Pour grape mixture into pie crust. Top with crust and bake at 450° for 10 minutes. Reduce oven to 350° and bake for an additional 20 minutes. Serve with vanilla ice cream.

LEMON PIE

COMPLIMENTS OF
CHEMUNG COUNTY HISTORICAL SOCIETY, ELMIRA, N.Y.

Average   **6 Servings**

2 lemons
1 cup plus 2 Tbsp. sugar
2 eggs
1 Tbsp. cornstarch *or* 1½
   tsp. flour
½ tsp. salt
1 8 inch pie shell, baked

Grate rind of lemons, taking care not to include any part of the white. Squeeze the juice; add one cup sugar and grated rind. Separate eggs and beat the yolks to foam. Put in cornstarch and salt. Have two cups of boiling water, turn all in and stir until thoroughly cooked; let cool. Pour into pie shell. Beat whites of eggs into a stiff froth, add 2 Tbsp. sugar, and spread over lemon mixture. Set in oven to brown (at 400° for about 10 minutes.) From *The Experienced Cook,* c. 1905.

HEAVENLY LEMON PIE

Your guests will bless you for serving this!

                                      8-10 Servings
Average   **Make Ahead**

CRUST:
1 cup sugar
¼ tsp. cream of tartar
4 egg whites

Sift together sugar and cream of tartar. Beat egg whites until stiff; add to sugar mixture. Line bottom of greased 9 or 10 inch pie plate. Fill just below rim with mixture. Bake at 275° for 1 hour. Cool.

FILLING:
4 egg yolks, beaten
½ cup sugar
3 Tbsp. lemon juice
1 Tbsp. lemon rind
2 cups heavy cream

Beat egg yolks; stir sugar, lemon juice and lemon rind into egg yolks. Cook in double boiler until thickened, stirring constantly, about 8-10 minutes. Let cool. Whip 1 cup heavy cream; fold into mixture. Fill pie shell. Chill 24 hours. Whip the other cup of heavy cream, and put on top of pie before serving.

PEAR CRUMBLE PIE
Average   **8 Servings**

1 9 inch pie shell, unbaked

FILLING:
8 Bartlett pears, pared
3 Tbsp. lemon juice
½ cup sugar
2 Tbsp. flour
1 tsp. lemon peel, grated

Slice 7 pears; cut remaining pears in sixths. Sprinkle pears with lemon juice. Mix sugar, flour and lemon peel; stir into sliced pears. Spoon into pastry shell. Arrange pear wedges atop sliced pears.

CRUMBLE TOPPING:
½ cup flour
½ cup sugar
½ tsp. ginger
½ tsp. cinnamon
¼ tsp. mace
4 Tbsp. butter
3 slices sharp processed
American cheese

Mix flour, sugar, ginger, cinnamon and mace. Cut in butter until crumbly. Sprinkle over filling. Bake at 400° for 45 minutes or until pears are tender. Remove from oven. Cut cheese slices in half diagonally and arrange on pie. Serve warm.

PEAR AND APPLE LATTICE PIE

8 Servings
Make Ahead
Average

6 ripe medium pears,
   peeled and thinly sliced
2 medium cooking apples,
   peeled and thinly sliced
½ cup sugar
¼ cup all-purpose flour
1 Tbsp. lemon juice
½ tsp. ground cinnamon
⅛ tsp. salt
Pie crust mix for one
   2-crust pie
2 Tbsp. butter or
   margarine, cut into
   pieces

In large bowl, combine all ingredients, except pie crust mix and butter; toss gently to mix. Set aside. Prepare pie crust mix according to directions on box. Shape pastry into 2 large balls, one slightly larger. Roll larger pastry ball into a circle about 2 inches larger than 9 inch pie plate. Line pie plate with pastry. Spoon mixture into pie shell. Roll remaining pastry into a 12 inch circle; cut into ¾ inch strips and place lattice style across top. Dot with butter in spaces. Bake at 425° about 40 minutes.

PEACH CREAM CHEESE PIE

Average

6-8 Servings
Make Ahead

2 Tbsp. cornstarch
¾ cup sugar
½ cup peach puree
½ cup water
2 Tbsp. lemon juice
3 oz. cream cheese,
   softened
¼ cup confectioners'
   sugar
1 9 inch pie shell, baked
4 cups peaches, sliced

In pan, combine cornstarch and sugar; blend in peach puree, water, and lemon juice. Bring to boil; cook and stir until thick and clear. Remove from heat and cool. Beat together cream cheese and confectioners' sugar until smooth. Spread evenly on baked pie shell. Spoon peaches over cream cheese mixture; pour cooled puree mixture over peaches. Chill.

GO BANANAS PIE

Easy

8 Servings
Make Ahead

2 cups coconut, shredded
⅓ cup butter, melted
1 3¾ oz. pkg. vanilla
   pudding and pie mix
1¾ cups milk
½ cup heavy cream,
   whipped
1¾ cups miniature
   marshmallows *or* 17
   large marshmallows,
   quartered
2 bananas, sliced

Combine coconut and butter in a skillet. Cook over low heat, stirring frequently, until coconut is toasted and golden brown. Press into a 9 inch pie plate and chill. Prepare pudding and pie filling mix as directed on package, using 1¾ cups milk. Cover with wax paper and chill. When chilled, fold in whipped cream and marshmallows. Slice bananas into pie shell and pour pie filling over bananas. Place a dab of whipped cream in the center, if desired. Chill several hours.

STRAWBERRY PIE

Easy

2 Pies
Make Ahead

8 oz. Cool Whip
1 8 oz. pkg. whipped
   cream cheese
½ cup sugar
2 8 inch pie shells, baked
1 21 oz. can strawberry
   pie filling

Mix Cool Whip, cream cheese and sugar thoroughly. Pour into pie crusts. Top with pie filling. Chill and serve.

STRAWBERRY GLACE PIE

Fresh strawberries at their best!

Easy

8 Servings
Make Ahead

1 cup sugar
2 heaping Tbsp. cornstarch
1 cup cold water
¼ cup strawberry gelatin powder (about ½ of a 3 oz. pkg.)
2 drops red food coloring
1 quart fresh strawberries, washed and hulled
1 9 inch pie shell, baked and cooled
Whipped cream

Combine sugar, cornstarch and cold water in 1 quart saucepan. Cook slowly, stirring frequently, until thick and clear. Stir in gelatin powder and food coloring. Slice strawberries into 9 inch crust. Put a few large whole strawberries on top. Pour sauce over and chill several hours. Serve with whipped cream.

LO-CAL STRAWBERRY CHIFFON PIE

Average

8 Servings
Make Ahead

1 cup crushed, unsweetened pineapple, undrained
10 strawberries, cut up
4-6 pkgs. artificial sweetener
1 pkg. diet gelatin
1 cup evaporated skim milk, chilled
1 Tbsp. lemon juice
1 tsp. vanilla extract
¾ tsp. almond extract
Strawberries for garnish

Bring pineapple to a boil; add strawberries, sweetener and gelatin. Stir until gelatin is dissolved. Whip milk and lemon juice in a chilled bowl, until frothy. Add extracts and beat until stiff. Slowly add gelatin mixture to whipped milk. Place into 9 inch pie plate and refrigerate. Garnish with additional strawberries.

CHOCOLATE BOURBON PIE

Average

8 Servings
Make Ahead

1 8½ oz. box chocolate
  wafers
½ cup butter or margarine,
  melted
21 large marshmallows
1 cup evaporated milk,
  heated
2 cups heavy cream,
  whipped
4 Tbsp. bourbon
Unsweetened chocolate,
  grated

Crush chocolate wafers. Stir wafer crumbs into melted butter. Pat mixture into 9 inch pie pan and bake at 350° for about 10 minutes, just to set. Cool. Melt marshmallows in hot evaporated milk, stirring over low heat. Cool. Fold 1 cup whipped cream into marshmallow mixture. Stir in bourbon. Pour into cooled chocolate wafer crumb-crust. Chill 3-4 hours. Top with 1 cup whipped cream. Sprinkle top generously with grated unsweetened chocolate.

CHOCOLATE MERINGUE PIE

Average

6-8 Servings
Make Ahead

1 9 inch pie shell, baked

FILLING:
1 3 oz. pkg. chocolate pie
  filling mix
2 cups milk
2 egg yolks
½ square unsweetened
  baking chocolate
2 Tbsp. brown sugar
2 Tbsp. margarine

Combine pie filling mix, milk, egg yolks, chocolate, sugar and cook according to filling directions. Add margarine and blend. Cool 5 minutes. Pour into baked shell.

TOPPING:
2 egg whites
4 Tbsp. sugar

Whip egg whites and sugar until stiff. Spread meringue over pie. Bake at 350° for 15 minutes or until meringue browns.

HELPFUL HINT

Make dessert meringue shells with leftover egg whites. Store egg whites in freezer for future use.

FREEZER CHOCOLATE PIE

Average

8 Servings
Make Ahead
Freeze

4 oz. semi-sweet
    chocolate
⅓ cup milk
2 Tbsp. sugar
3 oz. cream cheese,
    softened
3½ cups non-dairy
    whipped topping, thawed
6 oz. chocolate chips,
    chopped in food
    processor
1 8 inch graham cracker
    crust
Whipped cream
Chocolate curls

Heat chocolate and 2 Tbsp. milk in saucepan over low heat, stirring until chocolate melts. Beat sugar into cream cheese. Add remaining milk and chocolate mixture to cream cheese and beat until smooth. Carefully fold in thawed whipped topping and chocolate chips. Blend until no white topping shows. Spoon into graham cracker crust and freeze until firm, about 3 hours. Remove from freezer about 15 minutes before serving and garnish with whipped cream and chocolate curls.

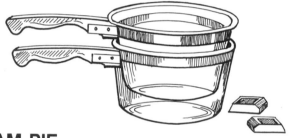

CHOCOLATE CREAM PIE

A lovely variation of an old pie!

Average

8 Servings
Make Ahead

1½ cups sugar
3 Tbsp. cornstarch
2 squares unsweetened
    chocolate
½ tsp. salt
3 cups milk
3 egg yolks, slightly
    beaten
1 Tbsp. butter
1½ tsp. vanilla
1 9 or 10 inch pie shell,
    baked
Whipped cream

Mix sugar, cornstarch, chocolate and salt in saucepan. Gradually add milk while stirring. Cook over medium heat, stirring constantly, until mixture thickens and boils. Boil 1 minute; add yolks. Boil 1 minute more. Blend in butter and vanilla. Pour immediately into pie shell. Chill for 2 hours. Garnish with whipped cream.

HOOSIER PIE

Average

4 Tbsp. butter, softened
1 cup sugar
3 eggs, beaten
¾ cup light corn syrup
1 tsp. vanilla
¼ tsp. salt
½ cup chocolate chips
½ cup pecans, chopped
2 Tbsp. bourbon
1 10 inch pie shell,
    unbaked
Whipped cream

Cream butter. Gradually beat in sugar. Add eggs, corn syrup, vanilla and salt. Blend well. Stir in chocolate chips, nuts and bourbon. Pour filling into pie shell. Bake at 375° for 40-45 minutes. Garnish top with whipped cream.

PECAN PIE

Average

8 Servings
Make Ahead
Freeze

1 9 inch pie shell, unbaked
4 Tbsp. butter
¼ cup dark Karo syrup
1¾ cups sugar
3 eggs, well beaten
Pinch of salt
1 tsp. vanilla
1 cup pecans, chopped

Prepare pie shell. Heat butter and syrup; add sugar slowly. Heat mixture over medium heat until it starts to bubble, but do **not** boil. Beat eggs. Add butter mixture to eggs, stirring; add salt, vanilla and pecans. Put into unbaked pie shell. Bake at 375° for 35 minutes.

CHERRY CHEESECAKE TARTS

Easy

1½ Dozen
Make Ahead

18 vanilla wafer cookies
16 oz. cream cheese,
    softened
¾ cup sugar
2 eggs
1 tsp. vanilla
Dash of cinnamon
1 21 oz. can cherry pie
    filling

Put a vanilla wafer in bottom of 18 foil cupcake cups. Mix cream cheese, sugar, eggs, vanilla and cinnamon. Fill each cup ⅔ full. Bake at 375° for 10 minutes. Cool. Top each tart with cherry pie filling and refrigerate.

RITZY CRACKER PIE

Have your guests guess what's in this pie!

Average

8 Servings
Make Ahead

3 egg whites
1 cup sugar
½ tsp. baking powder
16 Ritz crackers, broken
  by hand
½ cup walnut meats,
  ground coarse
¼ tsp. salt
Dash of vanilla
1 cup heavy cream
½ Tbsp. confectioners'
  sugar
Semi-sweet chocolate,
  grated

Beat egg whites until stiff; gradually add sugar, baking powder, crackers, nuts, salt and vanilla. Pour into buttered 8 or 9 inch pie plate. Prehead oven to 350°, reduce to 325°, and bake for 30-40 minutes. Cool. Mix cream and confectioners' sugar and beat until stiff. Smooth on pie shell and sprinkle with chocolate. Refrigerate **at least** 12 hours.

FOOLPROOF PIE CRUST

Average

5 Single Crusts
Make Ahead
Freeze

4 cups flour
1 Tbsp. sugar
2 tsp. salt
1¾ cups shortening (do
  not use butter or
  margarine)
½ cup water
1 large egg
1 Tbsp. vinegar

Put flour, sugar and salt in large bowl and mix well with fork. Add shortening and mix with fork until crumbly. In a small bowl, beat together with a fork, water, egg and vinegar. Add to flour mixture, stirring with fork until all ingredients are moistened. Divide dough into 5 portions and with hands shape each portion into a flat round patty ready for rolling. Wrap each in plastic and chill at least ½ hour. When ready to roll, lightly flour both sides of patty; put on lightly floured board or pastry cloth. Dough may be left in refrigerator for 3 days or freeze.

APPLE CRUNCH

Easy

6 Servings
Make Ahead

4 apples
¾ cup oatmeal
¾ cup brown sugar
½ cup flour
1 tsp. cinnamon
½ cup butter
Whipped cream or ice
  cream

Pare apples and slice thin; arrange slices in a greased 8 inch square pan or 9 inch pie plate. Combine oatmeal, sugar, flour and cinnamon. Cut in butter; sprinkle over apples. Bake at 350° for 35-40 minutes. Serve with whipped cream or ice cream.

MICROWAVED APPLE CRISP

Easy

6-8 Servings

6 cups apples, peeled and
  sliced
½ cup brown sugar,
  packed
½ cup all-purpose flour
⅓ cup brown sugar,
  packed
⅓ cup quick-cooking oats
4 Tbsp. butter, softened
½ tsp. cinnamon

In 8 inch square dish, place apples and ½ cup brown sugar. With pastry blender, mix flour, ⅓ cup brown sugar, oats, butter and cinnamon until crumbly; sprinkle over top of apples. Microwave at high for 10 minutes, rotating dish ½ turn after 5 minutes. Let stand a few minutes before serving. Good served with ice cream or whipped cream. Recipe may be varied by using other fresh or canned fruit.

HELPFUL HINT

To soften an open box of brown sugar, place 1 cup hot water in microwave along with box of sugar and cook, on high, for 1-3 minutes.

LUSCIOUS LAYERED BLUEBERRY DESSERT

Easy

10 Servings
Make Ahead

Approximately 14 whole
  graham crackers
1 6 oz. pkg. vanilla instant
  pudding mix
1 cup Cool Whip, thawed
1 21 oz. can blueberry pie
  filling

Line a 9 inch square pan with whole graham crackers. Prepare pudding according to package directions. Blend in Cool Whip. Spread ½ pudding mixture over crackers; add another layer of crackers; add rest of pudding mixture. Top with blueberry pie filling.

CHERRY PECAN CRUNCH

Easy

8 Servings
Make Ahead

1 8 oz. can crushed
  pineapple, undrained
1 21 oz. can prepared
  cherry pie filling
1 box yellow or white cake
  mix, dry
1 cup butter, melted
½ cup or more pecans,
  chopped

Put pineapple in 13x9 inch pan. Put cherry pie filling on top; then crumble cake mix over top. Do not mix or stir. Put butter over all and top with nuts. Bake according to cake directions.

CHERRIES IN THE SNOW

Easy

10-12 Servings
Make Ahead

1 tsp. vanilla
1 box Dream Whip (2
  pkgs.)
1 cup milk
8 oz cream cheese,
  softened
1 cup confectioners' sugar
1 angel food cake, baked
1 21 oz. can cherry pie
  filling

Mix vanilla with Dream Whip and milk. Make Dream Whip according to directions on box. Mix cream cheese and sugar; add to Dream Whip. Put **some** creamy mixture in 13x9 inch dish. Top with thin slices of cake. Add more creamy mixture. Alternate layers ending with cake. Put cherries on top and refrigerate at least 8 hours.

COEUR DE CREME

So good, it must be against the law!

Average

8-10 Servings
Make Ahead

16 oz. cream cheese,
  softened
½ cup confectioners'
  sugar
Seeds of ½ vanilla bean or
  ½ tsp. vanilla extract
2 cups heavy cream

Beat cream cheese until light and fluffy. Add sugar and vanilla; mix well. In separate bowl, whip cream until it mounds when dropped from spoon. Fold whipped cream into cheese mixture. Wet cheese cloth or Handi-Wipe and line a coeur de creme mold or plate-size basket (needs a mold with holes for drainage). Pour mixture into mold and cover; place on plate to drain and refrigerate for 6 hours.

SAUCE:
1 10 oz. pkg. frozen
  strawberries, thawed
½ cup red currant jelly
1 Tbsp. Framboise Liqueur
  (raspberry)
2 cups fresh strawberries

Place thawed strawberries in blender; add jelly and Framboise. Blend well. Pour over fresh whole berries. Serve over slices of coeur de creme.

STRAWBERRY DELIGHT

Average

10 Servings
Make Ahead

½ cup butter
1 cup flour
¾ cup nuts, chopped
12 oz. Cool Whip, divided
  in half
1 cup confectioners' sugar
8 oz. cream cheese,
  softened
1 tsp. vanilla
1 21 oz. can strawberry
  pie filling, or any other
  flavor pie filling
1 cup coconut, flaked

Melt butter and let cool; add flour and ½ cup nuts to make dough. Press into 9x13 inch pan. Bake at 350° for 15 minutes. Let cool **completely.** Beat ½ Cool Whip, sugar, cream cheese and vanilla until very light and fluffy. Spread over crust. Spread pie filling over cheese mixture. Top with remaining Cool Whip, then coconut and remaining nuts. Refrigerate several hours before serving. Any leftovers should be refrigerated.

ORANGES IN LIQUEUR

Easy

6 Servings
Make Ahead

8 large oranges
Rind of 2 oranges, finely
  grated
½ cup fine sugar
5 Tbsp. liqueur, *either*
  Cointreau or Grand
  Marnier

Cut peel and pith completely from all oranges. Cut oranges into thin slices; sprinkle with rind and sugar. Add liqueur and allow to chill for 2-3 hours or more.

RHUBARB CRUMBLE

Easy

6-8 Servings
Make Ahead
Freeze

1½ to 2 lbs. rhubarb (6
  cups) cut into 1 inch
  pieces
¼ cup sugar
½ tsp. cinnamon
¾ cup flour
4 Tbsp. margarine
½ cup brown sugar

Place rhubarb in buttered 8x12 inch dish. Sprinkle with sugar and cinnamon. Sift flour into bowl; add margarine and cut into flour with pastry blender. Add brown sugar and mix again until mixture is crumbly. Sprinkle evenly over rhubarb; mash down lightly. Bake at 400° for 30 minutes or until golden brown and crisp.

LO-CAL FRUITED FREEZE

Easy

1 Serving

½ cup evaporated skim
  milk, chilled
1 pkg. artificial sweetener
Choice of *one*:
  ½ cantalope, peeled,
    cubed and frozen
  ½ cup pineapple
    chunks, frozen
  ½ cup unsweetened
    applesauce
  12 strawberries, frozen
  ½ banana, frozen

Blend evaporated milk, sweetener and fruit. Eat immediately. This is good using the variety of fruits together.

CARAMEL ICE CREAM SURPRISE

Don't think of your hips when serving this!

Easy

10 Servings
Make Ahead
Freeze

½ cup brown sugar
½ cup quick oats
½ cup pecans, chopped
1 cup butter or margarine, melted
2 cups flour
1 12 oz. jar caramel ice cream topping sauce or use sauce of your choice
½ gallon vanilla ice cream, softened

Mix sugar, oats, pecans, margarine and flour. Spread and pat onto greased cookie sheet to ½ inch or less thickness. Bake at 400° for 10-15 minutes. Do not allow bottom to get crisp. Crumble while still hot. Spread ½ crumbs in 9x13 inch pan. Drizzle ½ sauce over crumbs. Spread ½ ice cream over top. Then repeat crumbs, ice cream and sauce. Freeze. Thaw slightly before cutting into squares for serving.

ICE CREAM CAKE DELUXE

Simple yet elegant!

Easy

12-14 Servings
Make Ahead
Freeze

SAUCE:
2 squares unsweetened chocolate
½ cup butter
2 cups confectioners' sugar
¾ cup evaporated milk

Slowly melt butter and chocolate in saucepan. Remove from burner, add sugar and evaporated milk alternately. Stir until smooth. Return to burner and simmer 8-10 minutes.

CAKE:
1 angel food cake
Mint ice cream
Whipped cream, tinted green

Split cake into 2 layers, making top layer smaller than bottom layer. Hollow out bottom layer, making a trench. Fill trench with ice cream. Place top layer over bottom layer. Wrap and freeze overnight. Frost with whipped cream before serving. Cut servings and spoon a generous amount of hot fudge sauce over each piece.

PEPPERMINT ICE CREAM PIE WITH HOT FUDGE SAUCE

Easy

**12 Servings
Make Ahead
Freeze**

PIE:
1 chocolate ready-made
   pie crust (Johnson's
   preferred) or homemade
   chocolate crust
½ gallon peppermint ice
   cream, softened

Fill crust with peppermint ice cream.
Return to freezer to harden.

HOT FUDGE SAUCE:
2 squares unsweetened
   chocolate
2 Tbsp. butter
2 Tbsp. flour
1 cup water
1 cup sugar
1 tsp. vanilla

Melt chocolate and butter together; add
flour, water, sugar and vanilla. Bring to
a boil; turn down heat and simmer 30
minutes, stirring frequently. To serve,
pour hot fudge sauce over pie.

CHOCOLATE RIBBON DESSERT

Easy

**20 Servings
Make Ahead
Freeze**

27 Oreo cookies, crushed
½ cup butter or margarine,
   melted
½ gallon chocolate chip
   ice cream, softened
1 12 oz. can chocolate
   fudge topping (Hershey's
   preferred)
12 oz. Cool Whip

Reserve ¼ cup Oreo crumbs for topping. Combine remaining Oreo crumbs
and butter and press into greased 9x13
inch pan. Freeze until hard for easier
handling. Spread ice cream over top.
Spread topping over ice cream and
cover with Cool Whip. Sprinkle reserved
Oreo crumbs over top. Freeze. Remove
from freezer 10 minutes before serving
to soften slightly.

PEACH MACAROON MOUSSE

Heaven with every bite!

Average

12 Servings
Make Ahead
Freeze

2 envelopes unflavored
  gelatin
½ cup cold water
¼ cup sugar
¼ cup Cointreau or Grand
  Marnier liqueur
1 quart vanilla ice cream,
  softened
1 cup macaroon cookie
  crumbs (Nabisco
  preferred)
1½ cups peaches, sliced
1 cup heavy cream
Whipped cream and
  peaches for garnish

In top of double boiler, combine gelatin and water and let sit for 5 minutes. Place over boiling water until dissolved. Remove from heat and stir in sugar and liqueur. Add ice cream, crumbs and peaches. Stir well. Beat cream and fold into mixture. Pour into greased 9 inch spring-form pan. Cover with foil and freeze. Remove from freezer 5-10 minutes prior to serving to allow to soften slightly. Just before serving, garnish with whipped cream and peaches.

PUMPKIN ICE CREAM DESSERT

A holiday dessert for a big crowd!

Easy

1½ Dozen
Make Ahead
Freeze

1 lb. can (2 cups)
  pumpkin, (*not* pie filling)
1 cup sugar
1 tsp. salt
1 tsp. ground cinnamon
1 tsp. ground ginger
½ tsp. ground nutmeg
1 cup pecans, chopped
  and toasted for 15
  minutes
½ gallon vanilla ice cream,
  softened
36 gingersnaps
Whipped cream

Combine pumpkin, sugar, salt and spices; add pecans. In a chilled bowl, fold pumpkin mixture into ice cream. Line a 13x9x2 inch pan with ½ gingersnaps; top with ½ ice cream mixture. Cover with remaining gingersnaps and then remaining ice cream. Freeze at least 5 hours. Garnish with whipped cream.

OLD-FASHIONED STRAWBERRY ICE CREAM

Average

1¼ Quarts
Make Ahead
Freeze

1 cup sugar
2 Tbsp. flour
Dash salt
1½ cups milk
2 eggs, slightly beaten
1½ cups strawberries,
   sieved or pureed
1½ cups heavy cream
1½ tsp. vanilla extract
1 tsp. almond extract

Combine ¾ cup sugar, flour and salt; set aside. Scald milk in top of double boiler; add small amount of milk to sugar mixture, stirring to make a smooth paste. Stir sugar mixture into remaining milk; cook, stirring constantly, until thickened. Cover and cook over low heat, for 10 minutes, making sure not to burn. Stir a small amount of hot mixture into eggs. Stir eggs into remaining hot mixture; cook, stirring constantly, 1 minute. Let cool. Combine strawberries, remaining ¼ cup sugar, cream and flavorings; stir into custard. Pour into container of 2 quart electric ice cream freezer; freeze according to freezer directions.

STRAWBERRY FLUFF

Average

6 Servings
Make Ahead
Freeze

1 10 oz. pkg. frozen
   strawberries
1¼ cups boiling liquid
   (juice drained from
   berries plus water)
1 3 oz. pkg. wild
   strawberry gelatin
1 pint vanilla ice cream,
   softened
Whipped cream for garnish
Fresh strawberries for
   garnish

Thaw berries according to directions on package. Drain juice from berries and add water to make 1¼ cups and boil. Mix in gelatin and berries and chill. When mixture is slightly thickened, fold in ice cream and chill for at least 1 hour or overnight. Top each serving with a spoonful of whipped cream and a fresh whole strawberry, if desired. May be molded and frozen.

HEATH BAR MOCHA DESSERT

Easy

12 Servings
Make Ahead
Freeze

2 pkgs. lady fingers, split
2 Tbsp. instant coffee
2 Tbsp. boiling water
½ gallon vanilla ice cream, softened
3 or 4 Heath Bars, crushed
1 cup whipping cream
3 Tbsp. cream de cacao

Line sides and bottom of spring-form pan with lady fingers. Dissolve coffee in boiling water and cool. Stir into softened ice cream. Add 3 crushed Heath Bars. Pour mixture over lady fingers. Freeze. Whip cream with cream de cacao and spread on top at serving time. Top with last crushed Heath Bar.

BUTTER CREAM TORTE

Average

10-12 Servings
Make Ahead
Freeze

2 cups vanilla wafers, finely crushed
1 cup butter, softened
2 cups confectioners' sugar, sifted
4 eggs
½ cup almonds, finely chopped
1 cup heavy cream
¼ cup *each* red and green Maraschino cherries, chopped
Whole Maraschino cherries for garnish

Spread 1 cup crushed wafers in bottom of 9 inch square pan. Combine butter with sugar and mix until creamy. (If using mixer set on low speed.) Add eggs, one at a time, while beating mixture vigorously (with mixer use high speed). Beat until well blended; slight separating of mixture is normal. Stir in almonds. Spoon mixture evenly over wafers in bottom of cake pan. Sprinkle additional ¾ cup crushed wafers on top. Beat cream until thick, and fold in cherries. Spread over wafers. Sprinkle additional ¼ cup wafers over layer of whipped cream and garnish with whole Maraschino cherries. Refrigerate 12 or more hours. To serve, cut with knife dipped in water.

BUTTERSCOTCH NUT TORTE

Average

12 Servings
Make Ahead

1 cup flour
½ cup butter, softened
½ cup walnuts, finely
  chopped
8 oz. cream cheese,
  softened
1 cup confectioners' sugar
12 oz. Cool Whip
2½ cups whole milk
1 3¾ oz. pkg. instant
  vanilla pudding mix
1 3¾ oz. pkg. instant
  butterscotch pudding
  mix

Mix flour with butter and put into greased 13x9 inch pan. Sprinkle walnuts over dough. Bake at 350° for 15 minutes. Cool. Blend cream cheese and sugar; add 1 cup Cool Whip. Immediately put this on top of dough. Beat milk and puddings according to package directions; let pudding thicken. Pour over cream cheese mixture. Spread remaining Cool Whip on top. Refrigerate overnight. May place in 9x9 inch pan for thicker servings.

MICROWAVED BREAD PUDDING

This is no ordinary bread pudding!

6 Servings
Make Ahead

Easy

4 cups bread cubes (4-5
  slices)
¼-½ cup brown sugar,
  packed
¼ tsp. salt
¾ cup raisins (optional)
2 cups milk
2-4 Tbsp. butter
2 eggs, beaten

Spread bread cubes evenly in 8 inch round dish. Sprinkle evenly with brown sugar, salt and raisins. Measure milk into 1 quart measuring cup; add butter. Microwave on high for 4 minutes, until butter is melted and milk is warm. Rapidly stir in eggs with fork and mix well. Pour over bread cubes in dish. Microwave on medium-high for 9-12 minutes, rotating dish ½ turn after 6 minutes. When cooked, center may still be slightly soft, but will set as pudding cools. Serve warm or chilled.

HELPFUL HINT

Bread placed in brown sugar will keep it soft.

CHOCOLATE MOCHA MOUSSE

Easy

4 Servings
Make Ahead

1 tsp. instant coffee
½ tsp. cinnamon
2 cups half and half
1 3 oz. pkg. instant
  chocolate pudding mix
2 Tbsp. brandy or creme
  de cacao
Whipped cream (optional)

Mix coffee and cinnamon with half and half. Add pudding mix and brandy. Follow the pudding package directions. Spoon into individual custard cups or 1 quart bowl. Chill and serve with a dollop of whipped cream.

CHOCOLATE MOUSSE

A chocolate-holic's undoing!

10 Servings
Make Ahead

Easy

1 lb. sweet chocolate
½ cup very strong coffee
10 eggs, separated
4 Tbsp. brandy
Whipped cream

Melt chocolate with coffee in double boiler. Cool. Beat egg yolks until light in color; add brandy and chocolate mixture and mix thoroughly. Beat egg whites until stiff and dry; fold into chocolate mixture. Pour into serving dishes and refrigerate overnight. Top with whipped cream.

HELPFUL HINT

Use metal or plastic spoon to stir chocolate, not a wooden one.

CHOCOLATE LADY FINGER DESSERT

Average

8 Servings
Make Ahead

1 6 oz. pkg. semi-sweet
  chocolate chips
2 Tbsp. water
2 Tbsp. sugar
4 egg yolks, beaten
4 egg whites, beaten stiff
Lady fingers
1 cup heavy cream,
  whipped and sweetened

In double boiler, melt chocolate, water and sugar. Cool. Add egg yolks and fold in egg whites. Line a 9 inch square pan with split lady fingers. Add a layer of chocolate mixture, then a layer of sweetened whipped cream, then a chocolate layer and end with whipped cream. Make a day ahead and refrigerate.

FOUR LAYER DESSERT

Party pretty and oh so easy!

Average

16 Servings
Make Ahead

CRUST:
1 cup flour
½ cup butter or margarine,
  melted
¾ cup nuts, chopped

2ND LAYER:
8 oz cream cheese
1 cup confectioners' sugar
½ 8 oz. container Cool
  Whip

3RD LAYER:
1 3 oz. pkg. instant
  chocolate pudding mix
1 3 oz. pkg instant vanilla
  pudding mix
2½ cups milk

TOPPING:
½ 8 oz. container Cool
  Whip
Nuts, chopped (optional)

Combine flour, butter and nuts; press into 8x10 inch pan. Bake at 375° for 20 minutes. Cool. Combine 2nd layer ingredients and spread over crust. Beat 3rd layer ingredients together according to package directions using 2½ cups milk. Spread on top of 2nd layer. Top with remainder of Cool Whip. Sprinkle with nuts, if desired. Chill.

298

CHOCOLATE CHARLOTTE

Hedonism at its tastiest!

Average

12 Servings
Make Ahead

3 cups German sweet
  chocolate, grated (about
  ¾ lb.)
½ cup cold water
⅓ cup sugar
9 eggs, separated
4 dozen lady fingers
1 cup heavy cream,
  whipped
Chocolate, grated for
  garnish

In upper part of double boiler, mix grated chocolate with water and sugar. Set over hot water and cook until sugar and chocolate melt and combine. Add 9 unbeaten egg yolks, one at a time, beating in each as added. Cook until mixture is custard consistency. Let cool. Beat egg whites until stiff. Add whites to cooled chocolate mixture. Line bottom and sides of an 8 or 9 inch spring-form pan with lady fingers. Pour half of the custard over bottom; add a layer of lady fingers. Add remaining chocolate custard. Refrigerate overnight. Top with whipped cream and grated chocolate before serving.

CREME A LA CREME

Sinfully rich, but oh so good!

Average

12 Servings
Make Ahead
Freeze

1 pkg. unflavored gelatin
¾ cup sugar
2 cups heavy cream
1 Tbsp. vanilla
2 cups sour cream

Put gelatin, sugar and heavy cream in a saucepan and let stand 5 minutes. Heat over low heat until gelatin dissolves. Let cool until lukewarm. Add vanilla and sour cream. Mix well. Pour into a 4 cup mold and refrigerate 2 hours. Unmold and serve with a nice variety of the following toppings: strawberries and brandy, raspberries and Kirsch, chopped pears and chocolate sauce, almonds and maple syrup, Mandarin oranges and honey, pineapple and creme de menthe.

CREAM PUFFS

COMPLIMENTS OF
CHEMUNG COUNTY HISTORICAL SOCIETY, ELMIRA, N.Y.

Average   **One Dozen Puffs**

PUFFS:
1 cup hot water
½ cup butter
1 cup flour, sifted
3 eggs

Boil water and butter together. While boiling, stir in flour. Take from stove and stir to a smooth paste. After this cools, stir in eggs, not beaten. Stir 5 minutes. Drop in tablespoons on a buttered pan and bake in a quick oven (400°-450°) for 25 minutes. Don't let them touch each other and don't open oven door more often than absolutely necessary.

CREAM:
3 Tbsp. flour or cornstarch
1 cup milk
½ cup sugar
1 egg
Vanilla

Dissolve cornstarch in a little milk. Put rest of milk on stove. When hot, stir in sugar and egg, beaten together. Add cornstarch and cook until thick. Flavor with vanilla. When both puffs and cream are cool, open one side of puffs and fill with cream. From *The Experienced Cook*, c. 1905.

GRANOLA DESSERT

Top with strawberries for the final touch!

Average

10 Servings
Make Ahead

2 cups granola, crushed if desired
¼ cup butter or margarine, melted
8 oz. cream cheese, softened
1 14 oz. can sweetened condensed milk
⅓ cup lemon juice
1 tsp. vanilla

Mix granola and butter thoroughly. Reserve ⅔ cup mixture for top. Press mixture into a greased 9x9x2 inch pan. Beat cream cheese until light and fluffy. Stir in milk gradually, until well blended. Blend in lemon juice and vanilla and pour over granola mixture in pan. Sprinkle with remaining granola mixture. Chill until firm, about 3-4 hours.

FLAN

Average

2 Tbsp. sugar
4 eggs
1 14 oz. can sweetened
   condensed milk
1 condensed milk can full
   of regular milk
1 tsp. vanilla

Melt sugar over direct high heat in top of double boiler until light brown; coat inside of pan. Mix eggs, both milks and vanilla in blender. Pour into sugar coated double boiler. Cover and cook over simmering water until flan is solid, even in the center, about 50-60 minutes. Remove and refrigerate. Turn onto serving platter after cooled.

CAN'T FAIL CUSTARD

Unbelievable! Makes a perfect custard every time!

5 Servings
Make Ahead

Easy

2 cups milk
2 eggs
⅓ cup sugar
½ tsp. vanilla
Nutmeg

Place milk, eggs, sugar and vanilla in a quart bowl. Mix until well blended. Pour into 5 custard cups. Sprinkle with nutmeg. Set cups in cold water in a pan with a tight fitting lid. Cover and bring to a boil. Turn off heat and let sit with cover on for 45 minutes.

MICROWAVED BAKED CUSTARD

4-6 Servings
Make Ahead

Easy

3 eggs
⅓ cup sugar
1 tsp. vanilla
⅛ tsp. salt
1½ cups milk
Nutmeg (optional)

In 1½ quart casserole, beat eggs, sugar, vanilla and salt with fork until well blended and sugar is dissolved. Place milk in glass measure. Microwave on high 3-4 minutes, stirring well. Add milk to casserole, cover, and microwave on low 10-13 minutes, rotating dish ¼ turn every 3 minutes until set. Sprinkle top with nutmeg before serving, if desired. Cool before serving.

FROZEN EGG NOG MOUSSE

Average

12 Servings
Make Ahead
Freeze

2 envelopes unflavored
  gelatin
1 quart fresh or canned
  egg nog
⅓ cup bourbon
2 tsp. vanilla
2 cups confectioners'
  sugar
2 cups heavy cream
½ cup slivered almonds,
  toasted
1 tsp. nutmeg
1 lb. jar fudge topping
  (optional)

In saucepan, sprinkle gelatin over 1 cup egg nog. Heat slowly, stirring until gelatin is dissolved. Remove from heat. In large bowl, combine gelatin mixture with remaining egg nog, bourbon and vanilla. Stir well. Chill until thickened, about 20-30 minutes. In bowl, beat sugar into cream until soft peaks form. Fold whipped cream into gelatin mixture. Stir in nuts and nutmeg. Freeze until firm, about 4 hours. Scoop into serving dishes and top with hot or cold fudge sauce, if desired. May be frozen in a 2 quart mold. When ready to serve, unmold and serve with fudge sauce.

FROZEN LEMON DESSERT

Average

10-12 Servings
Make Ahead
Freeze

CRUST:
1 cup coconut bar cookies,
  crushed (12-13)
2 Tbsp. butter, melted

Combine crushed cookies and butter. Sprinkle ¾ of cookie mixture in bottom of 9 inch square pan. Reserve rest to sprinkle on top.

FILLING:
2 egg yolks
1 tsp. lemon rind
⅓ cup lemon juice
⅔ cup sugar
Dash salt
2 egg whites
⅔ cup dry milk powder
⅔ cup water

Combine egg yolks, lemon rind, lemon juice, sugar and salt. Set aside. Whip egg whites, milk powder and water together until stiff peaks form, about 5-8 minutes. Then blend lemon mixture into egg white mixture and pour over crumbs. Sprinkle with remaining cookie crumb mixture. Cover and freeze.

LEMON MOUSSE

Average

¾-1 cup sugar
1 pkg. unflavored gelatin
1½ tsp. cornstarch
2 tsp. lemon peel, finely
    shredded
1 cup lemon juice
4 egg yolks, beaten
1½ cups heavy cream
2 Tbsp. orange liqueur
6 egg whites, stiffly beaten

In saucepan, combine sugar, gelatin, cornstarch and lemon peel. Stir in lemon juice and egg yolks. Cook and stir until thickened and bubbly. Remove from heat; cover surface with clear plastic wrap. Cool, then chill. Beat cream to soft peaks. Put chilled lemon mixture into blender. Add orange liqueur; cover and blend until smooth. Pour mixture into large mixing bowl; fold in whipped cream, then egg whites. Turn into serving bowl. Cover and chill 4-6 hours or overnight. Garnish with lemon slices, if desired.

LEMON FLUFF

10 Servings
Make Ahead

Average

1½ cups hot water
1 3 oz. pkg. lemon gelatin
½ cup honey or maple
    syrup or corn syrup
3 Tbsp. lemon juice
Rind of 1 lemon, grated
1 13 oz. can evaporated
    milk, *chilled overnight*
Approximately 36 vanilla
    wafers, crushed

Mix water and gelatin. When gelatin is partially set, (consistency of egg whites) gently beat until fluffy. Add honey, juice and rind; add ½ can **chilled** evaporated milk and beat. Add other ½ can evaporated milk and beat. Sprinkle ½ vanilla wafers on bottom of 8 inch spring-form pan. Pour lemon mixture on top; cover with rest of crushed vanilla wafers. Chill. This is best when made 2-3 days ahead, but can be made the same day it is served.

RASPBERRY MOUSSE

This is the stuff dreams are made of!

Average

1 10 oz. pkg. frozen
  raspberries, thawed
1 3 oz. pkg. raspberry
  gelatin
1 cup hot water
16 marshmallows
Lady fingers
1 cup heavy cream

Drain berries and set aside, but reserve juice. Combine raspberry juice, gelatin and hot water in medium-size saucepan and heat until gelatin dissolves. Add marshmallows and cook over medium heat, stirring often, until marshmallows melt completely. Pour into large bowl; chill until mixture is thick and syrupy. While gelatin chills, line bottom and sides of a spring-form pan with split lady fingers. Beat thickened gelatin until it doubles in bulk, turns pink and mounds slightly when dropped from a spoon; very gently fold in raspberries, reserving a few for garnish. If mixture gets too soft, chill a few minutes. Beat cream until stiff; gently fold into raspberry mixture. Spoon into pan and chill until set. Garnish with reserved raspberries.

LO-CAL STRAWBERRY CREAM

Easy

1 pkg. unflavored gelatin
1 pkg. strawberry D-Zerta
  gelatin
2 pkgs. artificial sweetener
6 oz. plain yogurt

Mix gelatins and 1 cup boiling water. Add 1 cup cold water (ice for faster results). Add sweetener. Let cool in refrigerator until partially set. Beat gelatin mixture and yogurt together Place in refrigerator to firm.

HOT FUDGE SAUCE

Easy

1½ Cups
Make Ahead

2 squares semi-sweet
  chocolate
⅔ cup evaporated milk
⅔ cup sugar
Scant ⅛ tsp. salt
1⅓ Tbsp. butter
⅔ tsp. vanilla

Mix chocolate, milk, sugar and salt together in heavy pan or double boiler. Cook over low heat until chocolate is melted. Remove from heat. Add butter and vanilla and continue to stir until butter is melted and sauce is smooth. Heat before serving.

SHINY CHOCOLATE FROSTING

Average

1½ Cups

2 Tbsp. butter
2 squares unsweetened
  chocolate
Dash of salt
1 cup confectioners' sugar
1 tsp. vanilla
2½ Tbsp. boiling water

In double boiler, melt butter with chocolate. Add salt, sugar and vanilla; stir. Add boiling water and mix until smooth. Pour over cooled cake. Spread quickly over top and sides. Covers two 8 inch layers thinly. Works very well on cupcakes as it gives them a nice shiny frosting.

NOTES

CJThorborg 82

CORNING GLASS CENTER
The world renowned Corning Glass Center exhibits the history of glass and demonstrates its scientific applications. The Center also houses the Steuben factory where workmen shape the magnificent Steuben crystal.

BARS, COOKIES AND CANDIES

APRICOT BARS

Delightful served warm!

Average

**2 Dozen
Make Ahead
Freeze**

¾ cup butter, softened
1 cup sugar
1 egg
1½ tsp. vanilla
½ tsp. salt
2 cups flour
1½ cups shredded
  coconut
1 8 oz. jar apricot
  preserves
1 cup walnuts, chopped

Cream together butter, sugar, egg and vanilla. Mix in salt, flour and coconut. Mix well. Reserve ¾ cup for topping. Spread rest into greased 9x11 inch pan. Spread apricot preserves over mixture. Sprinkle nuts over preserves. Crumble reserved ¾ cup dough over top. Bake at 350° for 30 minutes. Cool slightly and cut into squares.

ANISE SEED BARS

A perfect holiday cookie!

Average

**2 Dozen
Make Ahead
Freeze**

2½ cups flour
1 cup sugar
4 Tbsp. butter, softened
1 Tbsp. anise seed
2 tsp. baking powder
¼ tsp. salt
3 eggs

In large bowl, measure 1½ cups flour and remaining ingredients. Beat with electric mixer on low speed until blended; increase speed to medium and beat for 3 minutes. Stir in remaining flour and mix well. Wrap dough in wax paper and refrigerate for 1 hour or until firm. Preheat oven to 375°. Divide dough in half. On well floured surface, shape each half into 12x2 inch loaf. Place loaves on greased cookie sheet 3 inches apart. Bake for 20 minutes. Remove from oven and immediately slice into 1 inch bars. Turn bars on side making sure they do not touch each other. Return to oven and bake 15 minutes more or until golden brown.

307

GRAHAM CRACKER BROWNIES

Don't tell anyone how easy this is!

Easy

1½ Dozen
Make Ahead
Freeze

1 14 oz. can sweetened
   condensed milk
1½ cups graham cracker
   crumbs
1 6 oz. pkg. chocolate
   chips
½-1 cup walnuts, chopped

Mix all ingredients and put into **well
greased** 8 inch square pan. Bake at
350° for 30-40 minutes.

FROSTED BROWNIES

Be sure to hide one for yourself!

Average

4 Dozen
Make Ahead
Freeze

BROWNIES:
1 cup sugar
½ cup margarine
4 eggs
1 16 oz. can chocolate
   syrup (Hershey's
   preferred)
1 cup plus 1 Tbsp. flour
½ tsp. baking powder
⅛ tsp. salt
1 cup nut meats, chopped
   (optional)

Mix together sugar, margarine and
eggs. Add chocolate syrup. Sift together flour, baking powder and salt.
Add to sugar mixture. Add nuts, if
desired. Place into greased 12x16x1
inch jelly roll pan and bake at 350° for
20-25 minutes. Cool before frosting.

FROSTING:
6 Tbsp. margarine
6 Tbsp. milk
1½ cups sugar
½ cup chocolate chips

Combine margarine, milk and sugar in
medium saucepan. Bring to a boil. Boil
for 30 seconds. Remove from heat; add
chocolate chips. Beat until firm enough
to spread.

VACATION BROWNIES

Average

**1½ Dozen
Make Ahead
Freeze**

½ cup butter
2 squares unsweetened
  chocolate
1 cup sugar
2 eggs, separated
½ cup flour
½ cup walnuts, chopped
1 tsp. vanilla

Melt butter and chocolate. Add sugar and egg yolks, stirring in yolks one at a time. Add flour, nuts and vanilla and mix. Beat egg whites until stiff peaks form. Fold egg whites into chocolate mixture. Spread into a greased 8x8 inch pan. Bake at 350° for about 20-25 minutes. Cut while hot, but let cool before removing from pan, as they will crumble.

BROWNIE CONFECTIONS

Average

**1½ Dozen
Make Ahead**

FUDGE BROWNIES:

Bake your own favorite fudge brownies baked in 8 or 9 inch pan. (May use recipe on the Baker's Chocolate Box.)

MIDDLE:
4 Tbsp. butter, softened
2 cups confectioners'
  sugar, sifted
2 Tbsp. heavy cream
1 tsp. vanilla

Brown butter to a delicate brown. Blend with sugar. Stir in cream and vanilla until smooth. Spread on baked brownies.

TOPPING:
1 square unsweetened
  chocolate
1 tsp. butter

Melt chocolate and butter. Cool. Spread a very thin coating over confectioners' sugar mixture.

309

CHOCOLATE CHIP PEANUT BUTTER SQUARES

Average

4 Dozen
Make Ahead
Freeze

1 cup butter, softened
¾ cup brown sugar
¾ cup white sugar
2 eggs
½ tsp. vanilla
2 cups flour
1 tsp. baking soda
½ tsp. salt
1½ cups chocolate chips
1½ cups peanut butter
  chips

Cream butter, sugars, eggs and vanilla until light and fluffy. Combine flour, baking soda and salt; add to creamed mixture. Combine both chips and stir into batter. Spread mixture evenly onto greased jelly roll pan. Bake at 350° for 25 minutes. Cool in pan.

MAGIC BARS

Watch them disappear!

Easy

4½ Dozen
Make Ahead
Freeze

1½ cups Corn Flake
  crumbs
½ cup butter or margarine,
  melted
3 Tbsp. sugar
1 cup walnuts, coarsely
  chopped
1 cup semi-sweet
  chocolate chips
1½ cups flaked coconut
1 14 oz. can sweetened
  condensed milk

Make a crust of Corn Flake crumbs, butter and sugar. Mix crust in ungreased 13x9x2 inch baking pan. Press crust flat. Sprinkle walnuts evenly over crust. Scatter chocolate chips evenly over walnuts. Sprinkle coconut evenly over chocolate chips. Pour condensed milk evenly over all. Bake at 350° for 25 minutes, or until lightly browned around edges.

CHOCOLATE BUTTER CREAM SQUARES

Complicated

**3 Dozen
Make Ahead
Freeze**

CRUST:
½ cup butter or margarine
¼ cup granulated sugar
1 square unsweetened
  chocolate
1 egg, beaten
½ cup pecans, chopped
1 tsp. vanilla
2 cups fine graham
  cracker crumbs
1 cup flaked coconut

Blend first 3 ingredients over boiling water and add beaten egg. Cook 5 minutes stirring; add remaining ingredients. Remove from heat. Press crust into 9x9x2 inch greased pan and chill for 15 minutes.

CREAM FILLING:
½ cup butter, softened
2 Tbsp. instant vanilla
  pudding mix
3 Tbsp. milk
2 cups confectioners'
  sugar

Cream butter and pudding mix until fluffy. Add milk and confectioners' sugar. Beat until smooth. Spread onto crust and chill for 15 minutes.

CHOCOLATE TOPPING:
1 Tbsp. butter
4 squares semi-sweet
  chocolate

Melt butter and chocolate over low heat or double boiler. Spread over cream filling and chill until firm. Cut into 1½ inch squares. Remove from pan. May be frozen in foil. Must be refrigerated until served.

NUTTY CHOCOLATE OATMEAL BARS

Easy

3-4 Dozen
Make Ahead
Freeze

4 cups quick cooking
   oatmeal
1 cup brown sugar
¼ cup light corn syrup
⅔ cup margarine, melted
¼ cup peanut butter
1 tsp. vanilla

Mix all ingredients and place into greased 9x13 inch pan. Bake at 400° for 12 minutes.

TOPPING:
6 oz. chocolate chips
3 oz butterscotch chips
⅔ cup crunchy peanut
   butter

Melt chips; add peanut butter and spread on bars. Let cool and refrigerate for several hours before cutting.

CHOCOLATE MERINGUE BITES

Average

4 Dozen
Make Ahead

¾ cup butter or margarine,
   softened
1½ cups brown sugar,
   packed
½ cup white sugar
3 eggs, separated
1 tsp. vanilla
2 cups flour
1 tsp. baking powder
¼ tsp. baking soda
¼ tsp. salt
1 6 oz. pkg. chocolate
   chips
1 cup coconut
¾ cup nuts, coarsely
   chopped

Mix butter, ½ cup brown sugar, white sugar, egg yolks and vanilla. Beat for 2 minutes at medium speed, scraping bowl constantly. Blend flour, baking powder, baking soda and salt. Mix thoroughly. Pat dough into a greased 9x13 inch pan. Sprinkle with chocolate chips, coconut and nuts. Beat egg whites until frothy. Add 1 cup brown sugar gradually, beating until stiff. Spread over nuts. Bake at 350° for 35-40 minutes.

CRUNCHY FUDGE SANDWICHES

1½ Dozen
Make Ahead

Average

1 6 oz. pkg. butterscotch
  morsels
½ cup peanut butter
4 cups Rice Krispies
1 6 oz. pkg. semi-sweet
  chocolate morsels
2 Tbsp. butter
1 Tbsp. water
½ cup confectioners'
  sugar, sifted

Melt butterscotch morsels and peanut butter over low heat. Stir in Rice Krispies. Press ½ mixture into buttered 8 inch square pan. Refrigerate to set. Stir chocolate morsels, butter and water over low heat. Add sugar and spread over chilled Rice Krispie mixture. Top with remaining Krispies and chill until firm. Cut into squares.

BUTTER PECAN TURTLES

3 Dozen
Make Ahead

Average

CRUST LAYER:
2 cups flour
1 cup brown sugar
½ cup butter, softened
1 cup pecan halves

Combine flour, sugar and butter and mix until particles are fine. Pat firmly into **ungreased** 9x13x2 inch pan. Sprinkle pecans on top of unbaked crust.

CARAMEL LAYER:
⅔ cup butter
½ cup brown sugar

Combine butter and sugar in saucepan. Cook over medium heat, stirring constantly, until entire surface of mixture begins to boil. Boil ½-1 minute, stirring constantly. Pour caramel evenly over pecans and crust. Bake on center oven shelf at 350° for 18-22 minutes or until entire caramel layer is bubbly and crust light golden brown.

TOPPING:
1 cup chocolate chips

Immediately sprinkle chocolate chips over caramel layer. Allow chips to melt slightly (2-3 minutes). Slightly swirl chips as they melt; leave some whole for effect. Cool completely before cutting into bars.

ROCKY ROAD SQUARES

Easy

3 Dozen
Make Ahead

1 roll refrigerated chocolate chip slice 'n bake cookies (Pillsbury preferred)
4 Tbsp. butter
¼ cup plus 1 tsp. water
1 box fudge frosting mix (Pillsbury preferred)
1 cup miniature marshmallows
¼ cup walnuts, chopped

Slice cookie dough ¼ inch thick; place slices in bottom of greased 8 or 9 inch square pan. Bake at 375° for 20-25 minutes, until light golden brown. (Cookies will be puffy when removed from oven). Cool slightly. Melt butter in water; stir in frosting mix; mix until well blended. Remove from heat. Fold in miniature marshmallows and nuts; spread over cookie base. Allow cookies to set in refrigerator for at least 1 hour before serving.

COFFEE TOFFEE BARS

A true taste delight!

Average

2 Dozen
Make Ahead
Freeze

BARS:
1 cup butter or margarine
1 cup brown sugar
1 tsp. almond flavoring
1-2 tsp. instant coffee, dry
2¼ cups flour
½ tsp. baking powder
¼ tsp. salt
1 6 oz. pkg. chocolate chips
½ cup nuts, chopped

Combine butter, sugar and flavoring. Add dry ingredients, chips and nuts. Press into greased 13x9 inch pan and bake at 350° for 30-35 minutes. While warm, add glaze.

GLAZE:
1 Tbsp. butter or margarine, softened
¾ cup confectioners' sugar
⅓ tsp. almond flavoring
2 Tbsp. milk

Mix all ingredients until smooth. Glaze. Cut into small bars.

CARAMEL FUDGE SHORTBREAD

A delightful way to gain weight!

Average

3 Dozen
Make Ahead

SHORTBREAD:
¾ cup all-purpose flour
¼ cup sugar
½ cup butter or margarine,
    softened

Mix flour and sugar in bowl; add butter. With hands, knead butter into flour and mix until a firm dough is formed; knead until smooth. Flatten with hand into bottom of 11x7x1½ inch pan until even; prick all over with fork. Bake at 325° for about 10 minutes or until golden brown. Remove from oven and set aside until caramel is ready and shortbread has cooled a little.

CARAMEL:
½ cup butter or margarine
½ cup sugar
3 Tbsp. Tate and Lyle
    golden syrup or
    substitute light corn
    syrup
½ 14 oz. can sweetened
    condensed milk

Boil all ingredients together; reduce heat and simmer for 5 minutes, stirring constantly to prevent burning. Pour over shortbread. Allow to cool and set.

COATING:
4 oz. semi-sweet
    chocolate

Melt chocolate and spread evenly over caramel. When chocolate is just set, cut into **small** bars. If chocolate becomes too firm, it will break.

LEMON GLACEES

A lemon lover's downfall!

Average

1½ Dozen
Make Ahead
Freeze

CRUST:
⅓ cup butter, softened
1 cup flour
2 Tbsp. sugar

Cream butter and cut in flour and sugar until mixture resembles coarse crumbs. Press firmly into 9 inch square pan. Bake at 350° for 15-20 minutes, until set, but not browned.

FILLING:
½ cup brown sugar
¾ cup coconut
½ cup walnuts, finely chopped
2 eggs, beaten
¼ tsp. salt
⅛ tsp. baking powder
½ tsp. vanilla

In bowl, combine all filling ingredients. Spread over crust. Bake at 350° for 20-25 minutes. Frost immediately.

FROSTING:
2 tsp. lemon rind, grated
2 Tbsp. lemon juice
1 cup confectioners' sugar

While glacees are baking, place all frosting ingredients in bowl and mix until smooth. Frost. Cool and cut into squares.

 # LEMON SQUARES

Easy

2 Dozen
Make Ahead

CRUST:
1 cup flour
½ cup butter, softened
⅓-½ cup confectioners' sugar

Blend together flour, butter and sugar. Press into 8 inch square pan. Bake at 350° for 20 minutes.

TOP LAYER:
2 eggs
1 cup sugar
2 Tbsp. flour
2 Tbsp. lemon juice
Pinch of lemon rind
½ tsp. baking powder

Beat together eggs, sugar, flour, lemon juice, lemon rind and baking powder. Pour over crust. Bake at 350° for 25 minutes longer. Cool slightly and cut into squares.

VIENNA BARS

We hear this is Ronald Reagan's favorite cookie!

Average

3 Dozen
Make Ahead
Freeze

1 cup butter, softened
1½ cups sugar
1 tsp. salt
2 large egg yolks
2½ cups flour
½ cup currant or red
    raspberry jam
4 egg whites
2 cups nuts, finely
    chopped

In large bowl, combine butter with ½ cup sugar and mix until creamy. Beat in salt and egg yolks. Gradually add flour. When dough becomes hard to work, knead it with fingers until smooth. Spread dough into greased 17x12 inch jelly roll pan. Bake at 350° for 15-20 minutes, or until lightly browned. Remove from oven, cool slightly, and spread evenly with jam. Set pan aside. In a deep bowl, beat egg whites with electric mixer at top speed until stiff peaks form. Blend in nuts and remaining sugar. Spread egg mixture over jam, going right to the end of the pan. Return pan to oven and bake at 350° for another 25 minutes. Remove from oven and cool 15 minutes. While still warm cut into bars or squares.

CREAM CHEESE COOKIES

Average

4 Dozen
Make Ahead
Freeze

1 cup butter, softened
½ cup granulated sugar
3 oz. cream cheese,
    softened (Philadelphia
    preferred)
1 tsp. vanilla
2 cups flour
Granulated sugar

Mix all ingredients together and form into balls the size of walnuts. Dip into sugar to coat. Place on ungreased cookie sheet and mash with fork. Bake at 375° for 12-15 minutes.

APPLE SQUARES

Average

**1 Dozen
Make Ahead
Freeze**

4 Tbsp. butter or
   margarine, melted
½ cup brown sugar
1 egg
1 tsp. vanilla
1 cup flour
1 tsp. baking powder
¼ tsp. salt
¼ tsp. cinnamon
½-1 cup apples, chopped
½ cup nuts, chopped

Melt butter and add sugar, egg and vanilla. Stir in remaining ingredients. Spread into greased 8x8 inch pan. Bake at 350° for 30 minutes. Blueberries may be substituted for apples.

APPLE PIE SQUARES

Average

**1½ Dozen
Make Ahead**

CRUST:
½ cup butter, softened
½ cup margarine, softened
2 cups flour
3-4 Tbsp. ice water

Cut butter and margarine into flour until it reaches a cornmeal-like texture. Sprinkle in ice water. Mix until it forms a ball. Chill 20 minutes. Roll crust into a 10x15 inch sheet on a jelly roll pan.

FILLING:
1 cup granulated sugar
1 Tbsp. cinnamon
12 apples, peeled, cored
   and sliced into small
   wedges
Lemon juice
½ cup maple sugar
   (optional)

Combine granulated sugar and cinnamon. Layer apples in 4 rows on crust. Sprinkle with sugar mixture; then sprinkle with a little lemon juice. Bake at 450° for 20 minutes. Reduce oven to 350° and bake for 30 minutes more. Remove from oven and sprinkle with maple sugar, if desired. Cut into squares. Serve warm or cold.

WHOOPIE PIES

Wickedly delicious!

Average

3-4 Dozen
Make Ahead

COOKIES:
1 cup shortening
2 cups sugar
1 cup sour cream
1 cup hot water
1 cup cocoa
4 cups flour
1 tsp. salt
2 tsp. baking soda
1 tsp. baking powder
2 egg yolks (reserve
   whites)

Blend all ingredients. Drop from spoon onto greased cookie sheet. Bake at 400° for 7-10 minutes.

FILLING:
2 egg whites, not beaten
2 tsp. vanilla
4 Tbsp. flour
2 Tbsp. plus 4 cups
   confectioners' sugar
4 Tbsp. milk
1½ cups shortening

Thoroughly beat all ingredients, except 4 cups confectioners' sugar. Add 4 cups confectioners' sugar to make mixture spreading consistency. Spread between two cooled cookies, sandwich style.

DATE NUT JUMBLES

Easy

3 Dozen
Make Ahead

4 Tbsp. margarine
1 cup brown sugar
1 cup dates, chopped
1 egg, well beaten
1 tsp. vanilla
2 cups Rice Krispies
½ cup nuts, chopped
Coconut

Melt together margarine, sugar and dates. Cook and stir about 8 minutes or until bubbly; remove from heat. Add egg, vanilla, Rice Krispies and nuts. Mix well. Let cool until it can be handled. Grease hands to prevent sticking. Roll into 1 inch balls. Roll balls in coconut.

MONSTER COOKIES

Your own little monsters will love them!

Easy

12 Dozen
Make Ahead
Freeze

1 cup margarine, softened
2 cups peanut butter
2 cups sugar
1 lb. brown sugar
6 eggs
Dash of light corn syrup
8 oz. chocolate chips
8 oz. M&M's
4 tsp. baking soda
1 tsp. vanilla
½ cup nuts, chopped
Raisins (optional)
9 cups oatmeal

Mix all ingredients in **huge** bowl, adding the oatmeal last. Drop by heaping teaspoon onto ungreased baking sheet. Bake at 350° for 10-12 minutes. Be prepared to stand by your oven for a long time as this recipe makes lots of cookies.

PEANUT BLOSSOMS

Average

7 Dozen
Make Ahead
Freeze

1 cup granulated sugar
1 cup brown sugar
1 cup margarine, softened
1 cup creamy peanut
    butter
2 eggs
¼ cup milk
2 tsp. vanilla
3½ cups flour
2 tsp. baking soda
1 tsp. salt
2 10 oz. pkgs. chocolate
    kisses (Hershey's
    preferred)

Cream sugar, margarine and peanut butter. Beat in eggs, milk and vanilla. Mix flour, baking soda and salt, and stir into sugar mixture. Shape into walnut-size balls and roll in granulated sugar. Bake at 375° on ungreased cookie sheet for 10-12 minutes. Immediately press chocolate kiss into center of cookie.

SHORTBREAD

COMPLIMENTS OF
CORTLAND COUNTY HISTORICAL SOCIETY, CORTLAND, N.Y.

Easy

2 Round Short-breads or 32 Wedges

1 lb. sweet butter (do *not* use margarine)
1 cup confectioners' sugar
4 cups flour, sifted

Cream butter and add sugar gradually. Blend well but don't overwork. Slowly work in flour. Pat out to ¾ inch thickness on board "floured" with a mixture of confectioners' sugar and flour. The dough should be round in shape. Pinch edges and prick all over with a fork. Chill in freezer 15-30 minutes. Place on two cookie sheets. Preheat oven at 375°. Bake shortbread at this heat for 5 minutes. Reduce heat to 300° and bake for 45-60 minutes, until shortbread is golden, but not browned. Cut when warm. Recipe can be halved.

SCOTTISH SHORTBREAD

An international favorite!

Average

**2 Dozen
Make Ahead
Freeze**

1 cup all-purpose flour
⅓ cup cornstarch
8 Tbsp. butter, softened
¼ cup superfine sugar
(May substitute regular sugar processed in blender for 1 minute.)
Superfine sugar for garnish

Sift flour and cornstarch together. Cream butter, then beat in sugar. Blend in flour and cornstarch, one tablespoon at a time. Knead mixture together. Place on 7x11 inch jelly roll pan and press with palm of hand until even. Prick all over with fork. Sprinkle with extra sugar. Chill in refrigerator for 15 minutes. Bake at 325° for 35 minutes or until a pale golden brown. Cut into small finger-like pieces before shortbread has cooled. Cool in baking pan several minutes. Gently transfer to wire rack to finish cooling.

ROCHESTER GINGERSNAPS

COMPLIMENTS OF
ROCHESTER MUSEUM AND SCIENCE CENTER, ROCHESTER, N.Y.

Average   **8 Dozen**

1 cup molasses
1 cup sugar
½ cup shortening
1 tsp. cinnamon
½ tsp. ginger
½ tsp. baking soda
1 egg, beaten
3 cups flour
1 tsp. baking powder

Boil together molasses, sugar, shortening, spices and baking soda for 5 minutes or to 232° F. Cool and add beaten egg and flour, sifted with baking powder. Chill mixture in refrigerator for several hours. Roll out very thin on floured board; cut into strips one inch wide and four inches long. Place on greased baking pans or cookie sheet and bake in moderate oven at 400° F. for 6 minutes. From the *Royal Baking Powder Cookbook,* 1940.

SOUR CREAM GINGER COOKIES

Average

5 Dozen
Make Ahead
Freeze

½ cup butter, softened
1½ cups brown sugar
½ tsp. salt
1 cup dark molasses
1 Tbsp. ground ginger
1 egg
1 cup sour cream
4 cups flour
1 tsp. baking powder
1 tsp. baking soda
1 tsp. cinnamon
½ tsp. ground cloves

Cream butter, sugar and salt. Add molasses and ginger; stir in egg. Add sour cream and mix thoroughly. Sift flour, baking powder, baking soda, cinnamon and cloves together and add to butter mixture. Refrigerate several hours.
Drop cookie method: roll 1-2 tsp. dough into ball. Roll in granulated sugar. Place on greased cookie sheet. Bake at 375° for 10-15 minutes.
Rolled/cut cookie method: roll out on slightly floured board to about ½ inch thickness. Cut into desired shapes. Bake at 375° for 10-15 minutes on greased cookie sheet.

GINGER KRINKLES

Average

¾ cup butter
1 cup brown sugar
1 egg
4 Tbsp. molasses
2¼ cups flour
2 tsp. baking soda
1 tsp. cinnamon
1-2 tsp. ginger
½ tsp. salt
½ tsp. ground cloves
Granulated sugar for
   dipping

Mix all ingredients well and chill. Roll into 1½ inch balls and dip balls into sugar. Sprinkle each one with one or two drops of water. Bake at 350° for 10-12 minutes. Don't overbake.

SOFT MOLASSES COOKIES

Just like Grandma used to bake!

Easy

3 Dozen
Make Ahead
Freeze

2½ cups flour
1 tsp. ginger
1 tsp. cinnamon
¼ tsp. salt
½ cup butter, softened
½ cup sugar
½ cup molasses
1 egg
2 tsp. baking soda
2 tsp. hot water
¼ cup cold water
½-1 cup raisins

Sift together flour, ginger, cinnamon and salt. Beat butter, sugar, molasses and egg together in medium-size bowl until light and fluffy. Dissolve baking soda in hot water; stir into butter mixture. Add dry ingredients alternately with cold water. Stir in raisins and drop onto lightly greased cookie sheet. Bake at 400° for 10 minutes.

MOLASSES JUMBLES

Easy

**4 Dozen
Freeze**

3 eggs
⅔ cup sour milk (put 1
   tsp. lemon juice or
   vinegar in measure, fill
   to ⅔ cup with milk)
1 cup sugar
1 cup molasses
1 cup butter
2 tsp. baking soda
1½ tsp. cinnamon
5 tsp. coffee
5 cups flour
Raisins

Mix all ingredients, except raisins, in bowl. Drop from spoon onto cookie sheet. Place 3 raisins on top of each. Bake at 375° for 8-10 minutes.

PECAN TEA TASSIES

Average

**3 Dozen
Make Ahead
Freeze**

PASTRY:
8 oz. cream cheese,
   softened
1 cup butter or margarine,
   softened
2 cups flour

Cream the cream cheese, butter and flour. Refrigerate several hours. When chilled, form small balls and press into **miniature** muffin tins, bringing dough up around sides.

FILLING:
2 eggs
2 Tbsp. butter or
   margarine
1½ cups brown sugar
2 tsp. vanilla
⅔ cup pecans, chopped

Cream all filling ingredients, except pecans. Mix well; stir in pecans. Fill cups ¾ full. Bake at 350° for 25-30 minutes. Let cool for 5 minutes in pan before removing.

OVERNIGHT MACAROONS

Easy

6 Dozen
Make Ahead
Freeze

4 cups quick cooking
   oatmeal
2 cups brown sugar
1 cup salad oil
2 eggs, beaten
1 tsp. salt
1 tsp. almond extract

Combine oatmeal, sugar and oil and let sit overnight. The next morning, add eggs, salt and almond extract. Drop by teaspoon onto well greased baking sheet. Bake at 325° for 10 minutes. Cool slightly before removing from pan.

FILLED MACAROONS GLACE

Complicated

2 Dozen
Make Ahead

MACAROONS:
½ lb. almond paste
1 cup sugar
3 small or 2 large egg
   whites

Blend almond paste and sugar. Beat in egg whites until consistency is such that it holds shape. Place in small mounds on unglazed brown paper, 2 inches apart. Bake at 300° for 30-35 minutes. Put paper on damp dish-towel for a few minutes before removing macaroons. Indent slightly to hold filling.

FILLING:
1 cup butter, softened
2 scant cups sugar
2 Tbsp. instant coffee
1 Tbsp. to ½ cup hot
   water (depending on
   consistency)

Cream butter until light. Add sugar and coffee. Gradually add hot water. Mixture should be light and fluffly, not runny. Fill macaroons, mounding center slightly. Chill, then glaze.

GLAZE:
½ cup butter, melted
⅓ cup cocoa
1 cup sugar
2 Tbsp. boiling water
1 tsp. instant coffee
1 tsp. vanilla

Combine all ingredients and mix until smooth and runny. Cool slightly. Dip filling side of macaroons into glaze, using fingers. Glaze should not be very warm. Refrigerate until 1 hour before serving.

MERINGUE KISSES

Easy

2 Dozen
Make Ahead

2 egg whites
⅛ tsp. cream of tartar
⅛ tsp. salt
¾ cup granulated sugar
½ tsp. vanilla
½ cup nuts, chopped
(optional)

Beat egg whites, cream of tartar and salt until stiff. **Slowly** add sugar and vanilla. Add nuts, if desired. Drop by teaspoon onto greased baking sheet. Bake at 250° for 30-35 minutes.

 # LEMON WAFERS

Light and luscious!

Average

3 Dozen
Make Ahead
Freeze

1 cup butter, softened
½ cup sugar
2 egg yolks
1 tsp. lemon extract
1 lemon rind, grated
1¼ cups flour

Cream butter and sugar; add egg yolks one at a time. Add lemon extract and rind. Gently beat in flour. Drop by spoon onto baking sheet. Bake at 375° for 5 minutes.

THIMBLE COOKIES

You don't have to sew to love these!

Average

8 Dozen
Make Ahead
Freeze

1 cup sweet butter,
  softened
½ cup regular butter,
  softened
1 cup sugar
2 egg yolks
1 tsp. vanilla
3 cups flour
Jelly of any flavor or
  chocolate kisses
  (Hershey's preferred)

Cream butters and sugar; add egg yolks and vanilla. Blend in flour. Roll into 1 inch balls, flatten slightly with fork and indent center with thimble (or finger dipped in ice water). Fill center with jelly or kiss. Bake on greased cookie sheet at 350° for 15-18 minutes.

POTATO CHIP COOKIES

Average

3 Dozen
Make Ahead

½ cup butter, softened
½ cup margarine, softened
½ cup sugar
1¼ cups flour
½ cup potato chips,
   crushed (may use stale
   ones)
½ cup nuts, chopped
1 tsp. vanilla
Confectioners' sugar

In mixing bowl, place all ingredients, except confectioners' sugar, in order given, mixing well after each addition. Drop by teaspoon onto ungreased cookie sheet. Bake at 350° for 15 minutes. Cool 1-2 minutes on cookie sheet before removing as cookies are fragile. Sprinkle with confectioners' sugar.

WEDDING COOKIES

Average

3½ Dozen
Make Ahead
Freeze

1 cup butter, softened
½ cup confectioners'
   sugar
1 tsp. vanilla
1 cup walnuts, chopped
2 cups flour, sifted
¼ tsp. salt
Confectioners' sugar

Cream butter; add sugar gradually, creaming continuously. Add vanilla, nuts and flour, sifted with salt; mix well. Shape into balls about the size of walnuts. Bake on ungreased cookie sheets at 350° for 20 minutes. While warm, roll in confectioners' sugar.

LACY OATMEAL COOKIES

Delicate and delicious!

Average

3 Dozen
Make Ahead

2¼ cups oatmeal (Old-
   Fashioned)
2¼ cups light brown sugar
3 Tbsp. flour
½ tsp. salt
1 egg, slightly beaten
1 cup butter, melted
½ tsp. vanilla

Combine oatmeal, sugar, flour and salt. Add egg, butter and vanilla. Stir. Drop by teaspoon onto well greased and floured cookie sheet. Cookies should be well spaced. Bake at 325° for 10-12 minutes. Watch to prevent burning. Cool slightly before removing from sheet.

327

EXTRA SPECIAL CHOCOLATE CHIPS

Courtesy of Lee Davis, Sandwich Shop Manager,
at Evanston Hospital!

Average

3 Dozen
Make Ahead

1¼ cups shortening
1 cup granulated sugar
1 cup brown sugar, packed
3 eggs
2 Tbsp. vanilla
1 tsp. salt
3½ cups flour
1 tsp. baking soda
1 tsp. baking powder
2½ cups semi-sweet
   chocolate pieces
1½ cups walnuts, chopped

Cream together shortening and sugars until light and fluffy, about 5 minutes. Add eggs, vanilla and salt; beat 5 minutes more. Sift flour, baking soda and baking powder. Add to first mixture, stirring by hand; mix well. Stir in chocolate pieces and nuts. Drop by tablespoon onto ungreased baking sheet. Bake at 375° for 12-15 minutes.

CHOCOLATE DROP COOKIES

Average

4 Dozen
Make Ahead
Freeze

1 egg, beaten
1 cup brown sugar
1 tsp. vanilla
½ cup shortening, melted
2 squares unsweetened
   chocolate, melted
1⅔ cups flour
½ tsp. salt
½ tsp. baking soda
½ cup milk
½ cup walnuts, chopped
   (optional)

Beat egg until light; add sugar and mix well. Add vanilla, then shortening which has been mixed and melted with chocolate; blend well. Sift flour with salt and baking soda; add alternately with milk; add nuts. Drop by teaspoon onto greased baking sheet, 2 inches apart. Bake at 350° for 10-12 minutes. While warm, frost with butter cocoa frosting.

BUTTER COCOA
   FROSTING:
⅓ cup butter, melted
1½ Tbsp. cocoa
2 Tbsp. milk
½ tsp. vanilla
1½ cups confectioners'
   sugar

Mix all ingredients well and frost warm cookies.

EXCELLENT CHOCOLATE CARAMELS

COMPLIMENTS OF THE CANAL MUSEUM, SYRACUSE, N.Y.

1½ Pounds
Make Ahead

Easy

1 cup Baker's chocolate, grated
3 cups granulated sugar
Pinch of salt
Butter, the size of a walnut
1 cup hot water

Combine ingredients in order given. Boil them down for 10 minutes, stirring constantly. Pour into buttered tins and, with a silver knife, stir back and forth until you find it sugaring. Mark it off in squares and set away to cool. Taken from George Adie's, *State Scow Boat Log Book*, 1880.

CREAMY CARAMELS

Let the children help wrap!

2 Pounds
Make Ahead

Average

2 cups sugar
2 cups heavy cream, warm
1 cup light corn syrup
½ tsp. salt
⅓ cup butter
1 tsp. vanilla
½ cup pecans, chopped (optional)

Mix sugar, 1 cup cream, syrup and salt in large pan. Cook and stir for 10 minutes. Add rest of cream very slowly so mixture does not stop boiling. Cook 5 minutes longer. Stir in butter 1 teaspoon at a time. Cook **slowly**, stirring until a small amount forms a firm ball in cold water (about 245° on candy thermometer). Remove from heat, add vanilla and nuts, if desired. Mix gently. Pour into buttered 8x8 inch pan. Cool. Cut into 1 inch squares and wrap in wax paper.

329

FABULOUS FUDGE

Average

1 Pound
Make Ahead
Freeze

2 cups sugar
2 oz. unsweetened baking
  chocolate
2 Tbsp. corn syrup
⅔ cup milk
⅛ tsp. salt
2 Tbsp. butter
1 tsp. vanilla
½ cup walnuts or pecans,
  chopped (optional)

Combine first 5 ingredients. Cook over medium heat until a ball forms when dropped into cold water. Pour into bowl. Add butter and vanilla. Add nuts, if desired. Beat at high speed, slowing as mixture thickens. Pour onto wax paper and cut into pieces.

TWO-TONE FUDGE

Average

2½ Pounds
Make Ahead

2 cups brown sugar
1 cup granulated sugar
1 cup evaporated milk
½ cup butter
1 7½ oz. jar marshmallow
  cream
1 tsp. vanilla
1 6 oz. pkg. butterscotch
  morsels
1 cup walnuts, coarsely
  chopped
1 6 oz. pkg. semi-sweet
  chocolate morsels

Combine brown sugar, granulated sugar, evaporated milk and butter in saucepan. Bring to a **full** boil over moderate heat, stirring constantly. Boil 10 minutes, over moderate heat, stirring occasionally. Remove from heat. Add marshmallow cream and vanilla; stir until smooth. Divide mixture in half. To one half, add butterscotch morsels and ½ cup nuts. Stir until morsels are melted and mixture is smooth. To other half, add chocolate morsels and ½ cup nuts; stir until smooth. Pour butterscotch mixture into greased 9 inch square pan. Pour chocolate mixture over butterscotch mixture. Chill until firm. Cut into squares. Refrigerate any leftovers.

TAFFY CHOCOLATE FUDGE

Average

4 Dozen
Make Ahead

1 14½ oz. can evaporated
  milk
3 cups sugar
½ cup light molasses
½ tsp. salt
3 cups miniature
  marshmallows
2 12 oz. pkgs. chocolate
  pieces
2 tsp. vanilla
⅓ cup peppermint candy,
  crushed

Combine milk, sugar, molasses and salt in large pan. Bring to a boil; boil 5 minutes, stirring occasionally. Remove from heat; stir in marshmallows, chocolate pieces and vanilla. Stir until smooth and ingredients melted. Pour into buttered 13x9x2 inch pan. Let stand until top becomes set. Sprinkle candy over surface of fudge. Chill until firm. To serve cut into squares. Keep fudge chilled or fudge will become soft.

CHOCO-NUT FRUIT CONFECTIONS

Easy

5 Dozen
Make Ahead

1 8 oz. pkg. pitted dates
1 cup pitted prunes
1½ cups raisins
4 oz. semi-sweet
  chocolate
1 cup nuts, chopped
2 Tbsp. orange juice
Nuts, finely chopped
Confectioners' sugar
Shredded coconut

In a food processor, finely chop dates, prunes, raisins, chocolate and nuts. Add orange juice and mix well with hands. Form into small balls. Roll in finely chopped nuts, confectioners' sugar or shredded coconut.

HARD CHRISTMAS CANDY

Average

4½ Pounds
Make Ahead

3⅜ cups white sugar
1½ cups light corn syrup
1 cup water
Flavoring oil (Buy essential oils, not external use. About 2-3 tsp. of each flavor is needed.)
Food coloring (Use eye to determine amount.)
Confectioners' sugar

Put sugar, syrup and water in saucepan. Stir mixture over medium heat until sugar dissolves. Put candy thermometer in mixture and leave alone while it begins to boil and temperature rises. The temperature will remain about 212° for a long time, until water boils from mixture. When it reaches 310°, remove mixture from heat. Quickly add flavoring, then coloring. Pour onto foil (tear off 2 foot long pieces and lay on several thicknesses of newspapers to protect counter), or on warm buttered cookie sheet or marble slab. Sprinkle confectioners' sugar liberally on candy. It cools rapidly. Before it turns hard, but not so sticky it sticks to cutter, cut into ¼ inch squares with pizza cutter.

CHOCOLATE COVERED PRETZELS

Let the children loose on this recipe!

Easy

5 Dozen
Make Ahead

1 6 oz. pkg. semi-sweet chocolate pieces
1 Tbsp. vegetable shortening (Crisco preferred)
60 small pretzels

Melt chocolate with shortening over simmering water. Remove from heat, but keep over water. Drop pretzels one at a time into chocolate. Lift out and tap lightly to remove excess chocolate. Place on wire rack, over wax paper and dry.

BLUE RIBBON TOFFEE

Melts in your mouth and sticks to your hips!

Average

**3 Dozen
Make Ahead**

1 cup sugar
½ tsp. salt
¼ cup water
½ cup butter
12 oz. semi-sweet
   chocolate chips
1 cup walnuts, finely
   chopped

Combine sugar, salt, water and butter and heat to boiling. Cook, without stirring, until light crack stage (285°). Pour candy onto cookie sheet. Let cool. Melt chocolate chips. Spread half of the chocolate over candy and sprinkle with half the nuts. Let cool. Refrigerate. Turn candy over and spread with rest of chocolate and nuts. Cool. Break into pieces.

CHOCOLATE CARAMEL TURTLES

Just try and save some!

Average

**2 Dozen
Make Ahead**

½ lb. soft caramels
2 Tbsp. heavy cream
1 cup pecan halves
4 squares semi-sweet
   chocolate

Melt caramels with cream over hot water; cool about 10 minutes. Cover a cookie sheet with wax paper and place pecan halves on it in clusters of 3, arranged so that one will be the head for each turtle and 2 will be legs. Spoon caramel mixture in center of each group, leaving tips of pecans showing. Let stand ½ hour, until set. Partially melt semi-sweet chocolate over warm water. Remove from water, stir rapidly until completely melted. Let stand until lukewarm and then spread over caramel turtles.

333

NOTES

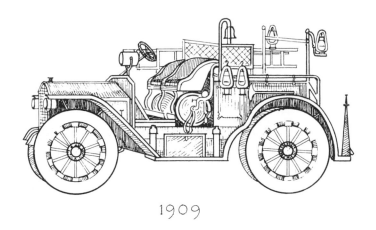

1909

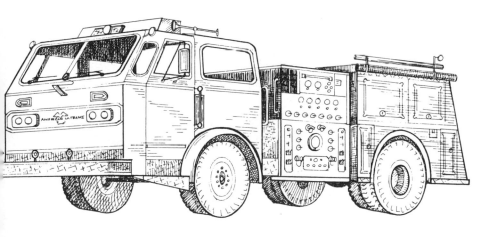

1978

CThorborg 82

FIRE ENGINES
"American LaFrance and Ward LaFrance truck companies, both founded by an Elmira family, are part of the city's rich history."

ON SUBSTITUTIONS

The recipes in *Thru The Grapevine* are complete. They need no more ingredients than are specified. On the other hand, one or two ingredients can be omitted and no harm done. Two or three herbs do well enough for four or five, one liqueur for two.

Substitutions arise from three motives:
Economy
Expediency
Preference

Substitutions for preference are the secret of infinite variety.

SUBSTITUTIONS

Arrowroot 1 Tbsp. = 2 Tbsp. flour (as thickening agent)

Baking powder 1 tsp. = ⅔ tsp. double action type or ¼ tsp. baking soda plus ½ tsp. cream of tartar

Chocolate 1 ounce (1 square) = 3 Tbsp. cocoa plus 1 tsp. to 1 Tbsp. shortening (less for Dutch cocoa)

Cornstarch 1 Tbsp. = 2 Tbsp. flour **or** 4 tsp. quick cooking tapioca (as thickening agent).

Flour Pastry flour: 1 cup = 1 cup all-purpose flour
or bread flour less 2 Tbsp.
Potato flour: 1 Tbsp. = 2 Tbsp. flour (as thickening agent)

Milk Fresh whole: 1 cup = ½ cup evaporated milk plus ½ cup water **or** ½ cup condensed milk plus ½ cup water (reduce the sugar in this recipe) **or** ¼ cup powdered whole milk plus 1 cup water **or** ¼ cup powdered skim milk plus 2 Tbsp. butter and 1 cup water.
Fresh skim: 1 cup = ¼ cup powdered skim milk plus 1 cup water
Sour or buttermilk: 1 cup = 1 cup lukewarm fresh milk (less 1 Tbsp.) plus 1 Tbsp. vinegar or lemon juice. Let stand 5 minutes.

IF YOU DON'T HAVE:	YOU CAN SUBSTITUTE:
1 cake compressed yeast	1 package or 2 tsp. active dry yeast
1 whole egg	2 egg yolks (in custards)
1 Tbsp. fresh chopped herbs	1 tsp. dried herbs
1 small fresh onion	1 Tbsp. instant minced onion, rehydrated
1 tsp. dry mustard	1 Tbsp. prepared mustard
1 clove garlic	⅛ tsp. garlic powder
1 cup tomato juice	½ cup tomato sauce plus ½ cup water
1 cup catsup or chili sauce	1 cup tomato sauce plus ½ cup sugar and 2 Tbsp. vinegar (for use in cooked mixture)
½ cup brown sugar	½ cup white sugar plus 2 Tbsp. unsulfured molasses
¼ cup superfine sugar	¼ cup granulated sugar processed in food processor or blender for 5-10 seconds

BON APPETIT!

INDEX

= members favorite recipes

N

Y

Z

NOTES

Update — Harvest 1987

Time has brought changes to the wineries of the Finger Lakes. Since our last Harvest Update, four of the wineries have closed: Rotolo and Romeo, Chateau Esperanza, Villa D'Ingianni, and the venerable Gold Seal Winery, which has seen its production turned over to the Taylor Wine Company. The Taylor company has been acquired by Seagram Distilleries and then sold again to a group known as Vintners International.

Corporate policies have influenced the changes we have seen. Emphasis on financial accountability at the large corporate-owned wineries has forced many of the grape growers either to give up production or to open wineries of their own. Two wineries, Finger Lakes Wine Cellars and Glenora, are in the process of becoming a single winery under the guidance of an outstanding winemaker, formerly with Gold Seal and Domaine Mumm in California.

Both Charles Fournier and Dr. Konstantin Frank have died but they leave a great tradition behind. Dr. Frank's Vinifera Wine Cellars is now Konstantin Frank and Sons and is run by his son, who also has Chateau Frank, a sparkling-wine cellar.

The Cayuga Wine Trail has gained three additions since our last printing: Hasmer Winery, Knapp Farms, and Swedish Hill Vineyard, all on the west shore of Lake Cayuga. All three farm wineries are owned by grape growers turned wine producers and each has its own special style and charm.

Cameron and Maren Hasmer's tiny 1000 case winery on Route 89 bottles Chardonnay, Riesling (dry), two Seyvals — dry and semi-sweet, and Apré, a Blush hybrid blend. Their winery is decorated with Maren's dried flower wreaths and grapevine wreaths which may be purchased. They've been growing grapes for fiteen years and opened their own winery in 1985. The forty acres of vineyards produce wines which are available in Syracuse and Ithaca, as well as at the winery.

Knapp Farms is north and west of Hasmer's, off Route 89 on the well-marked Wine Trail. The Knapps have been a grape growing family in this area for years, but Doug left to pursue a career in electrical engineering. In 1971, he returned to the Finger Lakes, started his own grape farm, and, as the industry changed, he and his wife, Sue, decided to open their own winery. Their first vintage was in 1982 and the tasting facility opened in 1985. Knapp Farms produces Chardonnay, Riesling, Cabernet Sauvignon, Pinot Noir (at present used for blending), Ravat, and house wines, red, white, and rosé. In the valut lie bottles of champagne, a Chardonnay — Pinot blend, not to be released for a few years. The twenty acre estate winery is planning to produce 30,000 gallons of wine this year under the direction of owner, grower, and wine maker Doug Knapp.

Swedish Hill Winery is on Route 414, north of Knapp Farms. Richard and Cynthia Peterson have been grape growers since 1969. With the encouragement of their son, David, a PHD in viticulture, they too joined the ranks of the farm wineries in 1986. Their tasting room is charming; a deck and picnic tables overlook the pond and grape vines run right to the entrance. The 5,500 gallon winery produces Chardonnay, Aurora, Catawba, Ravat, and Ventura, a Canadian hybrid. The Swedish flag waves in the breeze and the winery sponsors a Swedish Festival in June.

Among the new wineries on Seneca's east shore is Hazlitt's 1852 Vineyard. Jerry Hazlitt comes from a 135 year tradition of grape growing in the region. His interest in and knowledge of the region are reflected in the museum-like atmosphere of the tasting room. Filled with artifacts collected by the family and gifts from friends, the winery has a horseshoe-shaped bar, crafted from wood grown on the Hazlitt farm. The family staffs the tasting room where the award winning Chardonnay, a Semi-dry Riesling, Gewurstraminer, Baco, Cayuga, Lambertelle (a seyval variety) and the house wines are served with fresh popcorn! Jerry and Elaine's winery produces 6,000 gallons of wine a year and his skill as a winemaker has made each vintage a sell-out!

South of Hazlitt's on 414 is Chateau Lafayette Reneau, just north of Rolling Vineyards. Their tasting room, in a delightfully restored barn, has a view that rivals that of their neighbor to the south. This 7,000 gallon-a-year winery has Chardonnay, Riesling, Baco, Seybal, Ravat, and a house rosé. The tasting area is shared with country antique furniture and clothing attractively displayed and available for purchase.

On the west side of Seneca Lake the earliest farm wineries have been joined by three additions. Prejean Winery, Inc. (pronounce "pray/zhawn") is about twenty miles north of Watkins Glen on Route 14. Mr. Prejean, a transplanted Cajun, comes from the advertising world. Anticipating retirement, he and his wife, Elizabeth, started growing grapes in 1979 and opened the winery in May of 1986. High on the hills overlooking the lake, the tasting room, decorated with riddling racks and barrel ends, serves the product of the thirty-nine acre vineyard: Chardonnay, both dry and semi-sweet Riesling, and Gewurstraminer, Seyval, and Cayuga. Jim Prejean is an avid collector and user of cookbooks and, as are so many in the wine world, a firm believer in food and wine planning.

South of Prejean and just north of Hermann J. Wiemer Vineyards is Lake View Vineyards. A very new 2,000 gallon winery, Jurgen and Christa Loenholdt's venture is producing only Chardonnay and Riesling wine. At present, tastings are only by appointment and purchases only at the winery. Mr. Loenholdt is the owner of Eastern Grape Nursery and has been growing vinifera stock for some time.

Three miles north of Watkins Glen on Route 14 is the Giasi Winery in Rock Stream. The winery was opened in 1982 by Michael Giasi and since his death has been operated by his wife Vera and their son Paul. The tasting room, in a weathered barn, is hung with hand-colored old prints of wine related scenes and lit through antique stained glass windows. Giasi produces Chardonnay, Cayuga, Seyval, and house blends, all very dry — and an unusual demi-sec Cherry wine, ideal as a dessert wine or in creative recipes. Giasi wines are available in the New York City area and at the winery.

Cana Vineyards is another new winery, up in the hills overlooking Keuka Lake from the west. They are three miles north of Heron Hill and market Chardonnay, Riesling, Ravat, and Cayuga as well as a couple of house blends. Tom and Ann Pellechia have come up from New York City, motivated by insanity (he said with a chuckle) and their love for scenic beauty to grow grapes and make good wine. Tom is a multi-media producer and his first thrust is educating restaurants to train their personnel to know wine and to recommend and serve it properly. He also does training of winery and liquor store staffs that they may serve their customers more effectively. The wines of Cana are available only at the winery.

As you drive between Seneca and Keuka Lakes, drive to Dundee on Route 14A. Just north of town, turn right on Route 230 and three miles along you'll come to the charmingly restored Red Brick Inn (607) 243-8844. This houses both a bed and breakfast and a winery, Barrington Champagne Co. Ray Spencer, properly notified, can house you and fortify your spirit with the champagne from his 5000 bottle annual production. The Inn is lovely — and the wine is good.

Harvest Update 1991: "The New York State of Wine"

The Junior League of Elmira, Inc., asked me to write a brief column concerning the current status of the New York State Wine Industry. I am delighted to share my professional observations and thoughts, and will address three basic questions: what is the role that local wines currently share in the market; where is the industry headed; and why have New York wines become so successful?

Allow me to start by saying that a restaurant is simply *the best* sounding board for determining how enjoyable a wine is. There is no substitute for immediate, informed feedback on a wine's quality, affordability, and drinkability. At the restaurant I am in a most advantageous position to keep my finger on the pulse of the consumer and the industry. Statistically, Pierce's is one of the highest grossing restaurants in the Northeast in wine sales. Wine sales account for nearly 20 percent of yearly sales volume and, as a percentage of beverage alcohol, exceed spirits by over 40 percent. Of total yearly wine sales, over 80 percent is domestic, with New York and California sharing our market equally. These are figures that I would have dreamed unthinkable just ten years ago—and they tell me what is really happening in the market.

What role do New York State Wines currently share in the market? Beyond a shadow of a doubt, this industry has come of age. The wines have won consistent and widespread consumer acceptance, and are now recognized for their world-class quality. Just a few years ago, I encountered occasional skeptics who refused to believe that New York produced excellent wine. Not only does this problem no longer exist, but today knowledgeable and novice consumers alike actively seek these wines when dining out. What only a few years ago was guarded optimism is now full-fledged consumer loyalty. Why? Recall a very popular Gallo White Zinfandel commercial that ran on television about one year ago. Several young couples are at a party where the host serves an unidentified blush wine. Everyone sits in silence waiting for the usual, meaningless "wine chatter" to begin, when a brave lady steps forward and says, "Can't we just like it because it tastes good?" That really says it all. New York wines are today simply the right product at the right time. They are clean, fresh, and "understandable." Varietal labeling eliminates the guess work, and all-in-all the wines become very user-friendly. This phenomenon is not unique to New York but is true of domestic wines in general. A very good price-value relationship further enhances their role in the market.

Where is the industry headed? It is clearly on solid footing. The number of wineries *statewide* has more than doubled in the last ten years, and production continues to increase. I do not, however, expect to see a continuation of this rapid expansion. The industry is now properly sized to meet demand, and I predict a leveling off will occur. The increased expansion of Vinifera production will continue if quality becomes the key factor for success. Despite the difficulty therein and economic considerations, the swing to Vinifera is clearly the way the industry is headed, and I believe this will play a large role in continuing to expand sales and win new customers. White wines will continue to dominate Finger Lakes production, and Long Island will become *the* newest American "hot spot" in the production of outstanding red wine. Lastly, New York could become *the* sparkling wine region of North America. Everything is in place for this to happen except long-standing experience, which will come in time. If the popularity and sales of sparkling wines ever soar as the experts predict, this region will stand to benefit enormously.

Why have New York State Wines become so successful? The key to the industry's success is its maturity. Those of us in the restaurant business long enough witnessed a similar success in California in the early 1980s. As it was there, vineyard sites and plantings in New York have been refined to allow the best grapes to be grown in the best locations. Viticultural practices now bring out the best of each vintage, and the consistent quality of our wines, year after year, is testimony to this. Ten years ago one really had to look hard to find a great bottle of New York State Wine. Today, it is almost impossible to find a disappointing one.

Do I have any favorites? Sure, but the reader won't know what they are unless they come to dinner! And should you find yourself in our beautiful Finger Lakes community, do schedule a visit to one of the outstanding wineries. I am privileged to know many of the producers personally. They are a wonderful assortment of dedicated professionals whose trials and tribulations often take them far beyond the call of duty. May they enjoy continued success and prosperity!

Joseph Pierce, Jr.
Pierce's 1894 Restaurant

NOTES

THRU•THE GRAPEVINE
Junior League of Greater Elmira-Corning, Inc.
P.O. Box 3150, Elmira, New York 14905
Phone 607-732-9846

Please send me _____ copies of THRU•THE GRAPEVINE @ $18.95 per copy postpaid.
New York residents please add $1.19 sales tax per book. Individual gift wrapping:
$.50 per book.
Method of payment:
☐ Check or Money Order (payable
  to THRU•THE GRAPEVINE)
☐ MasterCard
☐ Visa
(Please list all digits from your card)

NAME _____

STREET _____

| | | | | | | | | | | | | | | | | | | |

Expiration Date | | | | |

CITY _____

_____
Authorized Signature

STATE_____ZIP _____

THRU•THE GRAPEVINE
Junior League of Greater Elmira-Corning, Inc.
P.O. Box 3150, Elmira, New York 14905
Phone 607-732-9846

Please send me _____ copies of THRU•THE GRAPEVINE @ $18.95 per copy postpaid.
New York residents please add $1.19 sales tax per book. Individual gift wrapping:
$.50 per book.
Method of payment:
☐ Check or Money Order (payable
  to THRU•THE GRAPEVINE)
☐ MasterCard
☐ Visa
(Please list all digits from your card)

NAME _____

STREET _____

| | | | | | | | | | | | | | | | | | | |

Expiration Date | | | | |

CITY _____

_____
Authorized Signature

STATE_____ZIP _____

THRU•THE GRAPEVINE
Junior League of Greater Elmira-Corning, Inc.
P.O. Box 3150, Elmira, New York 14905
Phone 607-732-9846

Please send me _____ copies of THRU•THE GRAPEVINE @ $18.95 per copy postpaid.
New York residents please add $1.19 sales tax per book. Individual gift wrapping:
$.50 per book.
Method of payment:
☐ Check or Money Order (payable
  to THRU•THE GRAPEVINE)
☐ MasterCard
☐ Visa
(Please list all digits from your card)

NAME _____

STREET _____

| | | | | | | | | | | | | | | | | | | |

Expiration Date | | | | |

CITY _____

_____
Authorized Signature

STATE_____ZIP _____

I would like to see this great cookbook in the following stores.

Store Name _____   Store Name _____

Address _____   Address _____

City, State, Zip _____   City, State, Zip _____

I would like to see this great cookbook in the following stores.

Store Name _____   Store Name _____

Address _____   Address _____

City, State, Zip _____   City, State, Zip _____

I would like to see this great cookbook in the following stores.

Store Name _____   Store Name _____

Address _____   Address _____

City, State, Zip _____   City, State, Zip _____